The Chartered Institute of Marketi

Professional Diploma in Marketing

STUDY TEXT

Project Management in Marketing

2010 EDITION

First edition September 2009
Second edition August 2010

ISBN 9780 7517 8942 3
(Previous ISBN 9780 7517 6815 2)

e-ISBN 9780 7517 9150 1

British Library Cataloguing-in-Publication Data
A catalogue record for this book
is available from the British Library

Published by

BPP Learning Media Ltd
Aldine House, Aldine Place
London W12 8AA

www.bpp.com/learningmedia

Printed in the United Kingdom

We are grateful to the Chartered Institute of Marketing for
permission to reproduce in this text the syllabus, tutor's
guidance notes and past examination questions.

Author: Glenn Haldane
With thanks to Kate Machattie for her input to this second edition
Template design: Yolanda Moore
Photography: Terence O'Loughlin

Your learning materials, published by BPP Learning Media Ltd,
are printed on paper sourced from sustainable, managed
forests.

Contents

Introduction

• Aim of the Study Text • Studying for CIM qualifications • The Professional Diploma Syllabus • Assessment • CIM's Magic Formula • A guide to the features of the Study Text • A note on Pronouns • Additional resources • Your personal study plan...v

Chapters

1 Aim of the Study Text

This book has been deliberately referred to as a 'Study Text' rather than 'text book', because it is designed to help you though your specific CIM Professional Diploma in Marketing studies. It covers Unit 4, Project Management in Marketing.

So, why is it similar to but not actually a text book? Well, the CIM have identified key texts that you should become familiar with. The purpose of this workbook is not to replace these texts but to pick out the important parts that you will definitely need to know in order to pass, simplify these elements and, to suggest a few areas within the texts that will provide good additional reading but that are not absolutely essential. We will also suggest a few other sources and useful press and CIM publications which are worth reading.

We know some of you will prefer to read text books from cover to cover whilst others amongst you will prefer to pick out relevant parts or dip in and out of the various topics. This text will help you to ensure that if you are a 'cover to cover' type, then you will not miss the emphasis of the syllabus. If you are a 'dip in and out' type, then we will make sure that you find the parts which are essential for you to know. Unlike a standard text book which will have been written to be used across a range of alternative qualifications, this Study Text has been specifically written for your CIM course, so if a topic appears in this book it is part of the syllabus and will be a subject the examiners could potentially test you on.

Throughout the Study Text you will find real examples of marketing in practice highlighted, as well as key concepts.

2 Studying for CIM qualifications

There are a few key points to remember as you study for your CIM qualification:

(a) You are studying for a **professional** qualification. This means that you are required to use professional language and adopt a business approach in your work.

(b) You are expected to show that you have 'read widely'. Make sure that you read the quality press (and don't skip the business pages), and read Marketing, The Marketer, Research and Marketing Week avidly.

(c) Become aware of the marketing initiatives you come across on a daily basis, for example, when you go shopping look around and think about why the store layout is as it is. Also consider the messages, channel choice and timings of ads when you are watching TV. It is surprising how much you will learn just by taking an interest in the marketing world around you.

(d) Get to know the way CIM write their exam papers and assignments. They use a specific approach which is referred to as The Magic Formula to ensure a consistent approach when designing assessment materials. Make sure you are fully aware of this as it will help you interpret what the examiner is looking for. (A full description of the Magic Formula appears later and is heavily featured within the chapters).

(e) Learn how to use Harvard referencing. This is explained in detail in our CIM Professional Diploma Assessment Workbook.

(f) Ensure that you read all assessment details sent to you from CIM very carefully. CIM are very strict with regard to deadlines eg. completing the correct paperwork to accompany any assignment or project and making sure you have your CIM membership card with you at the exam. Failing to meet any assessment entry deadlines or failing to complete written work on time will mean that you will have to wait for the next round of assessment dates and will need to pay the relevant assessment fees again.

3 The Professional Diploma Syllabus

The Professional Diploma in Marketing is aimed at anyone who is employed in a marketing management role, such as Brand Manager, Account Manager or Marketing Executive etc. If you are a graduate, you will be expected to have covered a minimum of a third of your credits in marketing subjects. You are therefore expected at this level of the qualification to be aware of the key marketing theories and be able to apply them to different organisational contexts.

The aim of the qualification is to provide the knowledge and skills for you to develop an 'ability to do' in relation to marketing planning. CIM qualifications concentrate on applied marketing within real work-places.

The complete qualification is made from four units:

* Unit 1 Marketing Planning Process
* Unit 2 Delivering Customer Value Through Marketing
* Unit 3 Managing Marketing
* Unit 4 Project Management in Marketing

CIM stipulate that each module should take 50 guided learning hours to complete. Guided learning hours refer to time in class, using distance learning materials and completing any work set by your tutor. Guided learning hours do not include the time it will take you to complete the necessary reading for your studies.

The syllabus as provided by CIM can be found on pages vii-xiii with reference to our coverage within this Study Text.

Unit characteristics

This unit will focus on the proactive development and delivery of a justified management process to support the initiation, implementation and control of marketing projects, including the use of research and information and preparing proposals and briefs to identify needs comprehensively.

The unit will also focus upon evaluating marketing project proposals and prioritising them on the basis of fit with market conditions, organisational capacity, competitor activity and strategic management, while concurrently managing the associated risk of implementing particular plans.

Ultimately, the unit will also cover the implementation of marketing proposals including an in-depth view of project management, but also integrating knowledge from the other units at this level.

By the end of this unit, students should be able to develop an effective business case within different organisational contexts and justify their project proposals in terms of fit with the marketing strategy, evaluation of risk and the effective use of organisational capacity and capability.

Overarching learning outcomes

By the end of this unit students should be able to:

* Identify the organisation's information needs, scope of research projects and resource capability to underpin the development of a business case to support marketing projects

* Develop an effective business case, complete with justifications, financial assessments and consideration of the organisation's resource capacity and capability to deliver

* Undertake a risk assessment programme with suggestions on how to mitigate for risks facing the organisation and the achievement of its business and marketing objectives

* Design, develop and plan significant marketing programmes, using project management tools and techniques, designed to deliver marketing projects effectively, in terms of quality, resource and delivery

* Integrate a range of marketing tools and techniques to support the development and implementation of a range of marketing projects

* Monitor and measure the effectiveness and outcomes of marketing projects through the end-to-end project process.

SECTION 1 – Using marketing information to develop a justified case for marketing projects (weighting 15%)

		Covered in chapter(s)
1.1	Critically assess the scope and type of marketing information required to develop effective business cases using both primary and secondary data: • Applied contextual research • Situational specific evidence • Gap analysis • Empirical prerogatives	1
1.2	Critically assess how organisations determine their marketing information requirements and the key elements of user specifications for the purposes of building a case: • Business intelligence • Product/process innovation • Culture • Source management • Output dissemination • Specialist sources • Consultancy/advice	1
1.3	Critically assess the scope, structure and characteristics of MIS and MkIS as marketing management support systems and evaluate their importance to business cases for marketing projects: • Corporate data • Operational data • Functional data • The data fuelled organisation • Data manipulation and utilisation • Confidentiality and integrity • Business databases	1
1.4	Develop a research brief to meet the requirements of an individually specific case for marketing: • Problem definition • Objectives • Information requirements • Data collection • Report parameters • Timescales • Resource allocation • Control and contingency	2
1.5	Critically evaluate a full research proposal to fulfil the brief supporting the information needs of the case and make recommendations for improvement: • Proposal scoring • Brief reviewing • The brief/proposal mechanic • Effort required for proposal versus available budget • Decision to use in-house or external agency resources • Utilisation of existing data	2

1.6	Identify and evaluate the most effective methods for presenting marketing information and making specific marketing recommendations relating to product/service development and implementation as part of the case: business function. Therefore a full range of professional presentation tools needs to be explored, adapted and applied in context.	2

- The marketing dashboard
- Graphs, charts and tables
- Pie charts
- Flow diagrams
- Spreadsheets
- Correlation and regression
- Strategic impact statements
- Effect and outcome metrics
- Investment and income budgets
- Measurement and control
- Project reports

SECTION 2 – Building a case for marketing projects (weighting 20%)

		Covered in chapter(s)
2.1	Define business case objectives for marketing plans and specific high expenditure marketing activities:	3

- Customer objectives
- Management objectives
- Profit objectives

2.2	Critically evaluate and assess the marketing potential for business case activities, including consideration of the assessments required to achieve the potential proposition:	3

- Projections
- Forecasting
- Pre/post trend extrapolation
- Historical data review
- Econometrics

2.3	Critically assess and evaluate customer groups relevant to the business case, matching their buying characteristics to the marketing proposition through the use of market research information:	3, 4

- Customer specific profiling
- Cross criteria scoring
- Contextualised positioning.

2.4	Determine the extent to which an organisation's marketing mix may need to be amended or adjusted to meet the requirements of the customer and broader stakeholders, and consider the impact of the change on the organisation:	4

- Management of the marketing mix
- Investment/divestment

2.5	Critically assess the resource capability and capacity to deliver the business case proposals and consider the competency and skill requirements of both internal and external resources to deliver the business case proposition: • Skills and competence • Role definition • Cross functionality • Agency management • Investment and income budgets • Recruitment	4
2.6	Present the business case and associated marketing plans for consultation and consideration, with full justifications for the proposed product/service initiatives and how they will support the delivery of marketing strategies and plans: • The marketing report • A structured presentation • Knowing the audience • Key impact indicators • Findings, prioritisation and conclusion	4

SECTION 3 – Assessing, managing and mitigating risk associated with marketing projects (weighting 25%)

		Covered in chapter(s)
3.1	Critically evaluate the importance of developing an understanding of risk assessments in organisations in order to protect long-term stability of a range of marketing projects: • Definition of risk • Risk perspective • Probability management • Risk culture • Strategic management	5
3.2	Critically evaluate the differences between the following types of organisational risk: • Strategic • Operational • Financial • Knowledge • Compliance • Project-based areas of risk	5
3.3	Analyse and assess the potential sources of risk, of both internal and external origins, directly related to a specific case and consider the impact of these risks on the organisation: • Internal strategic, operational, financial and hazard • External social, legal, economic, political and technological	5

3.4	Design a risk management programme appropriate to measuring the impact of risk in the context of marketing projects:	6
	• Risk audit	
	• Risk evaluation	
	• Risk report	
	• Risk treatment	
	• Risk monitoring	
3.5	Undertake risk assessments on marketing projects and assess the impact of short/long-term tactical changes to the marketing plan:	6
	• Customer assessment	
	• Management assessment	
	• Profit assessment	
3.6	Critically evaluate the different approaches organisations can take to mitigate risk in order to reduce its potential to harm the organisation or its reputation:	6
	• Organise for risk	
	• Incorporate risk management	
	• Risk avoidance	
	• Risk transfer	
	• Risk financing	
3.7	Critically assess the strategic impact of implementing proposed risk control measures versus the strategic impact of taking no action:	6
	• Business impact analysis	
	• Event tree analysis	
	• Threat analysis	
	• Scenario analysis and planning	
	• Assumption analysis	
	• Probability analysis	
3.8	Develop a range of methods for monitoring, reporting and controlling risk on an ongoing basis for project implementation:	6
	• Risk audits	
	• Risk management objectives	
	• Risk reporting	
	• Risk awareness	
	• Risk response	
	• Industry benchmarking	

SECTION 4 – Project management for analysis, planning, implementation and control (weighting 40%)

		Covered in chapter(s)
4.1	Critically evaluate different approaches to developing a culture of project planning within the marketing function and the organisation: <ul><li>Managing dynamics</li><li>The marketing/project interface</li><li>The project structured organisation</li><li>Planning, implementation and control</li><li>Policies, strategies and methodologies</li><li>Managing the project life cycle</li></ul>	7
4.2	Critically evaluate soft and hard projects in the context of marketing and consider the differences in terms of project implementation: <ul><li>Types of project</li><li>Strategic context</li><li>Operational context</li><li>Tactical context</li><li>Short/medium/long-term objectives</li><li>Quality, investment and delivery</li></ul>	7
4.3	Develop the main stages of a marketing project plan, identifying the activities, estimating time and cost, sequencing of activities, and assess the competency and skills required of the people needed to deliver the project: <ul><li>Project initiation</li><li>Scope and objectives</li><li>Beginning/end dates</li><li>Key/core deliverables</li><li>Methodology adaptation</li><li>Project limitations</li><li>Risk management</li><li>Outline budgeting</li><li>Project implementation</li><li>Schedules/schemes of work</li><li>Resource reviews</li><li>Personnel requirements</li><li>Project termination</li><li>Project evaluation</li></ul>	8
4.4	Critically assess the importance of and techniques for establishing the marketing project's scope, definition and goals relative to the organisational marketing plan: <ul><li>The project scoping document</li><li>Goals, objectives and critical success factors</li><li>In/out of scope</li><li>Risk highlights</li><li>Assumptions</li><li>Roles and responsibilities</li><li>Stakeholder management</li></ul>	8

4.5	Utilise a range of tools and techniques to support project planning, scheduling, resourcing and controlling of activities within the project to enable effective and efficient implementation:	9
	• Work breakdown structure	
	• Cost analysis	
	• Estimate forecasting	
	• Gantt charts	
	• Critical path analysis	
	• Histograms	
	• Phase management	
	• Feedback control systems	
4.6	Utilise a variety of methods, measurements and control techniques to enable effective monitoring and measuring of progress throughout the project to ensure that it is completed to specification, on time and within budget:	10
	• The project scorecard	
	• Objective review	
	• Budget review	
	• Update reporting	
	• Productivity	
	• Corrective action plans	
4.7	Critically assess the main techniques for evaluating effectiveness, success or failure of a marketing project on its completion:	10
	• Variance analysis	
	• Outcome matrices	
	• Profit/loss analysis	
	• Liquidity analysis	
	• Asset utilisation analysis	
	• Investment performance analysis	
	• Productivity analysis	
	• Value analysis	
	• Marketing mix analysis	
	• Lessons learned	

4 Assessment

The unit covered by this Study Text (Unit 8 *Project Management in Marketing*) is assessed by a work-based project requiring an in-depth study of a specific and focussed area of business activity. Tasks will require application to real settings and will be directly relevant to a work context.

5 CIM's Magic Formula

The Magic Formula is a tool used by CIM to help both examiners write exam and assignment questions and you to more easily interpret what you are being asked to write about. It is useful for helping you to check that you are using an appropriate balance between theory and practice for your particular level of qualification.

Contrary to the title, there is nothing mystical about the Magic Formula and simply by knowing it (or even mentioning it in an assessment) will not automatically secure a pass. What it does do however is to help you to check that you are presenting your answers in an appropriate format, including enough marketing theory and applying it to a real marketing context or issue. Students working through the range of CIM qualifications, are expected to evaluate to a greater extent and apply a more demanding range of marketing decisions as they progress from the lower to the higher levels. At the Chartered Postgraduate Diploma level, there will be an emphasis on evaluation whilst at the Introductory Certificate level the emphasis is on developing concepts.

Graphically, the Magic Formula for the Professional Diploma in Marketing is shown below:

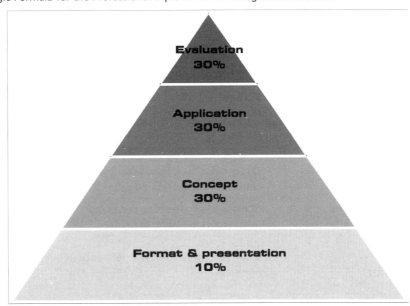

The Magic Formula for the Professional Diploma in Marketing

You can see from the pyramid that for the Professional Diploma marks are awarded in the following proportions:

- ## Presentation and format – 10%

  Remember you are expected to present your work professionally which means that it should ALWAYS be typed and attention should be paid to making it look as visually appealing as possible even in an exam situation. It also means that CIM will stipulate the format that you should present your work in. The assessment formats you will be given will be varied and can include things like reports to write, slides to prepare, emails, memos, formal letters, press releases, discussion documents, briefing papers, agendas, and newsletters.

- ## Concept – 30%

  Concept refers to your ability to state, recall and describe marketing theory. The definition of marketing is a core CIM syllabus topic. If we take this as an example, you would be expected to recognise, recall, and write this definition to a word perfect standard to gain the full marks for concept. Understanding marketing concepts is clearly the main area where marks will be given within your assessment.

- ## Application – 30%

  Application based marks are given for your ability to apply marketing theories to real life marketing situations. For example, you may be asked to discuss the definition of marketing, and how it is applied within your own organisation. Within this sort of question 30% of the marks would have been awarded within the 'concept' aspect of the Magic Formula. You will gain the rest of the marks through your ability to evaluate to what extent the concept is applied within your own organisation. Here you are not only using the definition but are applying it in order to consider the market orientation of the company.

- ## Evaluation – 30%

  Evaluation is the ability to assess the value or worth of something sometimes through careful consideration of related advantages and disadvantages or weighing up of alternatives. Results from your evaluation should enable you to discuss the importance of an issue using evidence to support your opinions.

  Using the example of you should be asking whether or not your organisation adopts a marketing approach: if you were asked to 'evaluate' this, provide reasons and specific examples of why you think they might take this approach, as well as considering why they may not take this approach, before coming to a final conclusion.

  You should have noticed that, for the Professional Diploma, you are expected to consider concept, application and evaluation in equal weighting in order to gain maximum marks in assessments.

6 A guide to the features of the Study Text

Each of the chapter features (see below) will help you to break down the content into manageable chunks and ensure that you are developing the skills required for a professional qualification.

Chapter feature	Relevance and how you should use it	Corresponding icon
Chapter topic list	Study the list, each numbered topic denotes a numbered section in the chapter.	–
Introduction	Shows why topics need to be studied and is a route guide through the chapter	–
Syllabus linked Learning Objectives	Outlines what you should learn within the chapter based on what is required within the syllabus	–
Format & Presentation	Outlines a key marketing presentation format with reference to the Magic Formula	
Concept	A key concept to learn with reference to the Magic Formula	
Application	An example of applied marketing with reference to the Magic Formula	
Evaluation	An example of evaluation with reference to the Magic Formula	
Activity	An application based activity for you to complete	
Key text links	Emphasises key parts to read in a range of other texts and other learning resources	
Marketing at work	A short case study to illustrate marketing practice	
Exam/ Assessment tip	Key advice based on the assessment	
Quick quiz	Use this to check your learning	
Objective check	Use this to review what you have learnt	

7 A note on Pronouns

On occasions in this Study Text, 'he' is used for 'he or she', 'him' for 'him or her' and so forth. Whilst we try to avoid this practice it is sometimes necessary for reasons of style. No prejudice or stereotyping according to sex is intended or assumed.

8 Additional resources

8.1 The CIM's supplementary reading list

We have already mentioned that CIM requires you to demonstrate your ability to 'read widely'. CIM issue an extensive reading list for each unit. For this unit they recommend supplementary reading. Within the Study Text we have highlighted, in the wider reading links, specific topics where these resources will help. CIM's supplementary reading list for this unit is:

Gray, C.F. and Larson, E.W. (2007) Project management: the managerial process, 4th edition, McGraw-Hill, Maidenhead.

Collier, P.M. (2009) Accounting for managers, 3rd edition, Chichester, John Wiley & Sons.

Creswell, J.W. (2008) Research design: qualitative, quantitative and mixed method approach, 3rd edition, Sage, Thousand Oaks.

Doyle, P. (2008) Value-based marketing: marketing strategies for corporate growth and shareholder value, 2nd edition, John Wiley & Sons, Chichester.

Easterby-Smith, M. et al (2008) Management research: theory and practice, 3rd edition, Sage, London.

Jankowicz, A.D. (2004) Business research projects, 4th edition, Thomson, London.

Jobber, D. (2007) Principles and practice of marketing, 5th edition, McGraw-Hill, Maidenhead.

Lewis, J.P. (2007) Mastering project management: applying advanced concepts to systems thinking, control and evaluation, resource allocation, 2nd edition, McGraw-Hill, Maidenhead.

McDaniel, C. and Gates, R. (2007) Marketing research essentials, 6th edition, John Wiley & Sons, Chichester.

Peter, J. P and Olsen, J.C. (2007) Consumer behaviour and market strategy, 8th edition, McGraw-Hill, Maidenhead.

Ward, K. (2003) Marketing finance: turning marketing strategies into shareholder value, Butterworth Heinemann, Oxford.

8.2 Assessment preparation materials from BPP Learning Media

To help you pass the entire Professional Diploma in Marketing we have created a complete study package. **The Professional Diploma Assessment Workbook** covers all four units for the Professional Diploma level. Practice question and answers, tips on tackling assignments and work-based projects are included to help you succeed in your assessments.

This unit is assessed by a work-based project.

Our A6 set of spiral bound **Passcards** are handy revision cards are ideal to reinforce key topics for the Delivering Customer value through Marketing pre-seen case study exam.

9 Your personal study plan

Preparing a Study Plan (and sticking to it) is one of the key elements to learning success.

The CIM have stipulated that there should be a minimum of 50 guided learning hours spent on each Unit. Guided learning hours will include time spent in lesson, working on fully prepared distance learning materials, formal workshops and work set by your tutor. We also know that to be successful, students should spend *at least* an additional 50 hours conducting self study. This means that for the entire qualification with four units you should spend 200 hours working in a tutor guided manner and at least an additional 200 hours completing recommended reading, working on assignments, and revising for exams. This study text will help you to organise this 50 hour portion of self study time.

Now think about the exact amount of time you have (don't forget you will still need some leisure time!) and complete the following tables to help you keep to a schedule.

	Date	Duration in weeks
Course start		
Course finish		Total weeks of course:
Submission date	Prep work to commence	Total weeks to complete project

Content chapter coverage plan

Chapter	To be completed by	Relevance to project?
1 Marketing information		
2 Briefing and presenting research		
3 Building the business case for marketing projects		
4 Delivering the business case for marketing projects		
5 Understanding risk		
6 Risk management		
7 Project planning and marketing		
8 The marketing project plan		
9 Project management tools and techniques		
10 Controlling and evaluating projects		

Chapter 1
Marketing information

Topic list

Introduction

Your syllabus provides guidance on 'development and context' for each of its four sections. The guidance for Section A includes the following remarks that are particularly relevant to this chapter.

This section of the syllabus allows the student to contextualise research around a specific undertaking. The emphasis here is on the ability to disseminate varying amounts of information from disparate sources, identify gaps and consequently rationale for primary research. As a result, candidates should be able to manipulate their findings and present a justified case for the development and management of a specific marketing project.

Syllabus-linked learning objectives

By the end of the chapter you will be able to:

Learning objectives	Syllabus link
1 Describe the nature of the information required to develop effective business cases	1.1
2 Explain how information requirements are defined	1.2
3 Explain how management and marketing information systems (MIS and MkIS) are used	1.3

1 The nature of a business case

  KEY CONCEPT

concept

A **business case** is required to justify any non-routine expenditure. In particular, any project requiring the allocation of scarce resources for its achievement will only be approved if a convincing business case can be created.

1.1 The business case

The essence of a business case is that it relates directly to the achievement of the **organisation's mission**. It should explain why the proposed work will improve the value added by the organisation in a cost-effective way. Thus, a plan to air condition an office cannot be justified in business terms by saying that it will improve working conditions, or even that it will improve the accuracy and diligence with which staff do their work.

 WORK BASED PROJECT TIP

Application

A possible approach to an effective business case might emphasise that a certain proportion of customer service failures are directly traceable to staff fatigue, short temper and poor motivation, which the improvement will tend to reduce. However, it would then be necessary to quantify the financial benefit of the improvement and show that it exceeded the cost involved.

A business case may vary in nature from an informal verbal summary to a fully-researched and detailed position paper. Matters dealt with are likely to include (at least) a consideration of the present position or problem; the desired future state; the possible solutions or courses of action; reasoning as to why the selected solution has been chosen (including financial analysis); and discussion of the risks involved.

1.2 Information and the business case

The preparation of a convincing business case for any project (not just marketing projects) thus revolves around customer impact and enhanced market success. These matters must be dealt with in a rigorous and quantified way, and that requires the acquisition, analysis and presentation of accurate information. Well-functioning information systems are, therefore, fundamental to this aspect of management, as to all others. Such systems can be expected to capture a wealth of data originating both internally and in the business environment. However, while well-designed MIS should be capable of the routine capture and dissemination of internal information, their capacity to do the same with external information is limited. It is for this reason that marketing research is so important. In this chapter we will discuss MIS and the information typically dealt with by them. In Chapter 2, we will consider marketing research.

1.3 Gap analysis

The concept of gap analysis is commonly associated with strategic planning and control. The '*gap*' is the shortfall in '*expected*' performance relative to '*required*' performance. Generally, the aim is to develop strategies to fill the gap, such as the launch of new products or the introduction of lean production. The gap analysis idea may also be applied to the problem of information adequacy. The information required to support a particular strategy, whether the overall corporate plan or a specific marketing project, can be specified in detail. This specification may then be compared with the information that is available or likely to be acquired, assuming present policies are followed. Information strategies to fill any gap between the two may then be designed and implemented.

2 Marketing management and information

  KEY CONCEPT concept

Information is required for **strategic**, **tactical** and **operational decisions** relating to matters such as markets and market share, products, prices, distribution, sales force organisation, advertising, customer attitudes, competitors' activities and environmental (SLEPT) factors.

Information is required for all levels of decision making within an organisation, be they strategic, tactical or operational. Decision-making levels, and the types of marketing and selling decisions taken at these levels, are shown in the following table.

Levels of decision making	Marketing and selling decisions
Strategic	Product/market decisions
	Product life cycles
	Product development
	Entry into new markets
	Investment in new technology to provide better information
	Database development
Tactical	Setting short term prices
	Discounting
	Promotional campaigns
	Advertising
	Distribution
	Product service levels
	Customer service levels
	Packaging
	Planning sales territories
	Short-term agency agreements

Levels of decision making	Marketing and selling decisions
Operational	Pricing, including discounting
	Competitor tracking
	Customer research
	Consumer research
	Distribution channels and logistical choices
	Sales and marketing budgets and sub-budgets, eg promotion/advertising
	Database management

Firms are becoming increasingly aware of the competitive advantage that may be achieved through the use of information. Information systems can affect the way the firm approaches **customer service** – the very essence of the **marketing concept** – and can provide advantages over competitor approaches. Superior customer service can only be achieved by being able to anticipate and satisfy customer needs. In order to meet this objective, **information** which is **up-to-date**, **accurate**, **relevant** and **timely** is essential.

The more information that a firm can obtain about competitors and customers, the more it should be able to adapt its product/service offerings to meet the needs of the market place through strategies such as **differentiation**. For example, mail order companies that are able to store data about customer buying habits can exploit this data by recognising patterns of buying behaviour, and offering products at likely buying times that are in line with the customer's profile.

Good information systems may alter the way business is done and may provide organisations with **new opportunities**.

2.1 Analysis, planning, implementation, control: APIC

Marketing management activities have been summarised using the acronym **APIC** (*Kotler*). This model is now quite old, but it is still relevant to the modern **project-based approach** to managing marketing activities.

Analysis	**P**lanning	**I**mplementation	**C**ontrol

(a) **Analysis**. The company must analyse its markets and marketing environment to find attractive opportunities and to avoid environmental threats. It must analyse company strengths and weaknesses, as well as current and possible marketing actions, to determine which opportunities it can best pursue. Marketing analysis feeds information and other inputs to each of the other marketing management functions. This is a description of the pre-initiation information needs of marketing projects.

(b) **Planning**. Marketing planning involves deciding on marketing strategies that will help the company attain its overall strategic objectives. Here we might simply substitute '*project*' for '*strategy*'.

(c) **Implementation**. Good marketing analysis and planning are only a start toward successful company performance – the marketing plans must be carefully implemented. It is often easier to design good marketing strategies than put them into action.

(d) **Control**. Many surprises are likely to occur as marketing plans are being implemented. The company needs control procedures to make certain that its objectives will be achieved. Companies want to make sure that they are achieving the sales, profits, and other goals set in their annual plans. This control involves measuring ongoing market performance, determining the causes of any serious gaps in performance, and deciding on the best corrective action to take to close the gaps. Corrective action may call for improving the ways in which the plan is being implemented or even changing the goals.

From time to time, companies should also stand back and look at their overall approach to the marketplace. The purpose is to make certain that the company's objectives, policies, strategies, and programmes remain appropriate in the face of rapid environmental changes.

To carry out these activities, **marketing managers need information**. They need to:

- Anticipate changes in demand
- Introduce, modify or delete products or services
- Evaluate profitability
- Set prices
- Undertake promotional activity
- Plan budgets
- Control costs

 ACTIVITY 1

 application

You should spend about ten minutes, before you carry on reading, thinking about information you use at work and then try and classify it into the major marketing and selling activities described under ACTIVITY in the table below. (Use a separate sheet of paper if necessary.) The second column headed INFORMATION should describe the type of information, for example: control chart, written report, oral report, telephone call, database and so on. The third column is for you to describe what you USE the information for. You may find that you use certain types of information to do more than one marketing or sales management activity, in which case feel free to list it more than once.

ACTIVITY	INFORMATION	USE
Analysing		
Planning		
Implementing		
Controlling		

2.2 The organisation's marketing information requirements

Here is a list of questions that managers of marketing projects might need answered.

(a) **Markets**. Who are our customers? What are they like? How are buying decisions made?

(b) **Share of the market**. What are total sales of our product? How do our sales compare with competitors' sales?

(c) **Products**. What do customers think of our product? What do they do with it? Are our products in a 'growth' or 'decline' stage of their life cycle? Should we extend our range?

(d) **Price**. How do our prices compare with others: higher, average, lower? Is the market sensitive to price?

(e) **Distribution**. Should we distribute directly, indirectly or both? What discounts are required?

(f) **Sales force**. Do we have enough/too many salespeople? Are their territories equal to their potential? Are they contacting the right people? Should we pay commission?

(g) **Advertising**. Do we use the right media? Do we communicate the right message? Is it effective?

(h) **Customer attitudes**. What do they think of our product/firm/service/delivery?

(i) **Competitors' activities**. Who are our competitors? Are they more or less successful businesses? Why are they more or less successful?

(j) **Environmental factors**. What factors impact on marketing planning?

Another way of viewing information needs in marketing management is to consider the **four key strategic questions**.

Question	Examples of information needed	Sources of information: forms of marketing research
Where are we now? Situation analysis	Current sales by product/market	Accounting system
	Market share by product/market	Customer database
	Competitors' market shares	Market analysis/surveys
	Customer attitudes and behaviour	Competitor intelligence
	Corporate image versus competitors' image	Customer surveys
	Company strengths and weaknesses	Internal/external analyses
Where do we want to be? Setting project objectives	Market forecasts by segment	Industry forecasts/surveys
	Environmental changes	PESTEL
	Growth capabilities	PIMS
	Opportunities and threats	Competitor research
	Competitor response	Product/market research
	New product/market potentials	
How might we get there? Shaping the project	Marketing mix evaluation	Internal/external audits
	Buying behaviour	Customer research
	New product development	Concept testing/test marketing
	Risk evaluation	Feasibility studies/competitor response modelling/focus groups/marketing mix research
	Alternative strategic options	
How can we ensure arrival? Controlling the project	Budgets	Internal accounting, production and human resource systems
	Performance evaluation	Marketing information systems
		Marketing audit
		Benchmarking
		External (financial) auditing

2.3 The role of information

Yet another useful approach is taken by Wilson (2006) who distinguishes four roles for marketing information.

(a)   **Descriptive information** answers questions such as which products are customers buying, where are they buying them?

(b)   **Comparative information** looks at how one thing compares with another, for instance how good is an organisation's after-sales support compared with its competitors?

(c)   **Diagnostic information** is intended to explain customer behaviour: why are they buying less of product A?

(d)   **Predictive information** attempts to determine the outcome of marketing actions. How would customers respond if this were made available in larger sized packs? and so on.

ACTIVITY 2

Try to assign the 'Examples of information needed' listed in the second column of the table illustrating the four key strategic questions to these categories: descriptive, comparative, diagnostic and predictive.

2.4 The Marketing Information System (MkIS)

KEY CONCEPT

concept

A **marketing information system** is built up from several different systems which may not be directly related to marketing. Typical components are an internal reporting system, a marketing intelligence system, a marketing research system and a decision and analytical marketing system.

In today's environment, marketing managers cannot operate unless there is lots of information coming into the organisation from a wide variety of sources such as commissioned research, third-party continuous research, databases, secondary sources of all descriptions, sales figures, customer surveys, environmental scanning and so forth.

KEY CONCEPT

concept

The collection, organisation and analysis of marketing information is the responsibility of a **marketing information system** (MkIS), which in itself is part of the hierarchy of information systems that exist within an organisation. The information collected, organised and analysed by an MkIS will typically include the following.

- Details on consumers and markets
- Sales – past, current and forecast
- Production and marketing costs
- Data on the operating environment: competitors, suppliers, distributors and so on

Kotler (1994) defines a marketing information system as a 'continuing and interacting structure of people, equipment and procedures to gather, sort, analyse, evaluate, and distribute pertinent, timely, and accurate information for use by marketing decision makers to improve their marketing planning, implementation and control.'

Three aspects of the information-gathering system are of special significance here.

(a)   **The speed of feedback**. The sooner the information is collected, the more accurate and useful it will be.

(b)   **The length of the planning horizon**. The planning horizon is getting shorter and there is no value in having quicker response times in the marketing function if these are not matched by quicker response times in other parts of the organisation. In the retail world, for example, scanning and EPOS systems mean that retailers know very quickly if a product on the shelves is selling or not.

(c)   **Planning how to do it** is becoming more important than planning **what to do**. To be able to react quickly to change, it is important to have a clear picture of how to respond in various eventualities so that when any given scenario emerges, action can be initiated rapidly.

2.5 Components of a MkIS

A MkIS is built up from several different systems which **may not be directly related to marketing**. It is likely to contain the following **components**.

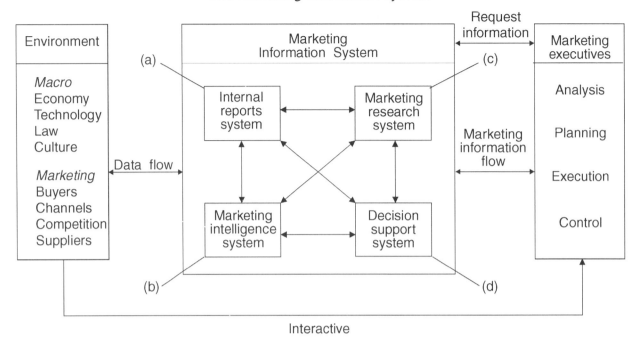

The marketing information system

Despite being designed a long while ago, Kotler's (1996) model of a marketing information systems remains true to this day because it is simple and clear.

2.5.1 Internal reporting system

The internal reporting system sits on top of the transaction processing system already discussed.

Although the data and records have been generated for some other purpose, they provide an invaluable insight into the current activity and performance of the company. Data such as sales records, invoices, production records and accounts can all be used in an internal reporting system. Many of these records are stored in computerised databases and therefore storage, retrieval and analysis is relatively quick and easy.

These records prove invaluable in an MkIS as the current operations of a business can be analysed and understood. It is good marketing practice to build any strategy or plan from an understanding of 'where we are now' and this system provides that understanding.

For example, these records may be used to provide an understanding of size and growth of customer segments, buying patterns, product profitability and many other areas.

2.5.2 Marketing intelligence system

 concept

A **marketing intelligence system** is a set of procedures and sources used by managers to obtain everyday information about pertinent developments in the marketing environment.

This system collects and stores everyday information about the external environment – information such as industry reports, competitors' marketing materials and competitors' quotes. Information collected here allows a company to build a more accurate profile of the external environment. The data may take the form of press cuttings, information derived from websites and so forth, but can also incorporate subscriptions to external sources of competitive data.

This could allow a company to calculate market sizes and growth patterns, competitor positioning and pricing strategy, and so on. This information may help in decision-making in many areas such as gap analysis, segmentation and targeting, market development and pricing strategy.

2.5.3 Marketing research system

This system uses marketing research techniques to gather, evaluate and report findings in order to minimise guesswork in business decisions. The system is used to fill essential information gaps which are not covered by the other components of the MkIS system. In this way it provides targeted and detailed information for the decision-making problem at hand.

A company might use marketing research to provide detailed information on new product concepts, attitudes to marketing communication messages, testing advertising effectiveness and understanding customer perceptions of service delivery.

2.5.4 Decision support system

This comprises analytical techniques that enable marketing managers to make full use of the information provided by the other three sources. This analysis may range from simple financial ratios and projections of sales patterns to more complex statistical models, spreadsheets and other exercises in extrapolation.

An example would be a price sensitivity analysis tool using internal data from sales records together with market share and pricing information on competitors to calculate the price sensitivity of products.

2.6 Marketing databases

Concept

In general terms, a database is an organised collection of data, typically held in digital form. Databases

Customer databases can contain a wide variety of information about the customer such as **contact details**, **transaction history**, **personal details** and **preferences** and so on. Information may come from a variety of sources besides transaction processing systems, including specialist geodemographic data and lifestyle information. Retailers are encouraging the collection of such data by introducing loyalty card which are swiped through the till at the checkout, and contain information about the customer and their purchases.

A **customer database** is *'A manual or computerised source of data, relevant to marketing decision making, about an organisation's customers.'* (Wilson 2006).

Database marketing has been defined as *'an interactive approach to marketing, that uses individually addressable marketing media and channels to: provide information to a company's target audience; stimulate demand; and stay close to them by recording and storing an electronic database memory of customer, prospects, and all communication and transactional data'* (Jobber 2010, p.549).

A marketing database can provide an organisation with lots of information about its customers and target groups. **Every purchase a customer makes has two functions**.

- Provision of **sales revenue**
- Provision of **information** as to future market opportunities

A typical customer database might include the following.

Element	Examples
Customer or company details	Account numbers, names, addresses and contact (telephone, fax, e-mail) details; basic 'mailing list' data, relationship to other customers. For business customers these fields might include sales contact, technical contact, parent company or subsidiaries, number of employees
Professional details	Company; job title; responsibilities – especially for business-to-business marketing; industry type
Personal details	Sex, age, number of people at the same address, spouse's name, children, interests, and any other relevant data known, such as newspapers read, journals subscribed to
Transaction history	What products/services are ordered, date, how often, how much is spent (turnover), payment methods
Call/contact history	Sales or after sales service calls made, complaints/queries received, meetings at shows/exhibitions, mailings sent, etc
Credit/payment history	Credit rating, amounts outstanding, aged debts
Credit transaction details	Items currently on order, dates, prices, delivery arrangements
Special account details	Membership number, loyalty or incentive points earned, discount awarded (where customer loyalty or incentive schemes are used)

The **sources** of information in a customer database, and the **uses** to which it can be put, are outlined in the diagram below.

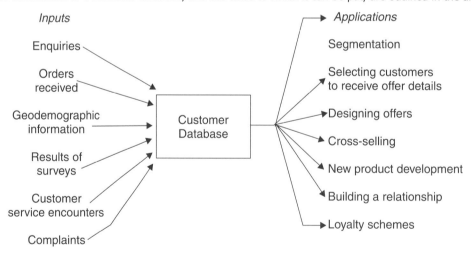

(a) The **majority** of customer information will be gleaned from the orders they place and the enquiries that they make. A relatively recent development in this area is the combination of cookies or user log-ins and server logging software, which enables **tracking and recording** of a customer's progress through a **website**, perhaps revealing interests that would otherwise have gone unnoticed.

(b) **Geodemographic** information relates to the characteristics of people living in different areas. Even simple post-code information can contain a lot of data about the customer.

(c) **Customer service** can be used to indicate particular concerns of customers. For example, in a DIY store, if customers have to ask service staff where items are stored, the volume of complaints might indicate poor signage and labelling.

(d) **Complaints** also indicate deficiencies in the product or the fact that customer expectations have been poorly communicated.

(e) The specific information held may **vary by type of market**. For example, an industrial database will hold data on key purchasers, influencers and decision makers, organisational structure, industry classification (SIC codes), and business size.

Customer data can be categorised into four groups :

(a) **Behavioural data** which is collected by the organisation as a result of their interactions with the customer (eg contact records, letters, complaints, competition entries, orders, payments, online enquiries, tracked web pages visited , discussion forums used, loyalty or membership cards swiped etc)

(b) **Volunteered data** is generated when customers complete forms, register with websites, request more information and provide their own details, respond to calls for more information, agree to be contacted by relevant third parties and update their online profiles.

(c) **Attributed data** is data generated as a result of a specific research project. This information is confidential and therefore individual respondents cannot be added to a database using their personal identity. The results of a research study, however, can be used to add more detail to your database. For example, a charity may have conducted some research into the type of communications message that is most likely to illicit a response from different groups of potential donors. If, for example, they found that a plea for help worked well with mothers aged between 20 and 40 years old then they could place a code next to individuals within that group on their database to show that they are best communicated using that type of message. Professional men aged 40 – 50 may have been found to respond more to altruistic appeals, and therefore males fitting this profile could be tagged accordingly. The next time the charity sent a piece of direct mail, they could then adapt their tone and send more targeted messages to the individuals on their database.

(d) **Profile data** is collected when it is linked with data from another source (eg lifestyle databases purchased, corporate databases, geodemographic profiles). Profiling is explored in more detail later.

Databases may be populated by information that the organisation collects for themselves or through information that is hired or purchased from third-party data providers.

2.7 The benefits of customer databases

Databases can provide **valuable information** to marketing management.

(a) Computer databases make it easier to collect and store more **data/information**.

(b) Computer software allows the data to be **extracted** from the file and **processed** to provide whatever information management needs.

(c) In some cases businesses may have access to the databases of **external organisations**. Reuters, for example, provides an on-line information system about money market interest rates and foreign exchange rates to firms involved in money market and foreign exchange dealings, and to the treasury departments of a large number of companies.

Other benefits of database systems might include:

(a) Increased **sales and/or market share** (due to enhanced lead follow-up, cross-selling, customer contact)
(b) Increased **customer retention** (through better targeting)
(c) Better use of **resources** (targeting, less duplication of information handling)

Databases enable marketing managers to improve their **decision making**.

- **Understanding customers** and their preferences
- Managing **customer service** (helplines, complaints)
- Understanding the **market** (new products, channels etc)
- Understanding **competitors** (market share, prices)
- Managing **sales operations**
- Managing **marketing campaigns**
- **Communicating** with customers

A database built for marketing purposes will, like the marketing function itself, be **future orientated**. It will be possible to **exploit** the database to **drive future marketing programmes**, not just to reflect on what has happened in the past.

2.8 User specifications for information

We will consider the place of a **research brief** in the marketing research process in more detail separately, but it is worth stressing from the outset how important it is that managers specify in advance what their information needs are. It can be very wasteful of time and money to collect answers to questions that did not need to be asked, or which were the **wrong questions** in the first place!

Key elements of user specifications will include the following.

(a) **Rationale**. How the need for information arises and what the users intend to do with the information when they have it, in other words what decisions will be taken.

(b) **Budget**. In general the benefits of collecting information should be greater than the costs of collecting it, but benefits in particular are not always easy to quantify. In any case, the budget may be limited by other organisational factors such as availability of cash or a head office allocation of, say, £5,000 per annum for marketing research purposes. Clearly, this will affect the scale and type of information search that can be carried out.

(c) **Timescale**. Quite obviously, if the decisions have to be made by May, for example, then the information needs to be collected and analysed before then. Once again this will have an impact on the sale and type of information search that can be carried out.

(d) **Objectives**. The precise information needed, set out as clearly as possible. For instance *'To determine customer response to a price reduction of £250 in terms of repeat purchasing, word-of-mouth recommendations and willingness to purchase our other products and services'*. The objectives should relate **only** to the rationale: it might be 'nice to know' what type of car customers drive, but if this will make no difference to the decisions that will be taken once the information has been collected, there is no need to know about customers' cars in the first place.

(e) **Methods**. This need only be an outline, setting out, for instance, the scale of the search, the mix of quantitative and qualitative information needed, the segments of the market to be included.

(f) **Reports**. How the final information should be presented. Considerations here might include style of reports, degree of summarisation, use of charts and other graphics, format for quantitative information (eg in Excel spreadsheets, for ease of further analysis).

3 Knowledge management

Knowledge is information within people's minds. It may or may not be recorded in the form of generally accessible information.

A **knowledge-based economy** is an economy based on application of knowledge. Organisations' capabilities and efficiency in using their knowledge override other, more traditional, economic factors such as land and capital.

Modern economies are, to a great extent, **knowledge-based**. The competitiveness of organisations depends on the accumulation of knowledge and its rapid mobilisation to produce goods and services.

(a)   Producing unique products or services or producing products or services at a lower cost than competitors is based on **superior knowledge**.

(b)   Knowledge is especially valuable as it may be used to create **new ideas**, insights and interpretations and for decision-making.

(c)   However, knowledge, like information, is of no value unless it is **applied**.

As the importance of knowledge increases, the success of an organisation becomes increasingly dependent on its ability to gather, produce, hold and disseminate knowledge.

 KEY CONCEPT   concept

Knowledge management involves the identification and analysis of available and required knowledge, and the subsequent planning and control of actions to develop knowledge assets so as to fulfil organisational objectives.

Knowledge assets are all the knowledge regarding markets, products, technologies, resources, skills, systems that a business owns or controls and which enable the business to achieve its objectives.

Knowledge can be analysed into two categories.

(a)   **Explicit knowledge** includes facts, transactions and events that are clearly stated and stored in management information systems. Explicit knowledge is created, manipulated, stored and retrieved by rationally-designed **systems and procedures**.

(b)   **Tacit knowledge** is expertise held by people within the organisation that has not been formally documented. It is a difficult thing to manage because it is **invisible**. The organisation may not even appreciate the extent to which it exists and the possessors may be reluctant to share it

We do not know what knowledge exists within a person's brain, and whether he or she chooses to share knowledge is a matter of choice. The **motivation to share** hard-won experience is sometimes low; the individual is 'giving away' their value and may be very reluctant to lose a position of influence and respect by making it available to everyone. Knowledge management is an attempt to address the two problems associated with tacit knowledge: invisibility and reluctance to share. It attempts to turn all relevant knowledge, including personal knowledge, into corporate knowledge assets that can be easily and widely shared throughout an organisation and appropriately applied.

3.1 Where does knowledge reside?

There are various actions that can be taken to try to determine the prevalence of knowledge in an organisation.

One is the **identification and development of informal networks** and communities of practice within organisations. These self-organising groups share common work interests, usually cutting across a company's functions and processes. People exchange what they know and develop a shared language that allows knowledge to flow more efficiently.

Another means of establishing the prevalence of knowledge is to look at knowledge-related business **outcomes**. One example is **product development and service innovation**. While the knowledge embedded within these innovations is invisible, the products themselves are tangible.

3.2 Customer knowledge within the organisation

Many business functions deal with customers, including marketing, sales, service, logistics and financial functions. Each function will have its own reasons for being interested in customer information, and may have its own way of recording what it learns or even its own customer information system. The diverse interests of different departments make it **difficult to pull together** customer knowledge in one common format and place and the problem is magnified because all have some political reason to keep control of (in other words **not share**) what they know about customers.

While much of this book is about the processes of **market research** (which generates **explicit knowledge**, often by going outside the organisation), it is also worth remembering the necessity to **motivate employees to record, share and use**

knowledge gained in a **less formal** manner. This includes experiential observations, comments made, lessons learned, interactions among people, impressions formed and so on.

Organisational means of encouraging sharing include emphasising it in the corporate **culture**, **evaluating** people on the basis of their knowledge behaviour and **rewarding** those who display good knowledge-sharing practice.

On a more practical level, **information and communications technology** can be of great assistance too, as we will see in the next section.

 MARKETING AT WORK application

Here are some examples of 'knowledge management' in business.

BP – introduced virtual teamworking (using videoconferencing) to solve problems.

Hewlett Packard – shares existing expertise to bring new products to the market faster.

Dow Chemical – exploits its patents to generate more revenue, by managing its patent portfolio more effectively.

4 Information systems formats and components

Information systems in all but the smallest organisations are conventionally divided into several broad categories.

(a)   **Transaction processing systems** do the essential number crunching.

(b)   **Expert systems** are used principally at the **operational** level and assist in structured problems that can be solved by applying the relevant business rules.

(c)   **Decision support systems** are used by **middle managers** for routine modelling, but also to analyse unstructured problem situations where there is no precedent that can be used as a universal guideline.

(d)   **Executive information systems** are used at **strategic** level, for unstructured problems, or to identify new opportunities.

4.1 Transaction processing systems

Transaction processing systems represent the lowest level in an organisation's use of information systems. Their primary function is to execute and record all the basic accounting functions required for the organisation to function, including those listed below.

*   Issue of invoices and authorisation of goods despatch
*   Receipt of cash and matching to invoices issued
*   Authorisation and recording of purchase orders
*   Authorisation, categorisation and payment of invoices received for both goods and services
*   Payroll computations

Transaction systems also provide a means of aggregating the value of transactions to provide totals. This is primarily required for basic accounting records but it also provides much basic information for day-to-day operational and financial management.

 KEY CONCEPT concept

Transaction processing systems are used for **routine tasks** in which data items or transactions must be processed so that operations can continue. Handling sales orders, purchase orders, payroll items and stock records are typical examples.

Transaction processing systems provide the **raw material** which can then be used at higher levels to generate information such as reports on cumulative sales figures to date, response to sales promotions, sales by type of customer, and so on: information that gives rise to marketing management decisions and new actions.

How much do you know about the accounting systems used in your organisation? You may have access to only a part of the system, but you should appreciate the range of marketing-and-sales-related information it contains and hopefully know how to extract reports on matters of relevance to your job. Find out as much as you can because this may provide you with practical insight useful for your assessment.

4.2 Expert systems

KEY CONCEPT

concept

Expert systems are computer programs that allow both experts and non-experts to benefit from expert knowledge, information and advice.

Expert systems are actually most commonly used to enable **non-experts** to behave as if they were experts. They take advantage of a database holding **specialised data** on, for example, **technical customer support** matters, and **rules** that can be predefined and applied by computer. This means that relatively untrained customer support staff can enter key data about a problem and the program will produce a decision or an answer about something on which an expert's input would normally be required. This is why, for instance, you can now get quick decisions on loan applications that used to have to be processed by highly qualified actuaries.

4.2.1 Expert systems and marketing management

Expert systems are also able to process very large amounts of interrelated data much more quickly and accurately than a human could, so experts use them too. Let's consider the marketing management goal of **precision marketing** (the mass-customisation model in which the marketing approach is matched precisely to the needs of the individual).

MARKETING AT WORK

application

In the USA, Sears-Roebuck targets those of its customers who have purchased domestic appliances without any associated maintenance cover, in a drive to sell them general maintenance contracts.

Precision marketing is problematic because of the difficulty of manipulating the vast quantities of data involved. Computers can easily handle the volume of data, although they cannot take decisions without being fed sets of rules to govern every possible situation.

In the past such rules have not been well enough defined. That is why customers sometimes receive inappropriate marketing communications, such as a promotional offer sent to a family that lives on the tenth floor of a tower block, asking them to think about how they'd feel if they opened their front door to find a brand-new car standing outside!

A well-designed expert system is a possible solution to this kind of dilemma. With an expert system, the computer can be taught how to make the necessary decisions using **artificial intelligence**. It may even 'learn from experience' in some circumstances.

There are other less complex applications which still allow some of the benefits of expert systems to be realised.

(a)   **Aggregation**. Customers are aggregated with others who share broadly similar behaviour patterns. This is the principle on which ACORN (A Classification of Residential Neighbourhoods) works. The precision is limited, but at least 'individual' approaches are possible at the group level.

(b) **Simple decisions**. Automatic decisions can be made to relate to relatively simple factors, as in the example of the Sears-Roebuck maintenance contracts. This approach can be developed incrementally, adding new decisions based upon simple combinations of factors revealed by experience.

 WORK BASED PROJECT TIP

Does your organisation use expert systems of any kind (it probably won't be called an 'expert system')? If so, make brief notes on how such systems are used. If not, try to think of ways in which expert systems might make your job easier and improve the service given to your customers.

4.3 Decision support systems

Decision support systems are used by management to assist them in making decisions on issues which are not as clear-cut as those that can be dealt with by expert systems. The objective is to allow the manager to consider a number of **alternatives** and **evaluate** them under a variety of potential conditions.

 KEY CONCEPT

concept

A **marketing decision support system** is a co-ordinated collection of data systems, tools and techniques with supporting **software and hardware** that is used for gathering and interpreting relevant information from the business and its environment, and which may be used as a basis for marketing decisions and actions. It is used by management to aid decision-making on unstructured, complex, uncertain or ambiguous issues.

In fact a simple **spreadsheet** 'what if' model, using data extracted from an accounting package, is one form of decision support tool. However, there are also many specialised software packages that enable **computer modelling** of **complex marketing management problems**.

4.4 Executive information systems

 KEY CONCEPT

concept

An **executive information system (EIS)** is an 'information system which gives the executive easy access to key internal and external data'.

An EIS is likely to have the following features.

(a) Provision of **summary-level data**, captured from the organisation's transaction processing or other systems.

(b) A facility which allows the executive to **'drill down'** from higher to lower levels of information for more details, usually using hyperlinks and clickable images, as on a website.

(c) **Data manipulation facilities** (such as comparison with budget or prior year data, trend analysis).

(d) **Graphics**, for user-friendly presentation of data.

The basic design philosophy of executive information systems is that they should:

(a) Be **easy to use,** as an EIS may be consulted during a meeting

(b) Make **data easy to access**, so that it describes the organisation from the executive's point of view, not just in terms of its data flows.

(c)   Provide **tools for analysis** such as forecasts and trends.

(d)   Provide **presentational aids** so that information can be converted into graphs, charts and tables at the click of the mouse.

4.5 The marketing dashboard

The **marketing dashboard** is an example of an executive information system that has sprung to recent notice. Typically, this presents a range of marketing-related information in vivid graphical form. There will also be a facility to 'drill-down' below the summary level in order to display greater detail. The marketing dashboard may be regarded as the means by which the **marketing information system** (MkIS) summarises and presents the most important elements of its content. (The MkIS is covered in detail later in this chapter.) A wide range of graphical devices is used to present information on a marketing dashboard, including pie charts, graphs and animated dials, tickers and moving tape gauges. The information presented can be tailored to local requirements but will often include such items as those shown below.

- Planned, committed and spent elements of marketing budgets
- A marketing calendar
- An overview of marketing projects
- Cost revenue and profit per sales transaction
- Lead conversion rate

E-commerce lends itself to this approach since so much data is captured automatically. An e-commerce marketing dashboard based on website selling might show such things as click-through rate from *Google* and other targeted advertising, page requests and downloads, top referral sites, server load and speed and frequency of visits by individual purchasers.

5   Systems that aid knowledge management

Any system – even a basic e-mail system – that helps and encourages people to work together and share information and knowledge will aid knowledge management. We have already covered expert systems, which may help to solve specific marketing problems, but marketing management is also likely to have the support of more general information sharing tools.

5.1 Groupware

  KEY CONCEPT    concept

Groupware is a term used to describe software that provides functions for the use of collaborative work groups.

Typically, groups utilising groupware are small project-oriented teams that have important tasks and tight deadlines. Perhaps the best-known general purpose groupware product is **Lotus Notes**. However, the components of **Microsoft Exchange** used on a networked system could also be considered to be a form of groupware, as could a CRM system.

Features might include the following.

(a)   A **scheduler** allowing users to keep track of their schedule and plan meetings with others.

(b)   An **address book**.

(c)   '**To do**' lists.

(d)   A **journal**, used to record interactions with important contacts, record items (such as e-mail messages) and files that are significant to the user, and record activities of all types and track them all without having to remember where each one was saved.

(e)   A **jotter** for jotting down notes as quick reminders of questions, ideas, and so on.

(f)   File sharing and distribution utilities.

There are clearly advantages in having information such as this available from a computer at the touch of a button, rather than relying on scraps of paper, address books, and corporate telephone directories. However, it is when groupware is used to **share information** with colleagues that it comes into its own. Here are some of the features that may be found.

(a) **Messaging**, comprising an **e-mail** in-box which is used to send and receive messages from the office, home, or the road and **routing** facilities, enabling users to send a message to a single person, send it sequentially to a number of people (who may add to it or comment on it before passing it on), or sending it to everyone at once.

(b) Access to an **information database**, and customisable **'views'** of the information held on it, which can be used to standardise the way information is viewed in a workgroup.

(c) **Group scheduling**, to keep track of colleagues' itineraries. Microsoft Exchange Server, for instance, offers a 'Meeting Wizard' which can consult the diaries of everyone needed to attend a meeting and automatically work out when they will be available, which venues are free, and what resources are required.

(d) **Public folders**. These collect, organise, and share files with others on the team or across the organisation.

(e) One person (for instance a secretary or a stand-in during holidays or sickness) can be given **'delegate access'** to another's groupware folders and send mail on their behalf, or read, modify, or create items in public and private folders on their behalf.

(f) **Conferencing**. Participation in public, online discussions with others.

(g) **Assigning tasks**. A task request can be sent to a colleague who can accept, decline, or reassign the task. After the task is accepted, the groupware will keeps the task status up-to-date on a task list.

(h) **Voting** type facilities that can, say, request and tally responses to a multiple-choice question sent in a mail message (eg 'Here is a list of options for this year's Christmas party').

(i) **Hyperlinks** in mail messages. The recipient can click the hyperlink to go directly to a Web page or file server.

(j) **Workflow management** (see below) with various degrees of sophistication.

Workflow is a term used to describe the defined series of tasks within an organisation to produce a final outcome. Sophisticated workgroup computing applications allow the user to define different **workflows** for different types of jobs. For example, when preparing a brochure, a document might be automatically routed between writers and then on to an editor, a proof reader and finally the printers.

At **each stage** in the workflow, **one individual** or group is **responsible** for a specific task. Once the task is complete, the workflow software ensures that the individuals responsible for the **next** task are notified and receive the data they need to complete their stage of the process.

5.2 Intranets

 KEY CONCEPT concept

An **intranet** is an internal network used to share information. Intranets utilise Internet technology and protocols. The firewall surrounding an internet fends off unauthorised access.

The idea behind an 'intranet' is that companies set up their own **mini version of the Internet.** Intranets use a combination of the organisation's own networked computers and Internet technology. Each employee has a browser, used to access a server computer that holds corporate information on a wide variety of topics, and in some cases also offers access to the Internet.

Potential applications include company newspapers, induction material, online procedure and policy manuals, employee web pages where individuals post details of their activities and progress, and **internal databases** of the corporate information store.

Most of the **cost** of an intranet is the **staff time** required to set up the system.

The **benefits** of intranets are diverse.

(a)   Savings accrue from the **elimination of storage**, **printing** and **distribution** of documents that can be made available to employees online.

(b)   Documents online are often **more widely used** than those that are kept filed away, especially if the document is bulky (eg manuals) and needs to be searched. This means that there are **improvements in productivity** and **efficiency**.

(c)   It is much **easier to update** information in electronic form.

Wider access to corporate information should open the way to **more flexible working patterns**, eg material available on-line may be accessed from remote locations.

5.3 Extranets

 KEY CONCEPT

 concept

An **extranet** is an intranet that is accessible to designated authorised users outside the company.

Whereas an intranet is accessible only to people who are members of the same company or organisation, an extranet provides various levels of accessibility to outsiders.

Only those outsiders with a valid username and password can access an extranet, with varying levels of access rights enabling control over what people can view. Extranets are becoming a very popular means for **business partners to exchange information** for mutual benefit.

Extranets, therefore, allow better use of the knowledge held by an organisation – by facilitating access to that knowledge.

6   Customer relationship management systems

Unfortunately, the label 'CRM' (customer relationship management) now tends to be applied (especially by software vendors) to any and all systems designed to support marketing and sales.

Traditional functional organisation structures tended to create stand-alone systems oriented to the separate requirements of the distinct departments responsible for the four main types of interaction with the customer: marketing, sales, fulfilment and after-sales. The modern philosophy is that a single system should store and allow access to all customer information wherever it is created or required for use. A CRM system is above all an **integrated system,** covering the entire sales and marketing process. It brings together a number of marketing and customer-facing systems within one system or homogeneous software application. The following features are usually associated with CRM:

*   Data warehouses
*   Customer service systems
*   Call centres
*   E-commerce
*   Web marketing
*   Operational systems (eg invoicing and payment)
*   Sales systems (eg mobile communications)

 ACTIVITY 3

application

Find out how an IT system based on a data warehouse works.

6.1 Self-support?

With an effective CRM system, whenever there is contact with customers, whether by letter or telephone or online, the customer should be recognised and dealt with appropriately: this will require that their contact histories are accessed, and that information and attention suitable to their individual requirements are provided. CRM software provides advanced suitable personalisation and customised solutions to customer demands, and gives marketing management a range of key information about each customer which can be applied to the current and future transactions.

However, some commentators would argue that it is now **customers** who **manage** the relationship with **companies**, and not the other way around.

7 Designing an effective system

When marketing management support systems are being designed, the following factors should be considered.

(a)   Users should **understand** the systems and be in a position to evaluate and control them. Management's **access** to the information must be **easy and direct** and the true meaning of the information provided must be clear.

(b)   The **cost** of data/information **gathering** should be **minimal**.

(c)   **Data gathering** should not cause excessive inconvenience to information sources. Preferably the data will be gathered without customers having to make any extra effort (for example, through analysis of supermarket checkout receipts which show consumer purchase patterns).

(d)   **Data gathering should be regular and continuous** since a small amount of data gathered regularly can build a considerable database. Regular data gathering produces more reliable results because it reduces the likelihood of bias of one kind or another.

(e)   The system must be **flexible**. It should be regularly **reviewed** and **improved** where possible.

Obviously the system needs to produce useful information in a useable format and it will only do so if the following matters are addressed.

(a)   **Irrelevant and/or inaccurate content** must be eliminated. (This is discussed in more depth in the next chapter). In particular a system that suggests answers that are clearly nonsense (for instance because business rules are badly defined) will not be trusted and not be used.

(b)   The system must allow for the easy and effective **storage and retrieval** of data and so consideration must be given to matters such as the following.

- Manual or computerised data, or both?
- The regularity of back-up
- Cross referencing of data
- Data protection legislation considerations

(c)   **Dissemination of the information**. Who needs to, or who should, receive information? Newsletters (or e-mail or an intranet) can be used for standardised regular information, but *ad hoc* reports should be available to senior managers on demand.

There will of course be **cost** and **organisational implications** of any marketing management support system.

(a)   **Training** of all staff will be necessary.

(b)   Staff with **specialist skills** might have to be recruited or contracted from outside.

(c)   **Software** and suitable networking and communications **hardware** may be very expensive.

(d)   Organisational considerations might include the **reallocation of duties** or **redundancies**.

As a quick example of a marketing management support system in action, let us visualise a company that has identified **quality service** as a strategic priority. To meet this goal, the system must be capable of performing a wide range of tasks, including the following:

(a)   Provide managers with **real time** information on how customers and staff **perceive the service** being given, on the assumption that **what is not measured can't be managed**.

(b)   Measure quality of both service and customer care so as to provide evidence that they do matter, the implication being that **what is seen to be measured gets done**.

(c)   Monitor how (if at all) the **customer base is changing**.

(d)   Perhaps, provide a basis on which marketing staff bonus payments can be determined, on the grounds that **what gets paid for gets done even better**.

Learning objectives	Covered
1 Describe the nature of the information required to develop effective business cases	☑ Justifies non routine expenditure ☑ Gap analysis
2 Explain how information requirements are defined	☑ Knowledge based economy ☑ APIC ☑ Descriptive, comparative, diagnostic and predictive information
3 Explain how management and marketing information systems (MIS and MkIS) are used	☑ Improve knowledge management-tacit and codified knowledge ☑ Transaction processing, expert systems, decision support systems, executive information systems ☑ CRM systems ☑ Effective systems

1   What is the essence of a business case?

2   What does Kotler say the activities involved in marketing management are, in broad terms?

3   What are the four roles of information, according to Alan Wilson?

4   What are the two main reasons why tacit knowledge is hard to manage?

5   What, typically, is the lowest level in an organisation's use of IT systems?

6   What is a 'marketing dashboard'?

7   A marketing information system has four typical components. Fill in the gaps.

    I .... R .... System

    M .... I .... System

    M .... R .... System

    A .... M .... System

8   List six ways in which groupware helps organisations to share information.

9   What is the most important thing that is achieved by CRM systems as opposed to earlier types of system?

1   The answer will be specific to your circumstances.

2   You should have found this fairly straightforward (eg current sales is descriptive information, competitors' market share is comparative, buying behaviour is diagnostic, forecasts and budgets are predictive). Some of the examples could be considered to fit into more than one category. This exercise is intended to fix the different roles of information in your mind.

3   A **data warehouse** receives data from transaction processing systems, such as a sales order processing system, and stores them in their most fundamental form, without any summarisation of transactions. Analytical and query software is provided so that reports can be produced at any level of summarisation and incorporating any comparisons or relationships desired. The value of a data warehouse is enhanced when **data-mining** software is used. True data-mining software discovers previously unknown relationships and provides insights that cannot be obtained through ordinary summary reports. These hidden patterns and relationships constitute knowledge that can be used to guide decision-making and to predict future behaviour.

1   It relates directly to the achievement of the organisation's mission. It should explain why the proposed work will improve the value added by the organisation in a cost-effective way.

2   APIC: Analysis, Planning, Implementation and Control

3   Descriptive, comparative, diagnostic and predictive

4   Tacit knowledge is hard to manage because the organisation cannot know that it exists (even the possessor of the information may not realise why it is that he or she is better at doing something than others), and because people may be reluctant to share it.

5   Transactions processing

6   A marketing dashboard is an example of an executive information system, typically using vivid graphics to display a range of information required to manage the marketing function

7   Internal Reporting System
Marketing Intelligence System
Marketing Research System
Analytical Marketing System

8   The features mentioned in the text of the chapter are: messaging, access to databases, scheduling, shared public folders, delegate access, conferencing, task assignment, voting, hyperlinks and workflow management.

9   Integration of information from all the systems that impact upon marketing.

References

Jobber, D (2010) <u>Principles and Practice of Marketing</u>, 6th edition, McGraw Hill, Maidenhead.

Kotler, P (1996) <u>Marketing Management: Analysis, Planning and Control,</u> 9th revised edition, Pearson, Harlow.

Wilson, A (2006) <u>Marketing Research: an Integrated Approach</u>, 2nd edition, Financial Times/Prentice Hall, London.

Chapter 2

Briefing and presenting research

Topic list

Introduction

In Chapter 1 we examined the main ways in which routine information is produced and handled by the organisation. In this chapter we are going to examine more closely the subject of marketing research, which is the active seeking out of information of marketing value. This will be largely examined from the point of view of the client organisation buying-in expertise from a marketing research agency. We include, in Sections 6, 7 and 8, extensive material on how research findings are presented. This will be useful in understanding the nature of the output from marketing research specialists and will also enhance your own general appreciation of how to go about presenting information.

Syllabus-linked learning objectives

By the end of the chapter you will be able to:

Learning objectives	Syllabus link
1 Prepare a marketing research brief for a given problem	1.4
2 Evaluate a marketing research proposal	1.5
3 Recommend effective methods for presenting marketing information	1.6

1   Marketing research: an introduction

Strictly speaking, **marketing** research is any kind of information gathering and analysis that aids the **marketing process** as a whole (a study of competitors' strengths and weaknesses, say) while **market** research is research into the characteristics of a **market** (France as opposed to India, say, or people aged under 30 as opposed to people aged over 65).

  KEY CONCEPT concept

Marketing research. 'The collection, analysis and communication of information undertaken to assist decision-making in marketing.' (Wilson, 2006) Marketing research includes market research, price research and so on.

To give you an idea of the **scope** of marketing research, the various components are summarised below.

Research type	Application
Market research	Forecasting demand (new and existing products)
	Sales forecast by segment
	Analysis of market shares
	Market trends
	Industry trends
	Acquisition/diversification studies
Product research	Likely acceptance of new products
	Analysis of substitute products
	Comparison of competitors' products
	Test marketing
	Product extension
	Brand name generation and testing
	Product testing of existing products
	Packaging design studies

Research type	Application
Price research	Competitor prices (analysis)
	Cost analysis
	Profit analysis
	Market potential
	Sales potential
	Sales forecast (volume)
	Customer perception of price
	Effect of price change on demand
	Discounting
	Credit terms
Sales promotion research	Analysing the effect of campaigns
	Monitoring/analysing advertising media choice
	Evaluation of sales force performance
	To decide on appropriate sales territories and make decisions as to how to cover the area
	Copy research
	Public image studies
	Competitor advertising studies
	Studies of premiums, coupons, promotions
Distribution research	Planning channel decisions
	Design and location of distribution centres
	In-house versus outsource logistics
	Export/international studies
	Channel coverage studies

1.1 Qualitative research

 KEY CONCEPT  Concept

Qualitative research is 'exploratory research that aims to understand consumers' attitudes, values, behaviour and beliefs'. (Jobber, 2010: p.251)

Qualitative research is particularly useful for new product research, marketing communications development and preliminary (exploratory) research prior to a more detailed, probably quantitative study.

1.1.1 New products or services

New products and services (and also proposed improvements to existing products and services) have the disadvantage that there is **no existing data** to measure, and perhaps **nothing more tangible than an idea** to present to people.

Qualitative research can help at the initial stages of development to help a company decide whether or not to continue with development at all, and later on, once there is a prototype of some kind, to find out what **further development** is necessary – what **other benefits** customers would like to see that could be included.

It may also help a company decide **what part of the market** to target: the idea may be very warmly received by some groups but generate no interest whatever amongst others.

1.1.2 Advertising and promotion

Qualitative research is fairly widely used in the **development** of marketing communications messages, to assess how consumers feel about a product or service and what sort of message they are most likely to respond to.

Qualitative methods can also be used to **pre-test** marketing communications messages, to make sure the message is understood and that no unintended messages are conveyed.

1.1.3 Other exploratory research

For existing products and services qualitative research may be used to find the answers to a variety of questions about customer attitudes and perceptions, segmentation and buying behaviour, often as a **preliminary** to help define the direction of **more detailed research**. For instance if ultimately you want statistical data about the decision-making process amongst different buyer segments you need to know what the different decision-making processes are in the first place, so you know what to measure.

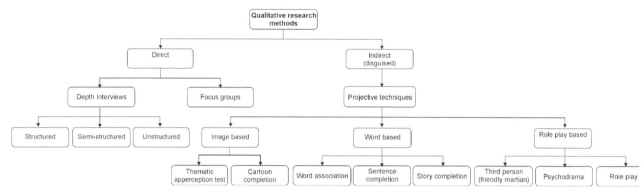

The main method of qualitative research is the **interview**. However, **focus groups** and **group discussions** are also ways of gathering qualitative information.

The key to qualitative research is to allow the respondents to say what they feel and think, in response to flexible, 'prompting' questioning, rather having than to give responses to set questions, or choosing from answers in a questionnaire.

1.2 Quantitative research

KEY CONCEPT

Concept

Quantitative research is structured to collect specific data regarding a specific set of circumstances.

1.2.1 Quantitative data collection methods

Questionnaires and surveys are key ways of collecting quantitative data, but it is important to select an appropriate survey method and to ask suitable questions. Surveys can be administered in a number of different ways, for example, face-to-face interviews, telephone interviews, mail surveys or Internet surveys. Organisations need to use an appropriate style of survey for the type of research they are carrying out. The following diagram highlights the alternative survey styles.

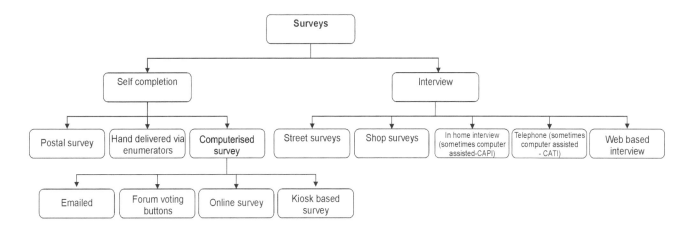

2 The stages of the marketing research process

If you read other books on marketing research you will find many slight variations on the suggested 'stages' of the market research process, partly depending on whether the book is written from the point of view of a client or a market research agency. There is fairly general agreement, however, that the process will entail the following stages, in this order. (The process spells **DODCAR**, if you like mnemonics!).

Stage 1   **Definition**: identify and define the **opportunity or threat**

Stage 2   **Objectives**: determine precisely what you need to know to deal with the opportunity or threat

Stage 3   **Design** the research and the methods to be used

Stage 4   **Collect** the **data**

Stage 5   **Analyse** the data

Stage 6   **Report** on the findings

Where an organisation is using an agency or agencies to do the research it will send out a **research brief** at the end of Stage 2, and the various agencies that are asked to tender for the work will then submit **research proposals** (in outline, at least) covering Stage 3, explaining how they would do the work and why they should be chosen. Research proposals are discussed at more length in the next chapter.

The organisation will **select its preferred supplier**(s) based on the contents and quality of their proposals (and on other factors such as cost, of course) and then Stage 3 will be undertaken in detail.

2.1 Stage 1: Identify and define the opportunity or threat

We have phrased the heading above so that it reminds you of SWOT analysis, since the identification of a need for market research will usually arise from strategic and marketing planning processes and reviews.

(a)   An **opportunity** is something that occurs in the organisation's environment that could be advantageous – a **change in the law**, say, or a **new technology** that could be exploited.

(b)   A **threat** is an environmental development that could create problems and stop the organisation achieving its objectives – a **new competitor**, perhaps, or an adverse change in **buying behaviour**.

In either case the organisation will **want to know more**. How can it best take advantage? What action is most likely to stave off or reverse the problem? The answers will depend on **how the market reacts** to different possible solutions, and the organisation can be much more sure about this if it conducts **research**.

Bear in mind that marketing research, however well organised, is not a substitute for decision-making. It can help to reduce the risks, but it will not make the decision. Professional marketing depends partially on sound judgement and reliable information, but it also needs flair and creativity.

2.2 Stage 2: Determine the objectives of the research

The objectives should set out the precise information needed, as clearly as possible. It is very wasteful of time and money to collect answers to questions that did not need to be asked or which were the wrong questions. The objectives should relate only to the problem or opportunity. They should be stated carefully, completely and precisely. The **SMART** mnemonic gives some clues, though there are several versions of just what this acronym stands for. Here is one reasonable possibility.

(a)   They should be as **specific** as possible: vague objectives will lead to inconclusive, vague research.

(b)   They should relate to **measurable** matters: quantified information should be the target, but even when a topic can only be dealt with in qualitative terms, the objectives should require as much quantification as possible.

(c)   They should be **attainable** with reasonable resources: objectives that are impossible to achieve are nonsensical.

(d)   They should focus on **results** rather than methods.

(e)   They should be **time-bound**: an overall time frame for the research should be agreed, with suitable progress gates incorporated.

Marketing research can sometimes be a waste of effort and resources.

(a)   The research undertaken may be designed without reference to the decisions that will depend on, or be strongly influenced by, the results of the research.

(b)   The research results may be ignored, misused, misunderstood, or misinterpreted. Sometimes this happens accidentally; more often it is deliberate because the results do not agree with some senior person's prejudices or established beliefs.

(c)   The research is poorly designed or carried out.

(d)   The results of the research are themselves inconclusive, giving rise to different opinions about what the research signifies.

With issues like this in mind, Wilson (2006) suggests **early consultation and involvement** of all the parties that will be involved in actioning the decisions taken as a result of the proposed research, for example by setting up a project team. This has the advantage that those closest to the project will probably have the best idea of what **knowledge** the organisation **already possesses**, and does not need to be researched. Also it means that the questions that **need** to be answered are more likely to get asked.

 ACTIVITY 1

application

Your company manufactures cruelty-free beauty products for a number of supermarket chains. You have been given responsibility for researching the market for a new line of cruelty-free cosmetics. List the likely research objectives.

 WORK BASED PROJECT TIP

Concept

Other matters that would be considered at this stage would be the available budget and the timescale for the work, and perhaps there would be outline thoughts about the methods to be used (for instance the scale of the research and the segments of the market to be included). All of this information, together with the requirements for the final report, would be included in the research brief if the work was now to be put out to tender.

2.3 Stage 3: Design the research and the methods to be used

The **category** of research must first be decided upon: the methods used will depend on that. Research may be **exploratory**, **descriptive** or **causal**.

2.3.1 Exploratory research

As the name suggests, **exploratory** research tends to **break new ground**. For instance, if your organisation has a **completely new idea** for a product or service which consumers have never been offered before, then exploratory research will be most appropriate in the first instance.

(a)   Potential consumers may be totally uninterested, in which case exploratory research will quickly show that it is best to **abandon the idea** before any more money is spent on developing it.

(b)   Consumers **may not understand** how the offer could benefit them, in which case exploratory research would show that it may be worth simplifying the product and introducing it to them in a different way, with different promotional techniques and messages.

(c)   On the other hand, consumers may not have responded because the **research methods used** were not appropriate, or because the wrong consumer group was chosen: exploratory research can help to define how more detailed research should be carried out.

Exploratory research may therefore be a **preliminary** to more detailed development of marketing ideas or a more detailed research project. It may even lead to abandonment of a product idea.

Research **methods** should involve as **little cost** and take as **little time** as possible. If use can be made of **existing research** by others then that is certainly desirable, as are methods that are not too labour and cost intensive such as **telephone** research or limited **Internet surveys**.

2.3.2 Descriptive research

Descriptive research aims to describe what is happening now (a single snapshot) or what has happened over a limited period of time (several snapshots).

(a)   Now (a **'cross-sectional study'**): 'At present 45% of the target market are aware of our product whereas 95% are aware of Competitor A's product'.

(b)   Over time (a **'longitudinal study'**): 'During the period of the in-store promotion (February to April) awareness of our product rose from 45% to 73%'.

In other words, descriptive research is useful for answering 'where are we now?' questions, and it can also be used to summarise how things have changed over a period in time. Published market research reports are examples of descriptive research: if you subscribe today you will find out 'where you were' when the report was last published, and if you wait a while for the next edition you will find out how you have progressed.

The main problem (for researchers) with longitudinal descriptive research is to ensure that their respondents are either the same people each time or, if that is not possible, that answers from very similar respondents are aggregated. Research **methods** are likely to include **telephone** research, with the consumer's agreement, and specially invited **panels** of respondents.

2.3.3 Causal research

Although descriptive research is very common and is much used it may not really tell us the **cause** of the event or behaviour it describes. To paraphrase Wilson (2006), virtually all marketing research projects fall somewhere along a continuum between purely descriptive and purely **causal**.

For example, the descriptive result 'During the period of the in-store promotion (February to April) awareness of our product rose from 45% to 73%' appears to suggest a reason for the change, but the only thing we know for certain is that two to three months have gone by. The change may be little or nothing to do with the in-store promotion. It may be due to a completely random factor such as temporary unavailability of a competitor's product, or uncontrolled and unmeasured actions taken by in-store staff, or to other promotional efforts such as TV ads.

The relationship between variables like this is not formally taken into account in descriptive research. **Causal** research attempts to identify and establish the relationship between all the variables, and determine whether one variable influences the value of others. **Experimental** research can be carried out, where one variable is deliberately changed to see the effect, if any, on other variables. The most obvious example is to see if lowering the price causes sales to rise.

Research **methods** might be similar to those for longitudinal descriptive research (panels of consumers for instance), but the information they are asked to provide will be more extensive and the time span may be longer. The researcher will need to consider the **sampling** method and parameters (how many people and of what type), where the people can be found, and the means of obtaining information (**interviews**, **questionnaires** and so on).

2.4 Stage 4: Collect the data

Data can be collected from either primary or secondary data sources.

(a) **Primary data** is information **collected specifically for the study** under consideration. Primary data may be **quantitative** (statistics), **qualitative** (attitudes etc) or **observational** videos of people browsing in a store, for instance).

(b) **Secondary data** is data collected for another purpose not specifically related to the proposed research, for instance, all the **internal** information in the company's marketing information systems and databases, or information such as **published research** reports, **government** information, **newspapers** and trade journals and so on.

2.5 Stage 5: Analyse the data

This stage will involve getting the data into analysable form by entering it into a computer and using statistics (for quantitative data) and other means of analysis and summary (qualitative data) to find out what it reveals.

 MARKETING AT WORK   application

Averages are misleading. Divide the total number of working testicles in the UK by its population and you arrive at the disconcerting conclusion that the average British citizen has one testicle. Averages also hide the true complexity of a market. Averages are predicated on ignoring and absorbing any and all variations or distributions in the data …

Averages are the enemy of market segments. More often than not a marketer will commission research that could reveal the presence of multiple market segments. But thanks to the application of the trusty average score, these segments remain hidden from view and any future marketing strategy. There is a common misconception that you must commission a special piece of research to reveal market segments. This is only true if you are applying averages to all your market research data. If you venture beyond the mean and into the heady territory of standard deviation and cluster analysis, any market research has the potential to reveal the presence of segments.

Averages are also peculiarly inappropriate to marketers because of their inherent focus on the mass at the expense of the target minority. For example, we can ask consumers how positive they feel about brand x on a scale of one (very unhappy) to seven (very happy). If we then apply an average to this data and receive a score of five, we probably conclude that we could do better.

However, the score could indicate a brand that is generally well thought of by most consumers (in which case it is unlikely to generate large market share when faced with more positively rated competitors), or a brand loved by 20% of the market and disliked by the rest (indicating a brand likely to be wildly successful).

2.6 Stage 6: Report on the findings

The final report is likely to take the form of a **presentation** given to an audience of interested parties and a detailed **written report** explaining and summarising the findings, with appendices of figures and tables and so on.

In putting together the research plan, decisions need to be made under the following headings.

Data sources	Primary data (data the organisation collects itself for the purpose)
	Secondary data (collected by someone else for another purpose which may provide useful information)
Type of data required	Continuous/*ad hoc*
	Quantitative (numbers)
	Qualitative (important insights)
Research methods	Observation
	Focus groups
	Survey
	Experiment
Research tools	Interviews (semi-structured, structured, unstructured; open vs closed questions)
	Questionnaires
	Mechanical tools (video, audio)
Sampling technique (if required)	Sampling unit
	Sample size
	Sample procedure
Contact methods	Telephone
	Mail
	Face-to-face

3 Ethical and social responsibilities

Marketing research aims to collect data about people. It could not take place at all if people were not willing to provide data, and that means that it is as much in the interests of the marketing research industry as it is of respondents for researchers to behave responsibly with the information collected.

3.1 Data protection

Most developed countries have specific legislation to protect the **privacy of individuals**. Many people feel unhappy about their personal details being retained by commercial organisations.

3.1.1 The Data Protection Act 1998

Data protection legislation was introduced in the UK in the early 1980s to try to prevent abuses. The latest provision is the **Data Protection Act 1998**.

The Act is concerned with **'personal data'**, which is information about **living, identifiable individuals**. This can be as little as a name and address: it need not be particularly sensitive information. If it is sensitive (discussed later) then extra care is needed. The Act gives individuals (**data subjects**) certain rights and it requires those who record and use personal information (**data controllers**) to be open about their use of that information and to follow 'sound and proper practices' (the Data Protection Principles).

3.1.2 The eight data protection principles

Data must be:

- Fairly and lawfully processed
- Processed for limited purposes
- Adequate, relevant and not excessive
- Accurate

- Not kept longer than necessary
- Processed in accordance with an individual's rights
- Secure
- Not transferred to countries that do not have adequate data protection laws

3.1.3 Fair processing for limited purposes

When an organisation collects information from individuals it should be **honest and open** about why it wants the information and it should have a **legitimate reason** for processing the data.

3.1.4 Adequate, relevant and not excessive; accurate and no longer than necessary

Organisations should hold **neither too much nor too little** data about the individuals in their list. For instance, many companies collect date of birth or age range information from their customers, but in many cases all they actually need to know is that they are over eighteen.

Personal data should be **accurate and up-to-date** as far as possible. Data should be **removed when it is no longer required** for audit purposes or when a customer ceases to do business with the organisation.

3.1.5 The rights of data subjects

Individuals have various rights including the following.

- The right to **be informed** of all the information held about them by an organisation.
- The right to **prevent** the processing of their data for the purposes of direct marketing.
- The right to **compensation** if they can show that they have been caused damage by any contravention of the Act.
- The right to have any inaccurate data about them **removed** or corrected.

3.1.6 Security

Organisations should make sure that they provide **adequate security** for the data, taking into account the nature of the data, and the possible harm to the individual that could arise if the data is disclosed or lost.

- Measures to ensure that **access** to computer records **by staff** is authorised (for instance a system of passwords).

- Measures to control **access** to records by **people other than staff**. For instance, care should be taken over the siting of computers to prevent casual callers to the organisation's premises being able to read personal data on screen.

- Measures to prevent the **accidental loss or theft** of personal data, for example backups and fire precautions.

3.1.7 Overseas transfers

If an organisation wishes to transfer personal data to a country outside the European Economic Area (EEA) it will either need to ensure there is adequate protection (e.g. a Data Protection Act) for the data in the receiving country, or obtain the consent of the individual.

3.1.8 Sensitive data

The Act defines eight categories of sensitive personal data. If an organisation holds personal data falling into these categories it is likely that it will **need the explicit consent** of the individual concerned. It will also need to ensure that its security is adequate for the protection of sensitive data.

The eight categories are:

- The racial or ethnic origin of data subjects
- Their political opinions
- Their religious beliefs or other beliefs of a similar nature
- Whether they are a member of a trade union
- Their physical or mental health or condition

- Their sexual life
- The commission or alleged commission by them of any offence
- Any details of court proceedings or sentences against them

3.1.9 Enforcement

If an organisation is breaching the principles of the Act, the Information Commissioner has various powers to force the organisation to comply, including issuing an enforcement notice, and the power to enter and search its premises, and examine equipment and documents. It is an offence to obstruct the Commissioner, and there are also fines and criminal penalties for holding data without being registered; for failing to comply with an enforcement notice; and for unauthorised disclosure of personal data.

3.2 Professional codes of practice

In addition to adhering to legislation, marketing researchers should act in the interests of the marketing research profession, and to help them do so a number of codes of practice have been developed by the various professional bodies. These do **not have legal status**, but breaches may result in **disciplinary action** by the professional body, including barring the transgressor from membership of the body.

The best known code is the ESOMAR code: the full document can be downloaded from the organisation's website: www.esomar.org.

4 The marketing research industry

4.1 Internal marketing research departments

Most organisations will have somebody who is responsible for marketing research, even if that simply means liaising with external agencies who actually carry out the work.

Larger organisations that have a regular need for marketing research information (particularly FMCG organisations) are likely to set up their own **marketing research department**.

4.2 Specialist agencies

As the name implies a specialist agency specialises in a particular type of work.

(a) Some agencies specialise in particular **markets** or market **sectors** or **regions**.

(b) Others specialise in a particular **research service** such as questionnaire design, or collection and analysis of qualitative information.

(c) **Field agencies** have specialised skills in **conducting** personal or telephone interviews and **administering** postal or e-mail surveys.

(d) **Data analysis agencies** can be employed to code up, read in or input data collected (in questionnaires, say, or perhaps recorded in personal interviews) and analyse it using state-of-the-art hardware (such as highly accurate scanners) and software (for instance highly specialised statistical packages).

(e) There are numerous **independent consultants** who will undertake a variety of tasks, usually on a **smaller scale**. Such people are typically ex-employees of larger research organisations or have gained their expertise in related disciplines such as IT or librarianship.

4.3 Syndicated research agencies

A syndicated service is one that is **not conducted for any specific client**. Regular research is conducted into areas that the agency knows for certain that many organisations will be interested in (for instance newspaper and magazine readership) and is then sold to anyone willing to pay the price.

Well-known examples of syndicated research agencies include **Datamonitor** (with products like MarketWatch: Drinks and MarketWatch: Food), and **Mintel** (www.mintel.co.uk) which has a huge number of regularly updated reports available on a subscription basis (eg *Agricultural Machinery, Nail Color and Care, Disposable Nappies and Baby Wipes*, and hundreds of others).

4.4 List brokers

A list broker **creates or acquires lists** of potential consumers **for the purpose of selling them on** to companies who are interested. Lists may be created from publicly available sources such as the telephone book or yellow pages or the electoral rolls but they will usually be **organised** for convenience, presented in **formats** that can be easily incorporated into clients systems, and **checked** for accuracy and currency. The client could possibly do this in-house, but it would be very **time-consuming**. Lists that have arisen as a result of some other exercise such as responses to mailshots or entry into a 'free' draw may also be **acquired** by list brokers.

4.5 Profilers

A profiler is able to take an organisation's database and **superimpose profiling information** (demographics, lifestyle and life stage information) on the basis of post codes. This allows the organisation's database to be segmented according to the criteria that are most appropriate to that organisation.

A profiler may also have access to other lists and be able to offer these to its clients, much like a list broker, except that the profiler has closer knowledge of the characteristics of the clients' existing customers and so the list may have more appropriate prospects.

4.6 Full service agencies

As the name implies a full service agency **offers all of the above services** and so will be able to conduct a research project from start to finish. Well-known international examples are **BMRB** (www.bmrb.co.uk), **Taylor Nelson Sofres** (www.tns-global.com) and **Ipsos** (www.ipsos.com).

In addition, many full service **advertising agencies** offer marketing research services as do firms of **management consultants** like McKinsey (www.mckinsey.com).

This is an extract from the Ipsos website (*www.ipsos.com*).

Research rooted in reality

We are an independent company which ranks fifth among global research companies. We are proud of this activity that we have been practicing for more than thirty years.

Our ambition: to make survey-based research one of the primary means to understand contemporary society and economy. And to make Ipsos a strategic partner for those who wish to better understand the world and play an active part in it, with lasting success.

Our experts are specialised in five areas of activity. Our teams are fully dedicated to their specialisation and work as close as possible to our clients' needs and expectations.

Our ambition is to grow faster than the market. This enables our company to strengthen its leading position in each of our areas of expertise and to preserve our independence and professionalism."

An excellent way to get a flavour of the marketing research industry is to visit the websites mentioned above and click on 'Services' (or 'Solutions', or whatever) to see the range of work carried out by different types of organisation. Don't restrict your web survey to large multinational companies. See if you can find links to the websites of smaller organisations in your own country.

5 Selecting a supplier

Very few organisations can shoulder the cost of a large full-time staff of marketing research workers, so market research is often outsourced.

5.1 External agencies versus in-house programmes

There are a number of advantages and disadvantages to each alternative.

(a) **Using an external agency**

   (i) **Advantages**

      (1) External agencies **specialising** in research will have the necessary expertise in marketing research techniques. This should allow them to develop a cost-effective research programme to a **tighter timescale**.

      (2) Skills in **monitoring and interpreting data** will allow the programme to be reviewed and modified as required.

      (3) Nationwide or global agencies will be able to offer much **broader geographical coverage**.

      (4) An external agency can provide an **objective input** without the bias which often results from a dependence on internal resources.

      (5) **Costs** can be determined from the outset, allowing better **budgetary control**.

      (6) When conducting **confidential research** into sensitive areas, there is less risk of information being 'leaked' to competitors.

   (ii) **Disadvantage**

      Agency knowledge of the industry will be limited: a serious drawback if the agency needs a disproportionate amount of time to familiarise itself with the sector.

(b) **In-house programme**

   (i) **Advantages**

      (1) **Costs can be absorbed** into existing departmental overheads.
      (2) It can **broaden the experience** and skills of existing staff.
      (3) It might promote a **team spirit** and encourage a 'results-oriented' approach.

   (ii) **Disadvantages**

      (1) There is a danger of **overstretching current resources** and adversely affecting other projects.

      (2) There is a risk of developing an **inappropriate programme**, yielding insufficient or poor quality data with inadequate analysis and control.

      (3) If additional **training or recruitment** is required this could prove expensive and time consuming.

      (4) **Bias** could result from using staff with pre-conceived views.

      (5) **Company politics** may influence the results.

(6) Considerable **computing resources** with appropriate software packages would be required to analyse the data.

(7) There may be a lack of **appropriate facilities**. For example, focus group research is often conducted off premises during evenings or weekends.

In view of the shortcomings of a purely in-house or external agency approach, a **combination** of the two might be more appropriate. For example, it might be deemed preferable to design the programme in-house but contract out certain aspects.

5.2 Choosing and using consultants

Choosing the right agency or consultant to work with is a key element in a successful working relationship. The external expert must become a trusted part of the team. It is important that the market researcher has the specialist knowledge and research service capabilities needed by the organisation. It helps if the agency has some knowledge of the market or business in which the company operates. Therefore, it may be worthwhile to develop a long-standing relationship with the research organisation, because their understanding of the company's business and the marketplace will develop over time.

5.3 The selection process

The selection process will generally involve the organisation sending out its **research brief** to a number of agencies and inviting each to submit a **research proposal**.

5.4 The research brief

The key to good research is the quality of the research brief prepared by the organisation commissioning the research.

A research brief will normally cover the following matters.

(a) **Background** – relevant information about the company, its products and services, its market place and so on.

(b) **Rationale** – how the need for information arose and what the users intend to do with it? What decisions will be taken?

(c) **Budget** – the benefits of collecting information should be greater than the costs of collecting it, but benefits are not always easy to quantify. The budget is always likely to be limited and this will affect the scale and type of information search that can be carried out. This item will probably not be revealed to possible external suppliers, since their response is likely to be based on how much research they are prepared to undertake for the price, rather than how they propose to meet the requirements of the brief.

(d) **Timescale** – commercial constraints may impose severe time limits. This will also have an impact on the scale and type of information search that can be carried out.

(e) **Objectives** – the precise information needed should be set out as clearly as possible.

(f) **Methods** – this need only be an outline, setting out, for instance, the scale of the search, the mix of quantitative and qualitative information needed, the segments of the market to be included, for example.

(g) **Reports** – how the final information should be presented. Considerations here might include style of reports, degree of summarisation, use of charts and other graphics, format for quantitative information (eg in Excel spreadsheets, for ease of further analysis).

5.5 Research proposals

Research proposals are prepared by research agencies in response to the research brief. In structure, a research proposal is similar to the research brief, but it will be much more detailed in certain parts.

(a) **Background**. This sets out the agency's understanding of the client company, its products and services, its market place and so on, and its understanding of why the research is required. If the agency has misunderstood the brief, this will be clear to the client.

(b)   **Objectives**. These will probably be much the same as those in the brief, although the agency's understanding of research techniques may have helped to define them more precisely still.

(c)   **Approach and method**. How the agency proposes to carry out the research, what methods will be used, where the sample will be taken from and so on.

(d)   **Reports**. How the final information will be presented, whether interim reports will be made, and so on.

(e)   **Timing**: how long the research will take and how it will be broken down into separate stages if appropriate.

(f)   **Fees and expenses**: this is self-explanatory.

(g)   **Personal CVs** of the main agency personnel who will be involved in the project.

(h)   **Relevant experience/references**: the agency will wish to assure the client that it is capable of carrying out the research, so it will include information about similar projects undertaken in the past, and possibly details of previous clients who are willing to testify to the competence of the agency.

Contractual details will set out the agency's terms of trade, and clarify matters such as ownership of the data collected.

5.6 Reviewing the research proposal

The research proposal should be reviewed very carefully, since it will form the basis of the contractual relationship with an external supplier and, even if internal resources are used, it must demonstrate that the proposed activity will meet the objectives set for the project.

Generally, a full assessment of a research proposal will inevitably spill over into an assessment of the agency making it, since it is necessary to be convinced not only that the details of the proposal are appropriate but also that the agency is capable of doing the work concerned, subject to the usual constraints of time, cost and quality. A proposal might thus be assessed against a number of criteria. Here are some examples.

(a)   The **methodology** proposed must be judged capable of achieving the overall objectives.

(b)   The agency must be considered **capable of carrying out its proposal**, both in its technical resources and in its ability to deploy and control their use.

(c)   The agency must be considered to be appropriately **stable** commercially and legally.

(d)   Proper attention must be paid to both **ethics and legal compliance**.

(e)   There must be proper and appropriate arrangements for **liaison and problem-solving** between the agency and the client.

(f)   **Time**, **quality** and **cost** constraints must be satisfied.

Assessment may be carried out on an entirely qualitative basis, especially when the bidding agencies are well-known to the client. However, some form of scoring may be useful where some of the bidders are unknown or the project requirements and selection criteria are particularly complex. When scoring is used, it is usual to weight each criterion and then score against the weight given. Thus, using the criteria outlined above, percentage weights might be allocated as shown below.

Criterion	Percentage weight
Methodology	30
Capability	25
Supplier stability	15
Compliance	10
Liaison	20

Any or all of the time, cost and quality constraints may be regarded as **imperatives**; that is they are absolute, non-negotiable factors and will be built into the contract on that basis, rather than being criteria for scoring.

6 Research reports

6.1 The audience thinking sequence

Wilson (2006) suggests that the researcher should take account of the typical 'thinking sequence' that people go through when others are communicating with them.

(a)   **Respect the client's importance**: in other words don't waste their time with irrelevant, badly structured or presented, over-long information.

(b)   **Consider the client's needs**: the client needs to make a marketing decision.

(c)   **Demonstrate how your information helps the client**: relate the research findings to the original objectives.

(d)   **Explain the detail that underpins your information**: why should your findings be believed? Because you have evidence that 'Nine out of ten dogs prefer ...' or whatever. This is the place for tables and charts, apt quotes from respondents and so on.

(e)   **Remind the client of the key points**.

(f)   **Suggest what the client should do now**: there will usually be a variety of options. It is the client's decision, but it is usual to give recommendations.

The researcher knows more about the subject matter of the report or presentation than the report user. It is important that this information should be communicated impartially, so that the report user can make his own judgements.

(a)   Any assumptions, evaluations and recommendations should be clearly signalled as such.

(b)   Points should not be over-weighted (or omitted as irrelevant) without honestly evaluating how objective the selection is.

(c)   Facts and findings should be balanced against each other.

(d)   A firm conclusion should, if possible, be reached. It should be clear how and why it was reached.

The researcher must also **recognise the needs and abilities of the audience**.

(a)   Beware of jargon, overly technical terms and specialist knowledge the user may not share.

(b)   Keep your vocabulary, sentence and paragraph structures as simple as possible, for clarity (without patronising an intelligent user).

(c)   Bear in mind the type and level of detail that will interest the user and be relevant to his/her purpose.

(d)   The audience may range from senior manager to junior operational staff to complete layman (a non-executive director, say). Your vocabulary, syntax and presentation, the amount of detail you can go into, the technical matter you can include and the formality of your report structure should all be influenced by such concerns.

6.2 Report layout and structure

Various techniques can be used to make the content of a research report easy to identify and digest.

- The material in the report should be in a logical order
- The relative importance of points should be signalled by headings
- Each point may be numbered in some way to help with cross-reference
- The document should be easy on the eye, helped by different font sizes, bold, italics, capitals, spacing and so on.

A typical report structure will use some or all of the conventions described below.

(a)   **Headings**. There should be a hierarchy of headings: there is an overall title and the report as a whole is divided into sections. Within each section main points have a heading in bold capitals, sub-points have a heading in bold lower-case and sub-sub-points have a heading in italics. (Three levels of headings within a main section is usually considered the maximum number that readers can cope with.) It is not necessary to underline headings.

(b) **References**. Sections are lettered, A, B and so on. Main points are numbered 1, 2 etc, and within each division paragraphs are numbered 1.1, 1.2, 2.1, 2.2. Sub-paragraphs inherit their references from the paragraph above. For instance the first sub-paragraph under paragraph 1.2 is numbered 1.2.1.

(c) **Fonts**. Word processors offer you a wealth of fonts these days, but it is best to avoid the temptation. It is often a good idea to put headings in a different font to the main text, but stop there.

A detailed report on an extensive research study may run to many pages, and may, therefore, require these elements.

(a) **Title page** (also giving contact information).

(b) A **list of contents**: the major headings and sub-headings. Most word processing software can produce these automatically.

(c) A **summary** of findings (to give the reader an initial idea of what the report is about). This is usually called the **executive summary**, the implication being that senior managers don't have time to read it all.

(d) **Introduction/problem definition**: this is likely to be very similar to the rationale and objectives set out in the research brief and proposal.

(e) **Research method (and limitations)**: again this is likely to be similar to the equivalent section in the proposal, although it must be updated if anything had to be changed during the implementation of the research or if the research did not go to plan (lower than expected response rates and so on).

(f) **Research findings**: this is the main body of the report.

(g) **Conclusions**: this section should point out the implications of the findings for the client with reference to the initial problem.

(h) Supporting **appendices**: these might include the questionnaire used or the original discussion document, more detailed tables of figures, lists of secondary sources used and so on. Appendices contain subsidiary detailed material, that may well be of interest to some readers, but which might lessen the impact of the findings if presented in full detail in the body of the report.

(i) Possibly, an **index**.

7 Presenting findings

7.1 Tables

Tables present data in rows and columns. This form of presentation makes it easier to understand large amounts of data. A railway timetable is a familiar example.

Tables are a simple way of presenting numerical information. Figures are displayed, and can be compared with each other: relevant totals, subtotals, percentages can also be presented as a summary for analysis.

A table is two-dimensional (rows and columns): so it can only show two variables: a sales analysis for a year, for example, might have rows for months, and columns for products.

 WORK BASED PROJECT TIP   Format and presentation

You are likely to present data in tabular form very often. Here are the key points to remember.

(a) The table should have a clear **title**.

(b) All columns and rows should be clearly **labelled**.

(c) Where appropriate, there should be **sub-totals** and a **right-hand total column** for comparison.

(d) A total figure is often advisable at the **bottom of each column** of figures also, for comparison. It is usual to double-underline totals at the foot of columns.

(e) **Numbers** should be **right-aligned** and they are easier to read if you use the **comma separator** for thousands.

(f)   **Decimal points should line up**, either by using a decimal tab or by adding extra noughts (the latter is preferable, in our opinion).

(g)   A grid or border is optional: see what looks best and is easiest to read.

(h)   Tables should not be packed with too much data. If you try to get too much in, the information presented will be difficult to read.

7.2 Line graphs

In business, line graphs are usually used to illustrate **trends over time** of figures such as sales or customer complaints. It is conventional to show **time** on the **horizontal** axis. By using different symbols for the plotted points, or preferably by using different colours, several lines can be drawn on a line graph before it gets too overcrowded, and that means that **several trends** (for example, the sales performance of different products) can be compared.

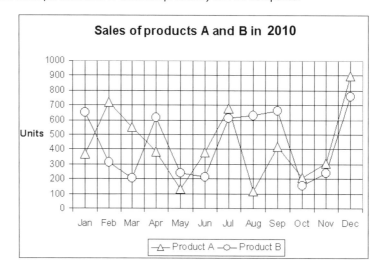

The scale of the vertical axis should be just large enough for you to tell with reasonable accuracy the sales figure at any given point during the period. In the example above we have used a scale of 100 and you can tell, for instance that sales of product A in April were a little less than 400.

7.3 Charts

7.3.1 Bar charts

The bar chart is one of the most common methods of visual presentation. Data is shown in the form of bars which are the same in width but variable in height. Each bar represents a different item, for example, the annual production cost of different products or the number of hours required to produce a product by different workteams.

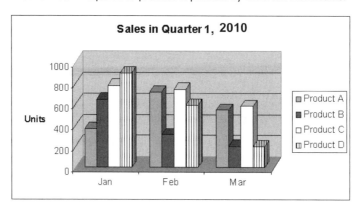

As you can see, here we are more interested in comparing a few individual items in a few individual months (although you can still get a visual impression of trends over time).

7.3.2 Pie charts

A pie chart illustrates the **relative** sizes of the things that make up a total.

Pie charts are most effective where the number of slices is small enough to keep the chart simple, and where the difference in the size of the slices is large enough for the eye to judge without too much extra information.

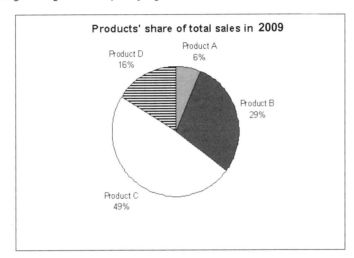

7.4 Flow charts, organisation charts and other labelled diagrams

Flow charts and organisation charts are useful ways of presenting and summarising information that involves a series of **steps** and **choices** and/or **relationships** between the different items.

On the following pages there are some examples of this type of presentation. If you choose any of these forms of presentation here are some points to bear in mind.

(a)   Be consistent in your use of layout and symbols (and colours, if used). For instance, in our flow chart example below a decision symbol is consistently a diamond with italic text; a YES decision consistently flows downwards; a NO decision consistently flows to the right.

(b)   Keep the number of connecting lines to a minimum and avoid lines that 'jump over' each other at all costs.

(c)   Keep the labels or other text brief and simple.

(d)   Hand-drawn diagrams should be as neat and legible as possible. If they are likely to be seen by a lot of people (not just your team) it is better to use a business graphics programme like Microsoft Visio.

(e)   Everyone can draw ... but only so well. If you are not expert you can waste an enormous amount of time playing with computer graphics. If it needs to be really beautifully presented and you are not an expert, sketch it quickly by hand, and then give it to a professional!

7.4.1 A flowchart

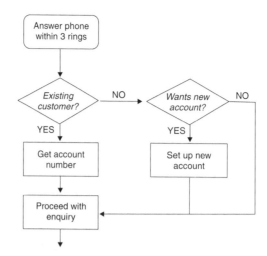

7.4.2 An organisation chart

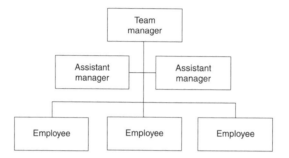

7.5 Pictograms

A pictogram is a simple graphic image in which the **data is represented by a picture or symbol**, with a clear key to the items and quantities intended. Different pictures can be used on the same pictogram to represent different elements of the data. For example, a pictogram showing the number of people employed by an organisation might use pictures of … people!

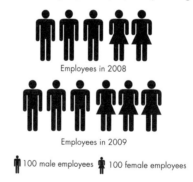

Employees in 2008

Employees in 2009

100 male employees   100 female employees

You can see quite easily that the workforce has grown and that the organisation employs far more female workers than before.

Pictograms present data in a simple and appealing way.

- The symbols must be clear and simple.
- There should be a key showing the number that each symbol represents.
- Larger quantities are shown by more symbols, not bigger symbols.

Bear in mind, however, that pictograms are **not appropriate** if you need to give **precise** figures. You can use portions of a symbol to represent smaller quantities, but there are limits to what you can do.

 *150 female employees*

 Over 100 employees, mostly male. But how many others and what sex are they?

7.6 Product positioning maps

Although they may be called **'maps'** these are really a form of **scatter diagram**. **Two key attributes** of a product are taken and competing products are graded to fit between the extremes of possessing an attribute or not possessing it.

For example, a package delivery service may be **fast** or **slow**, and it may deal with **large** or **small** packages.

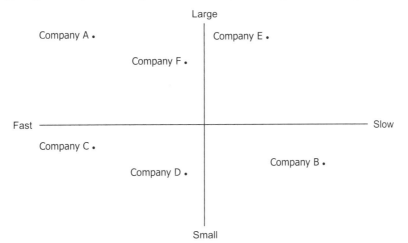

ACTIVITY 2  application

Interpret the diagram above.

7.7 Spreadsheets

Spreadsheets were originally developed as aids to calculation. They have since been developed into extremely sophisticated computer applications that can be used for a wide range of purposes that require computation and other manipulation of data. They are frequently used for purposes that involve very little computation, such as forms design and the presentation of tabulated data of all kinds. When they are used for computational purposes, great care must be taken with their design, since it is very easy when designing formulae to make syntax errors that are invisible to users.

8 Correlation and regression

WORK BASED PROJECT TIP Concept

Correlation and regression are two very simple aspects of statistical analysis. It is not appropriate for you to become practised in the relevant calculations, but you should understand the significance of the terms when they are used in a marketing research context.

8.1 Correlation

Two variables are said to be correlated if a change in the value of one variable is accompanied by a change in the value of another variable. This is what is meant by **correlation**.

Here are two examples of correlation.

*   A person's height and weight
*   The distance of a journey and the time it takes to make it

One way of showing the correlation between two related variables is on a **scatter diagram**, plotting a number of pairs of data on the graph. For example, a scatter diagram showing monthly selling costs against the volume of sales for a 12-month period might be as follows.

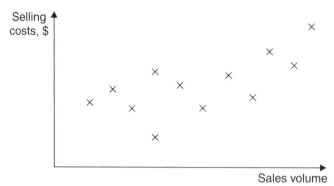

The **independent** variable (the cause) is plotted on the **horizontal** (x) axis and the **dependent** variable (the effect) is plotted on the **vertical** (y) axis.

This scattergraph suggests that there is some correlation between selling costs and sales volume, so that as sales volume rises, selling costs tend to rise as well.

Two variables might be perfectly correlated, partly correlated or uncorrelated. Correlation can be positive or negative.

These differing degrees of correlation can be illustrated by scattergraphs (scatter diagrams).

Perfect correlation

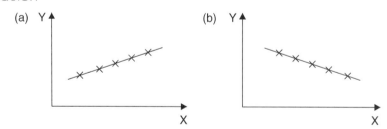

All the pairs of values lie on a straight line. An exact **linear relationship** exists between the two variables.

Partial correlation

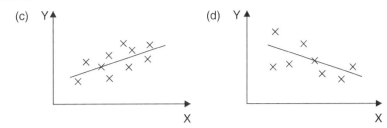

In (c), although there is no exact relationship, low values of X tend to be associated with low values of Y, and high values of X with high values of Y.

In (d) again, there is no exact relationship, but low values of X tend to be associated with high values of Y and vice versa.

No correlation

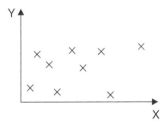

The values of these two variables are not correlated with each other.

Correlation, whether perfect or partial, can be **positive** or **negative**.

 KEY CONCEPT  concept

- **Positive correlation** means that low values of one variable are associated with low values of the other, and high values of one variable are associated with high values of the other.

- **Negative correlation** means that low values of one variable are associated with high values of the other, and high values of one variable with low values of the other.

The **degree of correlation** between two variables is measured by **Pearson's correlation coefficient, r**. The nearer r is to +1 or −1, the stronger the relationship. Pearson's coefficient is calculated using a complex formula. The correct use of this formula is a rather specialised technique and we will not discuss it further.

Correlation coefficient, $r = \dfrac{n\sum XY - \sum X \sum Y}{\sqrt{[n\sum X^2 - (\sum X)^2][n\sum Y^2 - (\sum Y)^2]}}$

Where X and Y represent pairs of data for two variables X and Y
   n = the number of pairs of data used in the analysis

The correlation coefficient, r must always fall between −1 and +1. If you get a value outside this range you have made a mistake.

- r = +1 means that the variables are **perfectly positively correlated**
- r = −1 means that the variables are **perfectly negatively correlated**
- r = 0 means that the variables are **uncorrelated**

Here is an example of the use of Pearson's correlation coefficient. A company wants to know if the money they spend on advertising is effective in creating sales. The following data have been collected.

Monthly advertising expenditure $'000	Sales in following month $'000
1.2	132.5
0.9	98.5
1.6	154.3
2.1	201.4
1.6	161.0

If we calculate the value of r we find it is 0.992. This is very close to 1, therefore there is a strong positive correlation and sales are dependent on advertising expenditure.

8.2 The coefficient of determination, r^2

Unless the correlation coefficient r is exactly or very nearly +1, −1 or 0, its meaning or significance is a little unclear. For example, if the correlation coefficient for two variables is +0.8, this would tell us that the variables are positively correlated, but the correlation is not perfect. It would not really tell us much else. A more meaningful analysis is available from **the square of the correlation coefficient, r**, which is called the **coefficient of determination, r^2**.

In the example above, r = 0.992, therefore r^2 = 0.984. This means that over 98% of variations in sales can be explained by the passage of time, leaving 0.016 (less than 2%) of variations to be explained by other factors.

Similarly, if the correlation coefficient between a company's output volume and maintenance costs was 0.9, r^2 would be 0.81, meaning that 81% of variations in maintenance costs could be explained by variations in output volume, leaving only 19% of variations to be explained by other factors (such as the age of the equipment).

Note, however, that if r^2 = 0.81, we would say that 81% of **the variations in y can be explained by variations in x**. We do not necessarily conclude that 81% of variations in y are *caused* by the variations in x. We must beware of reading too much significance into our statistical analysis.

8.3 Correlation and causation

If two variables are strongly correlated, either positively or negatively, this may be due to **pure chance** or there may be a **reason** for it. The larger the number of pairs of data collected, the less likely it is that the correlation is due to chance, although that possibility should never be ignored entirely.

If there is a reason, it may not be **causal**. For example, monthly net income is well correlated with monthly credit to a person's bank account, for the logical (rather than causal) reason that for most people the one equals the other.

Even if there is a causal explanation for a correlation, it does not follow that variations in the value of one variable cause variations in the value of the other. For example, sales of ice cream and of sunglasses are well correlated, not because of a direct causal link but because the weather influences both variables.

8.4 Lines of best fit

Correlation enables us to determine the **strength of any relationship between two variables** but it does not offer us any method of **forecasting** values for one variable, Y, given values of another variable, X.

If we assume that there is a **linear relationship** between the two variables and we determine the **equation of a straight line (Y = a + bX)** which is a good fit for the available data plotted on a scattergraph, we can use the equation for forecasting. We do this by substituting values for X into the equation and deriving values for Y.

There are a number of techniques for estimating the equation of a line of best fit.

The scattergraph method involves the use of judgement to draw what seems to be a line of best fit through plotted data. Suppose we have the following pairs of data about output and costs.

Month	Output '000 units	Costs £'000
1	20	82
2	16	70
3	24	90
4	22	85
5	18	73

(a) These pairs of data can be plotted on a **scattergraph** (the **horizontal** axis representing the **independent** variable and the **vertical** axis the **dependent**) and a line of best fit might be judged as the one shown below. It is drawn to pass through the middle of the data points, thereby having as many data points below the line as above it.

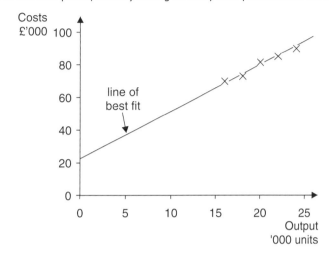

(b) A **formula for the line of best fit** can be found. In our example, suppose that we read the following data from the graph.

(i) When X = 0, Y = 22,000. This must be the value of **a** in the formula Y = a + bX.

(ii) When X = 20,000, Y = 82,000. Since Y = a + bX, and a = 22,000, 82,000 = 22,000 + (b × 20,000)

b × 20,000 = 60,000

b = 3

(c) In this example the estimated equation from the scattergraph is Y = 22,000 + 3X.

Once we have our equation we can use it to make forecasts. For example, using the same data, if we wanted to predict costs at a certain level of output (say 13,000 units), the value of 13,000 could be substituted into the equation Y = 22,000 + 3X and an estimate of costs made.

If X = 13, Y = 22,000 + (3 × 13,000)

∴ Y = €61,000

Predictions can be made directly from the scattergraph, but this depends on how accurately we can read the scale on our graph.

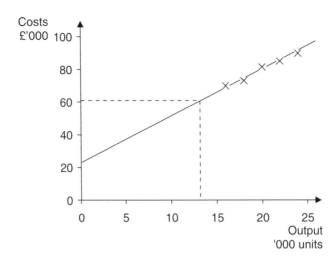

The prediction of the cost of producing 13,000 units from the scattergraph is €61,000. Note that this is an example of **extrapolation**, in that it relates to a point on the line of best fit that lies **outside the range of the original data** (16,000 to 24,000 units). If we had sought a cost estimate for a level of production that lay within that range, this would have been **interpolation**.

Extrapolation is considered to be less reliable that interpolation, since there is no evidence that the observed relationship holds true outside the observed range.

8.5 Linear regression analysis

Drawing the line of best fit in our example was fairly simple because the plotted points on our scattergraph were pretty nicely aligned. Unfortunately, this is rarely the case in real life. However, a mathematical technique called linear regression analysis or the method of least squares can be used to estimate a line of best fit. Once an equation for a line of best fit has been determined, forecasts can be made in the usual way. Once again, this is a rather specialised technique to use and we will not discuss it further.

The **least squares method of linear regression analysis** involves using the following formulae for a and b in Y = a + bX.

$$b = \frac{n\sum XY - \sum X\sum Y}{n\sum X^2 - (\sum X)^2}$$

$$a = \overline{Y} - b\overline{X}$$

Where n   is the number of pairs of data

   $\overline{X}$ is the mean X value of all the pairs of data

   $\overline{Y}$ is the mean Y value of all the pairs of data

Learning objectives	Covered
1 Prepare a marketing research brief for a given problem	☑ Scope of research
	☑ Stages of research
	☑ Ethical issues
	☑ Market Research industry
2 Evaluate a marketing research proposal	☑ Research suppliers
	☑ Research proposals
3 Recommend effective methods for presenting marketing information	☑ Research reports
	☑ Analytical tools
	☑ Presentation methods

1   What does DODCAR stand for?

2   List the eight data protection principles.

3   What are five disadvantages of in-house market research departments?

4   What is meant by 'rationale' in the context of a research brief?

5   Why should an agency include a discussion of the background to the project in a research proposal?

6   What kind of graphic is used to show how a variable changes over time?

7   A graphic aid used to show steps and relationships between processes and events is a .... chart.

8   If represents $100m, draw a pictogram for $550m.

9   .... correlation means that low values of one variable are associated with low values of the other, and high values of one variable are associated with high values of the other, while .... correlation means that low values of one variable are associated with high values of the other, and high values of one variable with low values of the other.

10   • Perfect positive correlation, r = ...
     • Perfect negative correlation, r = ...
     • No correlation, r = ...

11   If the correlation coefficient of a set of data is 0.95, what is the coefficient of determination and how is it interpreted?

1   We've not given you enough information to enable you to be too precise. You would have much more information in real life, of course. Your objectives might look something like this:

To collect information about the market for a new line of cruelty-free cosmetics with a view to drawing up and implementing a marketing plan.

(a)   The size of market, value, number of items sold, number of customers
(b)   The leading companies and their respective market share
(c)   The breakdown of market by type of cosmetic (lipstick, eye shadow and so on)
(d)   Current consumer trends in buying cruelty-free cosmetics (price, colour and so on)
(e)   Consumer preferences in terms of packaging and presentation
(f)   The importance to consumers of having a choice of colours within the range
(g)   The influence on consumers of advertising and promotion that emphasises the cruelty-free nature of products

Remember that objectives need to be SMART.

Research objectives	Example
Specific	Size of market for *cruelty-free* cosmetics not cosmetics in general
Measurable	Respective market share in percentage terms of leading players
Attainable	Good guidance on attitudes to cruelty-free products rather than absolute confidence
Results focussed	Interviewing technique is left to the experts
Time-bound	Information within three months so product can be marketed for Christmas

2   **Company details**

Company A specialises in delivering large packages quickly

Company B delivers smaller packages slowly

Company C delivers smaller packages quickly

Company D delivers fairly small packages slightly more quickly than average

Company E delivers very large packages very slowly

Company F delivers medium to large packages more quickly than average

1   Definition, Objectives, Design, Collect, Analyse, Report. In other words the marketing research process.

2   Data must be:

- Fairly and lawfully processed
- Processed for limited purposes
- Adequate, relevant and not excessive
- Accurate
- Not kept longer than necessary
- Processed in accordance with individual's rights
- Secure
- Not transferred to countries that do not have adequate data protection laws

3   **Five from**

(1)   There is a danger of **overstretching current resources** and adversely affecting other projects.

(2)   There is a risk of developing an **inappropriate programme**, yielding insufficient or poor quality data with inadequate analysis and control.

(3)   If additional **training or recruitment** is required this could prove expensive and time consuming.

(4)   **Bias** could result from using staff with pre-conceived views.

(5)   **Company politics** may influence the results.

(6)   Considerable **computing resources** with appropriate software packages would be required to analyse the data.

4   How the need for information arose and what the users intend to do with it.

5   To set out the agency's understanding of the client's problem and needs in order to avoid costly mistakes.

6   A line graph

7   Flow chart

8   💰 💰 💰 💰 💰 💰

9   Positive, negative

10
- $r = +1$
- $r = -1$
- $r = 0$

The correlation coefficient, r, must always fall within the range -1 to $+1$.

11   Correlation coefficient = r = 0.95

Coefficient of determination = $r^2 = 0.95^2 = 0.9025$ or 90.25%

This tells us that over 90% of the variations in the dependent variable (Y) can be explained by variations in the independent variable, X.

Jobber, D (2010) <u>Principles and Practice of Marketing</u>, 6th edition, McGraw Hill, Maidenhead.

Wilson, A (2006) <u>Marketing research: an integrated approach</u>, 2nd edition, Financial Times/Prentice Hall, London.

Chapter 3

Building the business case
for marketing projects

Topic list

Introduction

All business is essentially a matter of using resources in order to create value. Resources are, by definition, scarce and their use within business organisations is therefore carefully controlled. A major part of management work at any level thus consists of deciding how available resources would be best employed. A **business case** is a reasoned exposition justifying the commitment of resources. It may be prepared as part of the control process for investment and, indeed, will often form part of the basis for control. However, the most common purpose of a business case is to be detailed support for a bid for resources under the control of a particular decision-making group. Marketers are likely to encounter this scenario regularly, since much marketing work takes the form of discrete programmes and projects and even continuing activities, such as call centre operations, are likely to be subject to processes of annual budget and review.

Doyle's (2008) concept of value-based marketing provides a substantial foundation for the consideration of the marketing business case. We will therefore start off with a review of Doyle's analysis before continuing with a discussion of business case objectives and methods. We will then deal with forecasting. The syllabus requirement here is to

'critically evaluate and assess the marketing potential for business case activities, including consideration of the assessments required to achieve the potential proposition'.

Syllabus-linked learning objectives

By the end of the chapter you will be able to:

Learning objectives	Syllabus link
1 Define business case objectives for marketing plans and projects	2.1
2 Discuss and use forecasting techniques in the preparation of a business case	2.2
3 Use market research information to assess and evaluate customer groups relevant to the business case (market segmentation element)	2.3

1 Shareholder value analysis

Shareholder value analysis (SVA) is a method of approaching the problem of business control by focusing on the creation of value for shareholders. Independent financial analysts measure the **value offered by a company's shares** by considering the **market value** of all the shares in existence (the market capitalisation), in the light of the **company's prospects** for generating both cash and capital growth in the future. If the current market capitalisation is less than the estimate of actual value, then the shares are undervalued. Investment is necessary to produce either assets that grow in value or actual cash surpluses, so the process of shareholder value analysis is essentially one of estimating the likely effectiveness of the company's **current investment decisions**. It is thus both a system for judging the worth of current investment proposals and for judging the performance of the managers who are responsible for the company's performance.

In the past, marketing managers have tended to pursue purely **marketing objectives**, such as sales growth, market share, customer satisfaction and brand recognition. None of these marketing objectives *necessarily* translates into increased shareholder value, and as a result, marketing has suffered from a lack of perceived relevance to true business value. An emphasis on profitability as a measure of success has led to a certain amount of short-termism in strategic management, with an emphasis on **containing and reducing current costs** in order to boost current profits. Unfortunately, this approach tends to underestimate the longer-term effect of such action and can lead to corporate decline. Investment in **intangible assets** such as brands can make a positive contribution to long-term shareholder value.

1.1 Computing value

According to Doyle (2008), the extent of a company's success may be measured in two ways. The first is by using the concept of **economic profit** (trademarked by Stern Stewart and Company as *Economic Value Added*®). The expression **economic profit** is used to distinguish the measure from **accounting profit**, which is computed according to the strict rules of accountancy. These feature, in particular, the principle of **prudence**. This makes it impossible for accounting profit to recognise spending on pure research, for instance, as an investment in an asset, since there is no guarantee that it will ever produce anything worth having; the same would be true of much marketing spending on building long-term effectiveness.

Economic profit is created when the return on a company's capital employed exceeds the cost of that capital.

Economic profit = NOPAT − (capital employed × cost of capital)

NOPAT is net operating profit after tax. Cost of capital may be calculated as the **weighted average cost of capital**, which takes account of both the expectations of the shareholders who have provided **share capital** and the lenders who have provided **loans**. (Buying shares generally entails greater risk than making a loan, so shareholders generally demand higher returns than lenders. This is why a weighted average figure must be used.)

Economic profit is useful for examining the company's current and past performance, but is less useful for assessing future prospects. For that purpose it is more appropriate to use the **cash flow approach**. Be aware that both the economic profit method and the cash flow method should produce the same result when applied to a particular company.

The **cash flow approach** may be used to estimate the degree of economic value a company may be expected to create in the future. It is based on an estimation of likely future **cash flows**, both positive and negative, as indicated in the corporate plans. A cash flow is simply a sum of money paid or received by the company. This is easier to calculate than to compute future NOPAT because it is far less complex and depends on far fewer variables.

1.1.1 Discounting cash flows

Because the SVA technique depends very much on the estimation of future cash flows arising from current investments, it is necessary to use **discounting arithmetic** in order to make the necessary judgements. We provide an explanation of discounting in the Annex to this chapter.

Business risk. Some businesses are inherently riskier than others: the degree of risk can be measured by the degree of predictability that attaches to its expected cash flows. A low risk business will have steady income from period to period, without any unexpected highs and lows. A high-risk business will have returns that vary wildly and unexpectedly from period to period, though its total long-term return may be as great or greater than the low-risk operation. Generally, investors are risk averse and, as a result, they demand higher returns from high-risk businesses than from low-risk ones. The high-risk business must, therefore, use a higher cost of capital in its shareholder value analysis than the low-risk business.

ACTIVITY 1

application

Make a list of five generic types of business and sort them in order of riskiness. Remember, risk here is about the steadiness or otherwise of cash income.

1.2 Value-based management

Doyle (2003), tells us that business success should be measured by shareholder value analysis because of the property rights of shareholders and the 'pressures to oust management that does not deliver competitive returns'. Purely marketing objectives are no longer acceptable to investors or the analysts whose reports they rely on. What Doyle calls **value-based management** is based on three elements.

(a)   A **belief** that maximising shareholder returns is the objective of the firm.

(b)   The **principles**, or strategic foundations of value are first, to target those market segments where profits can be made and second, to develop competitive advantage 'that enables both the customer and the firm to create value'.

(c)   The **processes** 'concern how strategies should be developed, resources allocated and performance measured'.

SVA is particularly appropriate for judging strategic investment decisions and applies the same principles that have been used for appraising investment in such tangible assets as premises and plant for many years. It is necessary to consider both the cash costs of the strategic investment to be made, and the positive cash flows that are expected to be produced by it. These may then be discounted to a net present value (NPV) using an appropriate cost of capital, and a judgement made on the basis of the NPV. Any specifically marketing proposal, such as an enhanced advertising spend or a new discount structure may be assessed in this way, though it will almost certainly be necessary to take advice from the finance function on the process.

Estimating the value of such investments forms one part of basic shareholder value analysis. Doyle also recommends that when considering the total value of a business, it is also necessary to consider the probable **residual value** of the business in the more distant future, outside the normal planning horizon, which he suggests is five years. This assumes no special competitive advantage from current investments and simply uses the cost of capital as an estimate of future earnings.

1.2.1 Marketing assets

Value-based management means that purely marketing investment proposals will be judged as described above. It will be necessary for marketing managers to justify their spending requests in such terms, on the basis that such spending is not a cost burden to be minimised but an investment in intangible assets such as the four that Doyle suggests.

- Marketing knowledge
- Brands
- Customer loyalty
- Strategic relationships with channel partners

The obstacle that lies in the path of this approach to marketing use of SVA is the common perception that marketing spending is merely a cost to be controlled and minimised. The onus is on marketing managers to demonstrate that their budgets do in fact create assets that provide competitive advantage for the business and that the benefits exceed the costs.

1.3 Value drivers

Doyle suggests that it is possible to identify the factors that are critical to the creation of shareholder value. These he calls **value drivers**; he divides them into three categories.

- Financial
- Marketing
- Organisational

It is important to remember that **the financial drivers should not be targeted directly**: they are objectives, not the components of strategy. The company influences them by the proper management of the **marketing** and **organisational** drivers.

1.4 Financial value drivers

There are four drivers of financial value.

- Cash flow volume
- Cash flow timing
- Cash flow risk
- Cash flow sustainability

1.4.1 Cash flow volume

Clearly, the higher that positive cash flows are and the lower negative cash flows are, the greater the potential for creating value.

Profitability. In the most simple terms, profit margin is measured by net operating profit after tax (NOPAT). NOPAT can be increased in three ways.

(a) **Higher prices**. Marketing strategies such as building strong brands can enable the charging of premium prices. A particularly powerful route to higher prices is **innovation**, since desirable new products will normally justify increased prices.

(b) **Reduced costs**. Cost reduction depends on increased efficiency in all aspects of the business operation.

(c) **Volume increases**. Other things being equal, volume growth increases the absolute profit margin and may increase the profit rate as well.

Sales growth. If increases in sales volume can be achieved without disproportionate increases in costs or, in particular, excessive discounting, positive cash flows will naturally increase. Increased sales can also bring increased **economies of scale**, which will take the form of reduced costs of all types. Overheads are spread over greater volumes and purchasing discounts reduce the cost of sales.

Investment. Investment provides the resources necessary to do business. These include premises, equipment, stocks, transport and well-trained, experienced staff. However, ill-advised investment can destroy value faster than profitable investment can create it, so any proposal for investment must be judged on its potential for generating acceptable returns. The **net present value** (NPV) approach (described in the Annex to this chapter) is the investment appraisal method best suited to the shareholder value principle, in that any project that has a NPV greater than zero provides a return greater than the cost of capital used in the discounting arithmetic.

1.4.2 Cash flow timing

The further into the future a cash flow occurs, the lower its present value. If positive cash flows can be achieved in the near future and negative ones delayed, the company benefits. This is why companies and individuals put off paying their bills for as long as possible. Buying on credit and selling for cash is another approach.

Doyle (2008) gives five examples of ways that marketing managers can accelerate cash flows.

(a)   **Faster new product development** processes, including the use of cross-functional teams and conducting projects concurrently rather than consecutively.

(b)   **Accelerated market penetration** through pre-marketing campaigns, early trial promotions and word-of-mouth campaigns using early adopters.

(c)   **Network effects**: that is, achieving market status as the industry standard. This is a self-reinforcing, feedback effect in which success leads to even greater success. It was seen, for instance, in the videotape market when *VHS* displaced the technically superior *Betamax*. Aggressive marketing measures to build the installed base are required.

(d)   **Strategic alliances:** speeds up market penetration, normally by providing extra distribution effort.

(e)   **Exploiting brand assets**: new products launched under a suitable, established brand are likely to be more successful than others.

1.4.3 Cash flow risk

The higher the degree of **risk** associated with future cash flows, the greater the proportion of them that will not actually come to pass. High risk can produce low returns as easily as high ones. Apart from this overall averaging effect, there is the disadvantage associated with **infrequent large cash flows**: failure of such a cash flow to occur can have catastrophic consequences. Risk is also associated with timing: the further into the future that a cash flow is expected to occur, the greater the risk associated with it, since there is a greater likelihood of **changed conditions** affecting its eventual value and even whether or not it actually occurs.

Doyle (2008) suggests that the most effective marketing route to reduced cash flow risk is '*to increase customer satisfaction, loyalty and retention*' by deploying such techniques as loyalty programmes and measures to increase satisfaction. Building **good channel relationships** also helps, both by building an element of loyalty based on good service and by sharing information on demand patterns to smooth stock fluctuations.

1.4.4 Cash flow sustainability

A single positive cash flow is useful. A positive cash flow that is repeated at regular intervals is much more useful. Quite apart from the extra cash involved, sustainable cash flows make it easier to plan for the future. Positive cash flows derive from the creation of competitive advantage and a sustainable advantage will lead to sustainable cash flows.

There are many **threats to sustainable profits**, including aggressive competition from copies and substitutes and, particularly in B2B markets, the bargaining power of customers. Part of the role of marketing management is to counter such threats using techniques such as those outlined above in connection with reducing risk.

Sustainable advantage also offers a benefit in the form of **enhanced options** for future development. Just as financial options to buy and sell securities and currency have their own value, so a strategy that creates **real options** for future activity has a value over and above any immediate competitive advantage it may offer. A simple example is the development of a completely new product for a given market that can also be made viable in other markets at low incremental cost. *Richard Branson's* ability to use his brand *Virgin* with almost any consumer product is another example. There are network effects here too, in that as more and more dissimilar *Virgin* products become available, the brand's suitability for use with even more types of product grows.

1.5 Marketing value drivers

Doyle (2008) analyses four marketing value drivers. The first, choice of markets, is only applicable to the large, diversified organisation, but the remaining three apply to all companies.

1.5.1 Choice of markets

A large organisation operating a number of strategic business units (SBUs) must apply a continuing **portfolio analysis** to them. You will be familiar with such portfolio analysis tools as the BCG matrix and the GE business screen from your earlier studies, but you may only have considered their use at **the product level**. Nevertheless, it is both feasible and proper to apply the concept at **the SBU level** in order to determine priorities for investment and policies for exploitation. Doyle (2008) suggests a very simple, one-dimensional classification of SBUs.

(a) **Today's businesses** generate the bulk of current profits and cash, but probably have only modest growth potential. If successful, they attract modest investment for incremental developments; if performing badly they are put right rapidly or sold off.

(b) **Tomorrow's businesses** have high potential and require major investment.

(c) **Options for growth** are the seeds of more distant businesses; such as research projects, market trials and stakes in new, small businesses that are a long way from success. Recognising the worth of such ventures is a difficult task; in the world of venture capital, it is recognised that many good ideas will come to nothing in the end.

A large company needs a suitable mix of the three types of SBU each with its own appropriate strategic objectives, though there may be opportunities for **synergy**, such as the use of common brand names. SBUs that do not fit into one of the categories should be divested.

 MARKETING AT WORK
application

GE to sell 81% stake in airport security unit

General Electric has agreed to sell an 81% stake in its airport security business to *Safran,* the French manufacturer of aviation gear, for $580m.

The accord extends Safran's push into a security market that delivers less cyclical results than its aerospace operations and frees GE, which will retain a 19% stake in the division, to focus on its core fire- and intrusion-detection business.

Justin Baer, Financial Times, 24 April 2009

1.5.2 Target segments

Most customers are not worth selling to. The loyal, long-term customer that pays full price and requires little special service attention is the ideal – but very few fall into this category. Nevertheless, it is appropriate to target this class of customer specifically rather than simply to aim for a large customer base. Desirable customers display four important characteristics.

- They are **strategic** in that their needs match the company's core capabilities.
- They are **significant** in terms of their size or potential for growth.
- They are **profitable**.
- They are **loyal**.

1.5.3 Differential advantage

For purchases other than convenience purchases, customers must have a reason for buying from a particular supplier. **Differential advantage** is created when target customers decide to buy and to remain loyal. Doyle proposes four types of customer, each of which is suited by a particular strategic approach to creating differential advantage.

A strategy of **product leadership** is based on innovation and speed to market. It is the differential advantage that enables a company to sell to **customers who want the latest, most fashionable products**. A good example is *Sony*, with its continuing development of well-designed, expensive customer electronics.

Operational excellence is needed to offer a combination of **customer convenience** and the **lowest prices**. *Wal-Mart* and *Toyota* are good examples of this approach.

Brand superiority is based on careful marketing research and strong and consistent marketing communication. This approach works with customers who identify with the **brand's values** or seek the **reassurance** that brands provide.

A growing segment is made up of customers seeking customised solutions to their specific wants. The appropriate strategy here is **customer intimacy**. This approach is becoming more feasible as information technology developments improve the ability of companies to store and access details of customer habits, needs and preferences.

Note that concentration on one particular strategy does not mean that the others can be neglected. A level of **threshold competence** must be achieved in all four, with one being established as the field of **core competence**.

1.5.4 The marketing mix

The marketing mix is derived from the decisions made about choice of markets, target segments and differential advantage.

1.6 Organisational value drivers

Doyle declares that 'in most situations organisational capabilities and culture are more important than strategy', and goes on to make several comparisons between pairs of companies that use similar strategies in the same industries but with markedly differing degrees of success. The differences arise from the extent to which the companies involved are able to develop and deploy appropriate **core competences** and this in turn is highly conditional upon the **culture** of the organisation and the **attitudes** of the people working in it.

 MARKETING AT WORK application

One of the examples Doyle gives is the contrast between the relative performance of *Singapore Airlines* and *Sabena*. Both '*target business travellers travelling between major international hubs with a value proposition based on service. But Singapore Airlines has been much more successful in delivering high levels of customer service and achieving extraordinary customer satisfaction and loyalty.*'

An important variable is **organisational structure**. In the days of mass marketing, a vertically organised hierarchical form was appropriate for achieving economies of scale and expertise. Companies now seeking to cut overheads, achieve fast response to changing markets and competition and exploit the advantages of a mass customisation approach need something better. Increasingly, advances in IT are producing organisations based on **networks**.

(a)   **Internal networks** take the form of horizontally-oriented, cross-functional teams with responsibility for processes that deliver customer satisfactions. Communication flows freely, making the best use of resources whatever their functional label. This style of working reduces costs, speeds response and improves motivation.

(b)   **External networks** are created when companies withdraw from activities that are not fundamental to their specific value-creating strategy and **concentrate on their core competences**. They buy-in the services they no longer perform for themselves, using the core competences of other companies to support their own. This type of organisation arises under the pressure of new technologies, new markets and new processes that make it difficult for any organisation to do everything well.

The *McKinsey 7S* model, as illustrated below, was designed to show how the various aspects of a business relate to one another. It is a useful example of the way culture fits into an organisation. In particular, it shows the links between the organisation's behaviour and the behaviour of individuals within it.

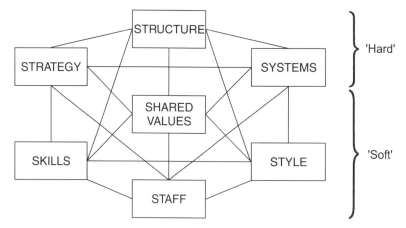

Three of the elements were considered 'hard' originally, but in today's context they are becoming more flexible.

(a)   **Structure**. The organisation structure determines division of tasks in the organisation and the hierarchy of authority from the most senior to junior.

(b)   **Strategy**. Strategy is way in which the organisation plans to outperform its competitors; it will be market-led.

(c)   **Systems**. Systems include the technical systems of accounting, personnel, management information and so on, with particular emphasis on how market-related information is distributed and used.

The McKinsey model suggests that the 'soft' elements are equally important.

(a)   **Shared values** lie at the heart of the organisation and are the guiding principles for the people in it. They are vital for developing the motivation to drive the organisation to achieve.

(b)   **Staff** are the people in the organisation. They have their own complex concerns and priorities. The successful organisation will recruit the right staff and develop their motivation to pursue the right goals.

(c)   **Style** is another aspect of the **corporate culture**, and includes the shared assumptions, ways of working and attitudes of senior management.

(d)   **Skills** are the core competences that enable the company to create value in a particular way.

The importance of the 'soft' elements for success was emphasised by Peters and Waterman in their study of 'excellent' companies.

1.7 Limitations of SVA

Doyle (2008) says that the 'essence of the shareholder value approach is that managers should be evaluated on their ability to develop strategies that earn returns greater than their cost of capital'. He goes on to assert that this approach is superior to traditional performance measures because it avoids emphasis on short-term results and is more appropriate than financial accounting measures for valuing businesses when intangibles such as brands and relationships with customers and suppliers are the primary assets. However, **SVA has its limitations** and managers should be aware of them.

Forecasting. SVA depends absolutely on the accuracy with which future cash flows can be forecast and these in turn depend on the normal parameters of planning such as sales forecasts. The danger is always that the managers responsible for these forecasts will display conscious or unconscious bias, either building slack into their forecasts to produce easily attainable targets or being over-optimistic to please their seniors.

Cost of capital. Calculating an accurate cost of capital is very difficult and the subject of much debate and research by financial management professionals. While the level of **loan interest** is clearly easily available, it can vary from loan to loan and in the case of overdraft finance may vary from time to time. The **cost of share capital** is much more difficult to compute since it is really only accessible through an examination of stock market behaviour and that is extremely complex. A further complication is the issue of **risk premium**. To some extent this is built into the cost of loan and share capital, but where money is allocated internally, management must make up their own minds. All these factors mean that choice of discount rate is very much a matter of judgement and the 'correct' rate may be unknowable to an accuracy of better than plus or minus several percentage points.

Estimating terminal value. When SVA is applied to a business strategy or project, two time periods are considered, divided by the normal planning horizon, which Doyle (2008) suggests should be five years. During the first five years, returns greater than the cost of capital are sought; thereafter, it is assumed that initial competitive advantage will have been eroded away and returns are expected to cover the cost of capital and no more. For this approach to work, it is necessary to estimate the present value of the cash flows from the five-year point onwards. There is no single, accepted way of doing this; business and financial judgement are needed and widely differing estimates can result.

Baseline business value. To calculate the **extra value** created by a given strategy it is necessary to compare two figures: the present value of the company if the strategy is pursued, and the present value if no change is made to current strategy. The latter is the baseline value. Once again, judgement is required in calculating this value, particularly since it may not be possible to maintain the current flow of profit simply by doing more of the same. Indeed, new strategies may be essential if the business is to avoid eventual liquidation.

Options for the future. Options to buy and sell securities, commodities and currencies have been a feature of financial markets for many years. Such options have prices and the way their value changes with time has also been the subject of much debate and research among finance professionals. Companies can create **real options** for themselves by their strategic decisions, but the valuation of such options is not currently possible using the techniques of SVA. A simple example of such an option would arise if a company decided to enter a new foreign market by means of direct exports. The market knowledge and contacts thus generated might well put the company in a strong position to undertake local manufacturing, should it wish to do so. The basic strategy of direct exporting could itself be valued by means of SVA, but it would not be possible to assign a value to the extra value created in the form of the option to manufacture locally.

Market valuation. The aim of the shareholder value approach to strategic management is to reward shareholders for providing financial resources to the company. These rewards take two forms: **dividends** and **capital appreciation**. Dividends are directly affected by the positive cash flows generated by successful strategies; capital appreciation, however, in the form of a rising share price, is not so clearly subject to this effect in the short-term. Longer-term future prospects for positive cash flows explain about 80% of market price movement, but in the shorter-term, markets are heavily influenced by a variety of other extraneous environmental influences. To reduce short-term share price volatility, company senior management must both investigate strategic forecasts very carefully and communicate their longer-term plans to the market.

2 Business case objectives

2.1 Goals, objectives and targets

All business activity must support and be consistent with the organisation's overall strategy. This applies as much to marketing plans and projects as to any other form of activity. One important aspect of this requirement for strategic consistency is that departmental and functional objectives should support the corporate mission. Shareholder value analysis will show how marketing activities can be expected to support the typical corporate objective of maintaining and enhancing shareholder wealth. Within the framework provided by overall value analysis of proposed activity, it is important that subordinate objectives are assessed for their contribution to supporting and enabling the overall departmental or functional objectives.

2.1.1 A hierarchy of objectives

A simple model of the relationship between the various goals, objectives and targets is a **pyramid** analogous to the traditional organisational hierarchy. At the top is the **overall mission**; this is supported by a **small number of wide-ranging goals**, which may correspond to overall departmental or functional responsibilities. Each of these goals is supported in turn by **more detailed, subordinate goals** that correspond, perhaps, to the responsibilities of the senior managers in the function concerned. As we work our way down this pyramid of goals we will find that they will typically become **more detailed** and will relate to **shorter timeframes**.

An important feature of any structure of goals is that there should be **goal congruence**; that is to say, goals that are related to one another should be **mutually supportive**. Goals can be related in several ways:

- **Hierarchically**, as in the pyramid structure outlined above.
- **Functionally**, as when colleagues collaborate on a project.
- **Logistically**, as when resources must be shared or used in sequence.
- In **wider organisational senses**, as when senior executives make decisions about their operational priorities.

A good example of the last category is the tension between long-and short-term priorities in such matters as the need to contain costs while at the same time increasing productivity by investing in improved plant.

 KEY CONCEPT  concept

The words *goal*, *objective* and *target* are used somewhat imprecisely and, to some extent, interchangeably. The suggestions we make below about the usage of these words are only tentative and you should read as widely as you can in order to make your own mind up about how to employ them.

A **goal** is often a longer term overall aspiration: Mintzberg defines **goals** as 'the intentions behind decisions or actions, the states of mind that drive individuals or collectives of individuals called organisations to do what they do.' Goals may be difficult to quantify and it may not be very helpful to attempt to do so. An example of a goal might be to raise productivity in a manufacturing department.

Objectives are often quite specific and well-defined, though they can also embody comprehensive purposes.

Targets are generally expressed in concrete numerical terms and are therefore easily used to measure progress and performance.

2.1.2 Management by objectives

We owe the concept of a hierarchy or cascade of objectives to the great management thinker and writer Peter Drucker, who outlined the system now known as **management by objectives** (MbO) in the middle of the twentieth century. MbO is still in use as a management tool, though no longer promoted as a universal solution. Its importance for this discussion of goals and objectives is that Drucker was the first to suggest that objectives should be SMART, thereby contrasting objectives with mission statements which tend to be more open-ended. This acronym originally stood for the qualities listed below.

Specific   **M**easurable   **A**chievable   **R**ealistic   **T**ime-related

Today, *realistic* is often replaced with *results–focused*, for two reasons.

(a)   The pursuit of innovation as a route to competitive advantage makes it very important that managerial attention is directed towards **achieving results** rather than just **administering established processes**.

(b)   Realistic means much the same thing as achievable, anyway.

There are other variants: *achievable* may be replaced with *attainable*, which has an almost identical meaning, and *relevant* (meaning appropriate to the group or individual concerned) has been proposed as a third option for *R*. Notice that whichever version you prefer, a SMART objective corresponds very closely with our description of the way the word *target* is commonly used.

Functions of objectives

(a)   **Planning**: objectives define what the plan is about.

(b)   **Responsibility**: objectives define the responsibilities of managers and departments.

(c)   **Integration**: objectives should support one another and be consistent; this integrates the efforts of different departments.

(d)   **Motivation**: the first step in motivation is knowing what is to be done. Objectives must be created for all areas of performance.

(e)   **Evaluation**: performance is assessed against objectives and control exercised.

2.2 Primary and secondary objectives

Some objectives are more important than others. In the hierarchy of objectives, there is a **primary corporate objective** and other **secondary objectives** which should combine to ensure the achievement of the overall corporate objective.

For example, if a company sets itself an objective of growth in profits, as its primary aim, it will then have to develop strategies by which this primary objective can be achieved. An objective must then be set for each individual strategy. Secondary objectives might then be concerned with sales growth, continual technological innovation, customer service, product quality, efficient resource management or reducing the company's reliance on debt capital.

Corporate objectives should relate to the business as a whole.

- Profitability
- Market share
- Growth
- Cash flow

- Customer satisfaction
- The quality of the firm's products
- Human resources
- Innovation

 MARKETING AT WORK  application

British Airways publicity once indicated the following corporate goals. What do you think of them? Which is most important? Will they have changed since the events of September 11 2001 and the subsequent turmoil in the airline industry?

- Safety and security
- Strong and consistent financial performance
- Global reach
- Superior services

- Good value for money
- Healthy working environment
- Good neighbourliness

'Overall, our aim is to be the best and most successful company in the airline industry.'

2.3 Financial objectives

For businesses in the UK, as Doyle (2008) says, the primary objective is concerned with the **return to shareholders**.

(a) A satisfactory return for a company must be sufficient to **reward shareholders adequately** in the long-run for the risks they take. The reward will take the form of **profits**, which can lead to **dividends** or to **increases in the market value** of the shares.

(b) The size of return which is adequate for ordinary shareholders will vary according to the risk involved.

 WORK BASED PROJECT TIP concept

There are different ways of expressing a financial objective in quantitative terms. Financial objectives would include the following.

- Profitability
- Return on investment (ROI) or return on capital employed (ROCE)
- Share price, earnings per share (EPS), dividends
- Growth

Profit and return on investment

Profit can be a misleading idea. As we saw in our discussion of shareholder value, when the word is used with precision, it relates to what is largely an accounting concept. In any event, a figure for profit is of little use without some idea of the resources used in generating it. Finance staff will therefore generally be more interested in **return on investment** than profit alone. Of course, commercial organisations must be profitable, but attention should be focused on the rate at which profit is generated from the resources used as compared with other possible uses for them. In particular, Doyle's (2008) analysis of **financial value drivers** in Section 1.3 above is very useful for considering financial objectives.

It is sometimes suggested that profit can be defined from a number of perspectives and does not exclusively relate to financial standards. You will find it difficult to convince the financially literate that this is the case.

Stock market indicators

Stock market indicators such as share price, earnings per share and dividend yield are often used by external financial analysts to assess corporate success. The problem with all of them is that they are subject to both internal manipulation and unconnected external forces.

Growth

There are some difficulties in accepting growth as an overall objective.

(a) **Growth of what?** In the long-run, some elements must be expected to grow faster than others because of the dynamics of the business environment.

(b) In the long-run, growth might lead to **diseconomies of scale** so that inefficiencies will occur.

Smaller companies will usually have a greater potential for significant rates of growth, especially in new industries, and growth will be a prime objective. Larger companies grow to achieve a size which will enable them to compete with other multinationals in world markets.

2.4 Customer objectives

Customer objectives in this context are **organisational objectives** that relate to customers, rather than the **objectives of the customers** themselves (though, clearly, there is a conceptual link between customer behaviour and what we can set out to achieve in relation to it). There are a vast number of specific objectives that might be set in this context.

For a **commercial organisation**, objectives relating to customers might include the following.

(a) Market share maintenance and enhancement
(b) Retention of key customers
(c) Changing the market profile by acquiring or shedding specific customer groups or customers from specific segments
(d) Improving the enquiry conversion rate
(e) Increasing the repeat purchase rate
(f) Dealing more effectively with customer complaints

A not-for-profit organisation such as a **charity** might have some customer objectives that were essentially similar to those of the commercial organisation, especially if it has a trading arm. It would also be likely to have objectives relating to its **client** and **donor** customer groups.

(a) Increasing client take-up of service in specific geographic areas or demographic groups
(b) Increasing donations per donor
(c) Retaining donors

ACTIVITY 2

application

Suggest some appropriate customer objectives for a local government education department.

2.5 Management objectives

The phrase 'management objectives' can mean two different things.

• Managers' objectives relating to their own work and how they do it.
• Objectives relating to the management of processes and projects – control, in other words.

2.5.1 Managers' objectives

Managers at all levels in all departments and functions will have a range of objectives relating to their roles and responsibilities. A very simple description of the manager's work was provided by the nineteenth century French management thinker Henri Fayol.

(a) **Planning**. Selecting the objectives and methods for achieving them, either for the organisation as a whole or for a part of it.

(b) **Organising**. Establishing the structure of tasks to be performed to achieve the goals of the organisation; grouping these tasks into jobs for an individual; creating groups of jobs within departments; delegating authority to carry out the jobs, providing systems of information and communication and co-ordinating activities within the organisation.

(c) **Commanding**. Giving instructions to subordinates to carry out tasks over which the manager has authority for decisions and responsibility for performance.

(d) **Co-ordinating**. Harmonising the activities of individuals and groups within the organisation. Management must reconcile differences in approach, effort, interest and timing.

(e) **Controlling**. Measuring and correcting activities to ensure that performance is in accordance with **plans**. Plans will not be achieved unless activities are monitored, and deviations identified and corrected as soon as they become apparent.

This analysis has, of course, been effectively superseded by more recent thinking about the nature of management, but it remains a useful description of the major roles and responsibilities of many managers. We could enhance the list by adding **communicating** and **motivating**.

We may reasonably anticipate that improvement objectives will flow from each of these aspects of managerial work. The need to plan, for example, might generate a need for project management software and the training to use it, possibly for the manager individually, possibly for chosen subordinates; the ever-present need for control and co-ordination might generate an objective of enhancing an under-performing MkIS; and so on.

2.5.2 Control objectives

Project control objectives and methods are covered in detail in Chapter 10.

3 Forecasting and the business case

 WORK BASED PROJECT TIP

Format and presentation

The preparation of any business case is likely to require an element of forecasting, even if it is only an assumption that things will continue much as they are. You should note that any assumptions made in forecasting should be clearly stated. Some definitions can usefully be outlined at this stage.

 KEY CONCEPT

concept

A **forecast** is a prediction of future events and a quantification of that prediction for the purpose of planning.

A **projection** is the expected future trend pattern, which is obtained by extrapolation. It tends to be concerned with quantitative factors, whereas a forecast includes judgements.

A variety of techniques is used in connection with forecasting. Different techniques are appropriate according to the **degree of uncertainty** perceived in the relevant forecast.

(a)   An approach based on **discounting** may be used when the amount and timing of future cash flows are assumed to be known with something **approaching certainty**.

(b)   Projects that are **repeated several times** lend themselves to the use of **expected values** and **decision trees**.

(c)   **Modelling** and **sensitivity analysis** are appropriate when there is **less confidence** about the range and distribution of potential outcomes: such techniques are employed in conjunction with decision rules that reflect the degree of risk aversion of the decision-makers.

(d)   It is important to remember that **certainty cannot be attained in any forecast**. Major, rapid changes, such as the collapse of the dot.com bubble and the global recession of 2008 simply are not knowable in advance.

3.1 Statistical projections

Statistical forecasts take past data and endeavour to direct it to the future, by **assuming** that **patterns or relationships which held in the past will continue to do so**. Many statistical techniques aim to reduce the uncertainty managers face. In **simple** or **static conditions the past is a relatively good guide** to the future.

Statistical forecasting techniques for static conditions

(a)   **Time series analysis**. Data for a number of months/years is obtained and analysed. The aim of time series analysis is to identify:

  (i)   Seasonal and other cyclical fluctuations
  (ii)   Long-term underlying trends

  For example, the UK's monthly unemployment statistics show a **headline figure** and the **underlying trend**.

(b)   **Regression analysis** as discussed earlier. Remember that the relationship between two variables may **only hold between certain values**. For example, you would expect ice cream consumption to rise as the temperature becomes hotter, but there is a maximum number of ice creams an individual can consume in a day, no matter how hot it is. Remember also the limited usefulness of **extrapolation** compared with **interpolation**.

(c)   **Econometrics** is the study of economic variables and their interrelationships, using computer models. In strict terms, econometrics is a branch of economics rather than a method of forecasting, but some short-term or medium-term econometric models might be used for that purpose.

  (i)   **Leading indicators** are indicators that change **before** market demand changes. For example, a sudden increase in the birth rate would be an indicator of future demand for children's clothes. Similarly, a fall in retail sales would be an indicator to manufacturers that demand from retailers for their products will soon fall. The number of new construction and house building starts in a period is often regarded as an indicator of future economic growth, as is purchasing activity in manufacturing.

  (ii)   The firm needs the ability to **predict the span of time between a change in the indicator and a change in market demand**. Change in an indicator is especially useful for demand forecasting when they reach their highest or lowest points (when an increase turns into a decline or *vice versa*).

(d)   **Adaptive forecasts** change in response to **recent** data.

3.1.1 Problems with statistical projections

(a)   Past relationships do not necessarily hold for the future.

(b)   Data can be misinterpreted, and **relationships assumed where none exist**. For example, sales of ice cream rise in the summer, and sales of umbrellas fall – the link is the weather, not any correlation between them.

(c)   Forecasts do not account for special events (eg wars), the likely response of competitors and so on.

(d)   The variation and depth of business cycles fluctuate.

(e)   In practice, statistical forecasters **underestimate uncertainty**.

3.2 Judgemental forecasts

Judgemental forecasts are used principally for the long-term, covering several decades. However, because of the limitations of short-term forecasting they are used for the short-term too. Effectively, they are based on **hunches or educated guesses**. Sometimes, these prove surprisingly accurate. At other times they are wide of the mark.

(a) **Individual forecasting**. A company might forecast sales on the basis of the judgement of one or more executives.

    (i) **Advantages** are that it is cheap and suitable if demand is stable or relatively simple.

    (ii) The **disadvantage** is that it is swayed most heavily by **most recent** experience rather than trend.

(b) **Genius forecasting**

    An individual with expert judgement might be asked for advice. This might be the case with the fashion industry; although demand might be hard to quantify, an ability to understand the mind of the customer will be very useful.

(c) In practice, forecasts might be prepared by an interested individual who has read the papers, say, and has promoted an item for management attention.

3.3 Modelling

At various points in this text, you have been given frameworks or models to structure your thinking.

 KEY CONCEPT   concept

A **model** is anything used to represent something else.

- *Descriptive:* describing real-world processes
- *Predictive:* attempting to predict future events
- *Control:* showing how action can be taken

A model is a simplified representation of reality, which enables complex data to be classified and analysed. Their relevance to building a future orientation depends on **how well they are used** and a **recognition of their limitations**.

3.4 Consensus forecasts

3.4.1 Jury forecasts

A panel of experts and/or executives prepare their own forecasts and a consensus forecast emerges from this.

(a) **Advantages**: expert opinions are sought and obtained.

(b) **Disadvantages**. The jury might **dilute** the best. The **group dynamics** will interfere with the decision. Each expert might differ and, in a face-to-face situation, the more forceful or confident would win the argument.

3.4.2 Delphi method

The Delphi method is a systematic forecasting method which relies on a panel of experts. The experts answer questionnaires in two or more rounds. After each round, a facilitator provides an anonymous summary of the experts' forecasts, as well as the reasons they provided for their judgments. Thus, experts are encouraged to revise their earlier answers in light of the replies of other members of their panel.

Delphi has been widely used for business forecasting and is characterised by the following features.

Structuring of information

The initial contributions from the experts are collected in the form of answers to questionnaires and the comments relating to those answers. The panel director controls the interactions among the participants, avoiding the negative effects of face-to-face panel discussions.

Regular feedback

Participants comment on their own forecasts, the responses of others, and on the progress of the panel as a whole. At any moment they can revise their earlier statements. On of the problems with regular group meetings is that participants tend to stick to previously stated opinions and often conform too much to the group leader. The Delphi method prevents this.

Anonymity

Usually all participants in Delphi forecasts maintain anonymity. This stops them from dominating others in the process, frees them to some extent from their personal biases, minimises the "bandwagon effect", allows them to freely express their opinions, encourages open critique and admitting of errors by revising earlier judgments.

3.5 Statistical versus judgemental and consensus forecasts

David Mercer identifies the relative advantages and disadvantages of each method.

Use of forecasts	Statistical	Judgement
Changes in established patterns	Past data is no guide	Can be predicted but could be ignored
Using available data	Not all past data is used	Personal biases and preferences obscure data
Objectivity	Based on specific criteria for selection	Personal propensity to optimism/pessimism
Uncertainty	Underestimated	Underestimated, with a tendency to over-optimism
Cost	Inexpensive	Expensive

3.5.1 Using both methods

Judgemental forecasting is **speculative**. However, speculation may be necessary to identify changing patterns in data or weak signals reflecting or presaging social changes.

3.6 Market forecasts and sales forecasts

Market forecasts and sales forecasts complement each other. The market forecast should be carried out first of all and should cover a longer period of time.

 KEY CONCEPT  concept

Market forecast. This is a forecast for the market as a whole. It is mainly involved in the assessment of environmental factors, outside the organisation's control, which will affect the demand for its products/services.

(a) Components of a market forecast.

    (i) The **economic review** (national economy, government policy, covering forecasts on investment, population, gross national product, and so on).

    (ii) **Specific market research** (to obtain data about specific markets and forecasts concerning total market demand).

    (iii) Evaluation of **total market demand** for the firm's and similar products (for example, profitability and market potential).

(b) **Sales forecasts** are estimates of sales (in volume, value and profit terms) of a product in a future period at a given marketing mix.

3.6.1 Research into potential sales

KEY CONCEPT

Sales potential is an estimate of the part of the market that is within the possible reach of a product.

Factors governing sales potential

- The price of the product
- The amount of money spent on sales promotion
- How essential the product is to consumers
- Whether it is a durable commodity whose purchase is postponable
- The overall size of the possible market
- Competition

Whether sales potential is worth exploiting will depend on the cost which must be incurred to realise the potential.

4 Assessing customer groups

The business case explains how a proposed activity will add value. Ultimately, it is the reaction of the customer that will determine whether or not an activity was worthwhile. Careful targeting of specific customer groups is an essential feature of marketing activity and a business case must explain which customers are to be targeted, why and how. This will require the acquisition and presentation of appropriate marketing research information.

4.1 Segmentation

A market is not a mass, homogeneous group of customers, each wanting an identical product. Market segmentation is based on the recognition that every market consists of potential buyers with different needs, and different buying behaviour. It is relevant to a **focus strategy**.

KEY CONCEPT

Market segmentation may therefore be defined as 'the subdividing of a market into distinct and increasingly homogeneous subgroups of customers, where any subgroup can conceivably be selected as a target market to be met with a distinct marketing mix'. (Kotler)

There are two important elements in this definition of market segmentation.

(a) Although the total market consists of widely different groups of consumers, each group consists of people (or organisations) with **common needs and preferences**, who perhaps react to market stimuli in much the same way.

(b) Each market segment can become a **target market for a firm**, and would require a unique marketing mix if the firm is to exploit it successfully.

4.1.1 Reasons for segmenting markets

The overall purpose of market segmentation is to be able to make sensible marketing decisions.

Reason	Comment
Better satisfaction of customer needs	One solution won't satisfy all customers
Growth in profits	Some customers will pay more for certain benefits
Revenue growth	Segmentation means that more customers may be attracted by what is on offer, in preference to competing products
Customer retention	By targeting customers, a number of different products can be offered to them
Targeted communications	Segmentation enables clear communications as people in the target audience share common needs
Innovation	By identifying unmet needs, companies can innovate to satisfy them
Segment share	Segmentation enables a firm to implement a focus strategy successfully

Steps in segmentation, targeting and positioning identified by Kotler

Step 1   Identify **segmentation** variables and segment the market

Step 2   Develop segment profiles   ]   Segmentation

Step 3   Evaluate the attractiveness of each segment   ]   Targeting

Step 4   Select the **target** segment(s)

Step 5   Identify **positioning** concepts for each target segment   ]   Positioning

Step 6   Select, develop and communicate the chosen concept

 ACTIVITY 3   application

Jot down possible segmentation variables for adult education, magazines, and sports facilities.

4.1.2 Identifying segments

(a) One basis will not be appropriate in every market, and sometimes two or more bases might be valid at the same time.

(b) One basis or 'segmentation variable' might be 'superior' to another in a hierarchy of variables. There are thus primary and secondary segmentation variables.

 MARKETING AT WORK   application

An airport cafe conducted a segmentation exercise of its customers. It identified a number of possible segments.

- Business travellers
- Airport employees
- Groups
- Single tourists

However, further analysis revealed that running through each of these categories was the same fault line.

- Those 'in a hurry'
- Those with time to spare

For marketing purposes, this latter segmentation exercise was more useful, and the firm was able to develop an 'express menu' for those in a hurry.

Jobber (2009) identifies three main approaches to segmenting consumer markets.

(a) **Behavioural**. This is the fundamental form of segmentation, in that it is consumer behaviour that has direct implications for marketing decisions.

(b) **Psychographic**. Psychographic segmentation is appropriate when it is believed that consumers' purchasing behaviour correlates with their personality or lifestyle variables.

(c) **Profile**. Profile variables such as social class are required in order to define and communicate with target markets.

The implication of this is that initial segmentation is carried out in terms of behavioural or psychographic categories, with the assessment of profile variables forming a second phase, primarily for purposes of communication. However, Jobber (2009) says that, in practice, profile segmentation will be a first step, with subsequent testing for behavioural differences between the groups identified.

4.2 Behavioural segmentation

Behavioural segmentation segregates buyers into groups based on their attitudes to and use of the product. There are five main segmentation bases.

(a) **Benefits sought**. Benefits might be a simple as flavour in a food product or pleasure from watching a DVD or as complex as the status and image conferred by certain unusual and luxury goods. The degree of a consumer's sensitivity to price is also an important benefit segmentation variable.

(b) **Purchase occasion**. Purchase occasion covers such aspects of behaviour as whether the purchase is seasonal, daily, impulse, as a gift, part of weekly grocery shopping or for convenience.

(c) **Purchase behaviour**. Purchase behaviour includes the degree of brand loyalty and how long the consumer takes after product launch to adopt the product.

(d) **Usage**. Segmentation can be based on the extent of use of the product, whether heavy, moderate or light. It can also be based on the occasion of use: for example, whether consumed alone, in a family setting or as part of a wider social group.

(e) **Perceptions, beliefs and values**. Segmentation may be based on consumers' attitudes to the market and to individual products.

Benefit segmentation of the toothpaste market

Segment Name	Principal benefit sought	Demographic strengths	Special behavioural characteristics	Brands dis-proportion-ately favoured	Personality character-istics	Lifestyle characteristics
The sensory segment	Flavour, product appearance	Children	Users of spearmint flavoured toothpaste	Colgate, Stripe	High self-involvement	Hedonistic
The Sociables	Brightness of teeth	Teens, young people	Smokers	Macleans, Ultra-Brite	High sociability	Active
The Worriers	Decay prevention	Large families	Heavy users	Crest	High hypochon-driasis	Conservative
The independent segment	Price	Men	Heavy users	Brands on sale	High autonomy	Value-oriented

4.2.1 Risk reduction

A benefit of a product is that it **reduces risk**. Toothpaste reduces the risk of tooth decay, for example. This is relevant to the worriers in the table above. **Perceptions** of risk are often very subjective. **Attitudes to risk** are useful in that they **offer segmentation opportunities**.

(a) Research has indicated high, medium, and low risk segments for producers of professional services by organisations such as consultants and market research agencies.

(b) **Risk can also affect how a product is positioned**. For example, it has been suggested that the feminine image of wine might mean that certain segments are inhibited by drinking it.

MARKETING AT WORK application 

The credit card market in the UK is becoming increasingly fragmented. Newcomers tend to offer lower interest rates than the mainstream competitors such as Barclaycard. The newcomers target or cherry-pick certain groups of customers with a good credit history, and who are motivated mainly by price.

Other card operators offer different customer benefits, by linking their cards to charitable organisations, so that some of the commission on each transaction goes to charity.

4.3 Psychographic segmentation

Psychographic segmentation is not based on objective data so much as how people see themselves and their **subjective** feelings and attitudes towards a particular product or service, or towards life in general.

Jobber (2009) suggests that the main bases of psychographic segmentation are **lifestyle** and **personality** characteristics.

Lifestyle dimensions			
Activities	*Interests*	*Opinions*	*Demographics*
Work	Family	Themselves	Age
Hobbies	Home	Social issues	Education
Social events	Job	Politics	Income
Vacation	Community	Business	Occupation
Entertainment	Recreation	Economics	Family size
Club membership	Fashion	Education	Dwelling
Community	Food	Products	Geography
Shopping	Media	Future	City size
Sports	Achievements	Culture	Stage in lifecycle

Source: Joseph Plummer,
'The Concept and Application of Lifestyle Segmentation',
Journal of Marketing (January 1974), pp. 33-37.

Three distinct types of social behaviour exist.

- **Tradition directed** behaviour is easy to predict and changes little
- **Other directedness** is behaviour influenced by the action and views of peer groups
- **Inner directedness** is behaviour uninfluenced by views of others

The research agency Taylor Nelson also identifies three main groups with sub groups.

(a) **Sustenance driven group**

(i) **Belongers**. What they seek is a quiet undisturbed family life. They are conservative, conventional, rule followers. Not all are sustenance driven.

(ii) **Survivors**. Strongly class-conscious, and community spirited, their motivation is to get by.

(iii) **Aimless**. Comprises two groups, (a) the young unemployed, who are often anti-authority, and (b) the old, whose motivation is day-to-day existence.

(b) **Outer directed group**

(i) The balance of the belongers.

(ii) **Conspicuous consumers**. They are materialistic and pushy, motivated by acquisition, competition, and getting ahead. Pro-authority, law and order.

(c) **Inner directed group**

(i) **Self-explorers**. Motivated by self-expression and self-realisation. Less materialistic than other groups, and showing high tolerance levels.

(ii) **Social resistors**. The caring group, concerned with fairness and social values, but often appearing intolerant and moralistic.

(iii)   **Experimentalists**. Highly individualistic, motivated by fast moving enjoyment. They are materialistic, pro-technology but anti-traditional authority.

Variations on the lifestyle or psychographic approach have been developed, analysing more precisely people's attitudes towards **certain goods or services**. The value of this approach is that it isolates potential consumer responses to particular product offerings.

 MARKETING AT WORK   application

The Henley Centre for Forecasting has outlined four different kinds of consumers in the market for technological and media products.

(a)   *Technophiles* (24% of the population) 'are enthusiastic about technology in a general sense and also show a high level of interest in applications of new technology. They are concentrated among the under-35s, are more likely to be male than female, and are more likely to belong to social grade C1 than AB'.

(b)   *Aspirational technophiles* (22% of the population) 'are excited in a general sense about technology but are much less interested in its applications. They are more likely to be male than female, and are concentrated in the AB social grade'.

(c)   *Functionals* (25% of the population) 'claim to be uninterested in technology but are not hostile to its applications, especially those areas which offer an enhancement of existing services. These consumers are more likely to be family ... and are most numerous among the over 45s'.

(d)   *Technophobes* (28% of the population) 'are hostile to technology at all levels and are sceptical about whether technology can offer anything new. Technophobes are concentrated in the over-60 age group, are more likely to be female than male, and are distributed fairly evenly through the social grades'.

4.4 Profile segmentation

Profile segmentation is of fundamental importance for marketers: the segmentation variables are clear and easily applied and the resulting segmentation is appropriate for the design of marketing communication strategy. The need to communicate means that even where target segments have been identified using behavioural or psychographic variables, there may be a need to re-analyse, in profile terms, in order to be able to communicate with them.

There are three main types of profile segmentation, though the approaches are generally combined with one another in modern practice.

*   Demographic
*   Socio-economic
*   Geographic

4.5 Demographic segmentation

Demographic segmentation involves classifying people according to objective variables about their situation, including age, sex and life cycle stage.

4.5.1 The family life cycle

The **family life cycle (FLC)** is a summary demographic variable that combines the effects of age, marital status, career status (income) and the presence or absence of children. It is able to identify the various **stages through which households progress**. The table below shows features of the family at various stages of its life cycle. Particular products and services can be target-marketed at specific stages in the life cycle of families.

It is important to remember that the model of the family life cycle shown in the table displays the **classic route** from young single to older unmarried. In contemporary society, characterised by divorce and what may be the declining importance of marriage as an institution, this picture can vary. It is possible and not uncommon to be young, childless and divorced, or young and unmarried with children. Some people go through life without marrying or having children at all. Individuals may go through the life cycle belonging to more than one family group. At each stage, whether on the classic route or an **alternative path**, needs and disposable income will change. Family groupings are, however, a key feature of society.

There has been some **criticism** of the traditional FLC model as a basis for market segmentation in recent years.

(a)   It is modelled on the **demographic patterns of industrialised western nations** - and particularly America. This pattern may not be universally applicable.

(b)   As noted above, while the FLC model was once typical of the overwhelming majority of American families, there are now **important potential variations** from that pattern, including:

(i)	Childless couples	–	because of choice, career-oriented women and delayed marriage
(ii)	Later marriages	–	because of greater career-orientation and non-marital relationships: likely to have fewer children
(iii)	Later children	–	say in late 30s. Likely to have fewer children, but to stress quality of life
(iv)	Single parents	–	(especially mothers) because of divorce
(v)	Fluctuating labour status	–	not just in work or retired, but redundancy, career change, dual-income
(vi)	Extended parenting	–	young, single adults returning home while they establish careers/financial independence; divorced children returning to parents; elderly parents requiring care; newly-weds living with in-laws
(vii)	Non-family households	–	unmarried (homosexual or heterosexual) couples
		–	divorced persons with no children
		–	single persons (often due to delaying of first marriage and the fact that there are more women than men in the population)
		–	widowed persons (especially women, because of longer life-expectancy)

An alternative or modified FLC model is needed to take account of consumption variables such as:

(a)   Spontaneous **changes** in brand preference when a household undergoes a **change of status** (divorce, redundancy, death of a spouse, change in membership of a non-family household).

(b)   **Different economic circumstances** and extent of consumption planning in single-parent families, households where there is a redundancy, dual-income households.

(c)   **Different buying and consumption roles** to compensate/adjust in households where the **woman works**. Women can be segmented into at least four categories - each of which may represent a distinct market for goods and services:

- Stay-at-home homemaker
- Plan-to-work homemaker
- 'Just-a-job' working woman
- Career-oriented working woman

4.6 Socio-economic segmentation

Age and sex present few problems but social class has always been one of the most dubious areas of marketing research investigation. Class is a highly personal and subjective phenomenon, to the extent that some people are class conscious or class aware and have a sense of belonging to a particular group. JICNAR's social grade definitions (A-E), which correspond closely to what are called Social Classes I-V on the Registrar General's Scale, are often used in quota setting.

| Registrar General's Social classes | JICNAR | | Characteristics |
	Social grades	Social status	of occupation (of head of household)
I	A	Upper middle class	Higher managerial/professional eg lawyers, directors
II	B	Middle class	Intermediate managerial/administrative/ professional eg teachers, managers, computer operators, sales managers
III (i) non-manual	C$_1$	Lower middle class	Supervisory, clerical, junior managerial/ administrative/professional eg foremen, shop assistants
(ii) manual	C$_2$	Skilled working class	Skilled manual labour, eg electricians, mechanics
IV	D	Working class	Semi-skilled manual labour, eg machine operators
V			Unskilled manual labour, eg cleaning, waiting tables, assembly
	E	Lowest level of subsistence	State pensioners, widows (no other earner), casual workers

From 2001, the UK Office for National Statistics used a new categorisation system, reflecting recent changes in the UK population.

New social class	Occupations	Examples
1	Higher managerial and professional occupations	
1.1	Employers and managers in larger organisations	Bank managers, company directors
1.2	Higher professional	Doctors, lawyers
2	Lower managerial and professional occupations	Police officers
3	Intermediate occupations	Secretaries/PAs, clerical workers
4	Small employers and own-account workers	
5	Lower supervisory, craft and related occupations	Electricians
6	Semi-routine occupations	Drivers, hairdressers, bricklayers
7	Routine occupations	Car park attendants, cleaners

4.7 Geographic segmentation

Geographic segmentation is appropriate when there are observable differences in consumption that correlate with geographic location. Jobber (2009) gives the example of beer, which is preferred with a foamy head in the north of England, whereas southerners prefer their beer flat. In Germany, a relatively large number of local brewers produce beer that satisfies local tastes. Geographic and, especially, national cultural differences are also important in marketing communications.

4.8 Geodemographic segmentation

Geographic and demographic information is combined in geodemographic segmentation. Social class information may also be included. For example, the ACORN system divides the UK into 17 groups which together comprise a total of 54 different types of areas, which share common socio-economic characteristics.

(a) The 17 ACORN groups are as follows.

The ACORN targeting classification: abbreviated list		% of population
A	*Thriving (19.7%)*	
A1	Wealthy achievers, suburban areas	15.0
A2	Affluent greys, rural communities	2.3
A3	Prosperous pensioners, retirement areas	2.4
B	*Expanding (11.6%)*	
B4	Affluent executives, family areas	3.8
B5	Well-off workers, family areas	7.8
C	*Rising (7.8%)*	
C6	Affluent urbanites, town and city areas	2.3
C7	Prosperous professionals, metropolitan areas	2.1
C8	Better-off executives, inner city areas	3.4
D	*Settling (24.1%)*	
D9	Comfortable middle-agers, mature home-owning areas	13.4
D10	Skilled workers, home-owning areas	10.7
E	*Aspiring (13.7%)*	
E11	New home-owners, mature communities	9.7
E12	White collar workers, better-off multi-ethnic areas	4.0
F	*Striving (22.7%)*	
F13	Older people, less prosperous areas	3.6
F14	Council estate residents, better-off homes	11.5
F15	Council estate residents, high unemployment	2.7
F16	Council estate residents, greatest hardships	2.8
F17	People in multi-ethnic, low-income areas	2.1

(b) As an example of a more detailed breakdown, group E ('Aspiring') contains the following groups.

E	*Aspiring (13.7% of population)*	
E11	*New home-owners, mature communities (9.7%)*	
11.33	Council areas, some new home-owners	3.8
11.34	Mature home-owning areas, skilled workers	3.1
11.35	Low-rise estates, older workers, new home-owners	2.8
E12	*White collar workers, better-off multi-ethnic areas (4.0%)*	
12.36	Home-owning multi-ethnic areas, young families	1.1
12.37	Multi-occupied town centres, mixed occupations	1.8
12.38	Multi-ethnic areas, white collar workers	1.1

Unlike geographical segmentation, which is fairly crude by area, geodemographics enables similar groups of people to be targeted, even though they might exist in different areas of the country. These various classifications share certain characteristics, including:

- Car ownership
- Unemployment rates
- Purchase of financial service products
- Number of holidays
- Age profile

4.9 Segmentation of the industrial market

Segmentation may apply more obviously to the consumer market, but it can also be applied to industrial markets (also known as organisational markets).

Industrial markets can be segmented with many of the bases used in consumer markets such as geography, usage rate and benefits sought. Additional, more traditional bases include customer type, product/technology, customer size and purchasing procedures.

(a)　**Geographic location**. Some industries and related industries are clustered in particular areas. Firms selling services to the banking sector might be interested in the City of London.

(b)　**Type of business** (eg service, manufacturing)

　　(i)　**Nature of the customers' business**. Accountants or lawyers, for example, might choose to specialise in serving customers in a particular type of business. An accountant may choose to specialise in the accounts of retail businesses, and a firm of solicitors may specialise in conveyancing work for property development companies.

　　(ii)　**Components manufacturers** specialise in the industries of the firms to which they supply components.

　　(iii)　**Type of organisation**. Organisations in an industry as a whole may have certain needs in common. Employment agencies offering business services to publishers, say, must offer their clients personnel with experience in particular desktop publishing packages. Suitable temporary staff offered to legal firms can be more effective if they are familiar with legal jargon. Each different type of firm can be offered a tailored product or service.

　　(iv)　**Size of organisation**. Large organisations may have elaborate purchasing procedures, and may do many things in-house. Small organisations may be more likely to subcontract certain specialist services.

(c)　**Use of the product**. In the UK, many new cars are sold to businesses, as benefit cars. Although this practice is changing with the viability of a 'cash alternative' to a company car, the varying levels of specification are developed with the business buyer in mind (eg junior salesperson gets an Escort, Regional Manager gets a Mondeo).

Wind and Cardozo (1974) developed a two-stage framework.

(a)　*Stage 1* calls for the formation of macrosegments based on organisational characteristics such as size, SIC (Standard Industrial Classification) code and product applications.

(b)　*Stage 2* involves dividing these macrosegments into microsegments based on the distinguishing characteristics of decision-making units. They identify five general segmentation bases moving from the outer towards the inner in the following sequence: demographic, operating variables, purchasing approaches, situational factors and personal characteristics of the buyer.

Jobber (2009) describes a microsegmentation stage based on six variables

(a)　**Buyer's choice criteria**. Buyers are likely to use different criteria and priorities when making purchase decisions. Cost quality and service and their relative importance are important choice criteria.

(b)　**Decision-making unit (DMU) structure**. The composition of the DMU is likely to vary as is the influence wielded by the various stakeholder groups involved.

(c)　**Decision-making process**. The time taken to make the purchased decision is linked to the size and structure of the DMU. An extended and complex decision process requires greater marketing effort.

(d)　**Buy class**. Purchases by organisations are of three types.

　　(i)　The **straight rebuy** is a repeat purchase from an approved supplier.

　　(ii)　The **new task** occurs when a need for a new type of product arises and there is little experience of its purchase.

　　(iii)　The **modified rebuy** requires the purchase of a standard product and the various sources of supply are well-known, but there has been a problem that has led to a modification of the standard purchasing procedure.

Buy class thus affects the complexity of the purchasing behaviour.

(e)   The structure of the **purchasing organisation** within the customer entity influences the purchasing decision. The basic distinction is between centralised and decentralised purchasing. Centralised purchasing tends to be in the hands of internally influential, specialist buyers who know the market in detail and buy in bulk, obtaining significant price discounts as a result. Such purchasing organisations are best dealt with by a national account sales force, while less expert decentralised buying, where the buyers have less influence, can be handled by local territory representatives.

(f)   A high degree of **innovation** in the customer organisation makes it a good target for the launch of new products.

Learning objectives	Covered
1 Define business case objectives for marketing plans and projects	☑ Shareholder value
	☑ Economic profit and cashflow
	☑ Value-based management
	☑ McKinsey 7S
	☑ Types of objectives
2 Discuss and use forecasting techniques in the preparation of a business case	☑ Forecasting
	☑ Statistical projections
3 Use market research information to assess and evaluate customer groups relevant to the business case (market segmentation element)	☑ Segmentation variables

1   What is the fundamental belief that Doyle believes is one of the foundations of value-based management?

2   Which four marketing value drivers does Doyle identify?

3   What are the four drivers of financial value?

4   Organisations need to find a way of differentiating themselves from their competition so that customers decide to buy from, and remain loyal to, them. Which differentiating strategy allows organisations to combine customer convenience with the lowest price?

(a)   Product leadership
(b)   Brand superiority
(c)   Operational excellence
(d)   Customer intimacy

5   How does the Delphi method of expert forecasting work?

6   What is the importance of having a number of segmentation bases?

7   Which segmentation deals with the stages households pass through?

8   What categories have been traditionally used to segment industrial customers?

1.   Here are some suggestions, starting with the least risky.

- Carry-out food shops
- Pub
- Horticulture
- Grocery supermarket chain
- Estate agency
- Machine tools manufacture
- Minerals extraction
- Cinema film production
- Oil exploration

2.   The first problem with this activity is to establish who you think the customers of such a department might be. There are probably several groups, but note that it is important here not to confuse 'customers' with the wider category 'stakeholders'.

- Children of school age
- Their parents
- Potential adult education students

Just considering the first category, we might suggest the following objectives.

- Increasing the exam success rate
- Reducing the unauthorised absence rate
- Increasing the number of optional study subjects taken up
- Increasing the take up of healthy school meals

3.   (a)   Adult education

- Age
- Sex
- Occupation
- Social class
- Education
- Family life cycle
- Lifestyle
- Leisure interest and hobbies

(b)   Magazines and periodicals

- Sex (Woman's Own)
- Social class (Country Life)
- Income and class aspirations (Ideal Home)
- Occupation (Marketing Week, Computer Weekly)
- Leisure interests (Railway Modeller)
- Political ideology (Spectator, New Statesman)
- Age

(c)   Sporting facilities

- Geographical area (rugby in Wales, skiing in parts of Scotland, sailing in coastal towns)
- Population density (squash clubs in cities, riding in country areas)
- Occupation (gyms for office workers)
- Education (there may be a demand for facilities for sports taught at certain schools, such as rowing)
- Family life cycle or age (parents may want facilities for their children, young single or married people may want facilities for themselves)

1   The objective of the firm is the maximisation of shareholder returns.

2   Marketing value drivers are choice of market; targeting of desirable customers; differential advantage derived from customer satisfaction; and a fully integrated marketing mix.

3   • Cash flow volume
     • Cash flow timing
     • Cash flow risk
     • Cash flow sustainability

4   C.   **Operational excellence**. Doyle proposes that product leadership, brand superiority operational excellence and customer intimacy on four strategic approaches to creating differential advantage. Operational excellence is needed to offer a contribution of customer convenience and the lowest prices.

5   Anonymous participants respond to a questionnaire containing tightly-defined questions. The results are collated and statistically analysed, then returned by the organiser to each expert. The experts respond again, having considered each other's opinions and analyses.

6   One basis will not be valid for every market and sometimes two or more bases might be valid at the same time

7   The family life cycle

8   Location, type of business, use made of the product, type and size of organisation

Baer, J. (2009) *'GE to sell 81% stake in airport security unit'* Financial Times, 24th April 2009, London.

Doyle, P. (2003) *'Strategy as Marketing'*, in Cummings, S. and Wilson, D. Images of Marketing (ed), Blackwell Publishing Limited, London.

Doyle, P. (2008). Value-based Marketing (2nd edition), John Wiley and Sons Ltd, London.

Jobber, D. (2009). *Principles and Practice of Marketing* (6th ed), McGraw-Hill, Maidenhead.

Wind, Y. and Cardozo R. (1974) *'Industrial Marketing Segmentation'*, Industrial Marketing Management, March, pp. 153 – 166.

Annex: Discounting cash flows

Discounting is a basic tool of financial analysis that is also widely used in other business techniques, so we will start off by showing you how it works.

The **basic principle of compounding** is that if we invest £X now for n years at r% interest per annum, we should obtain £S in n years time, where £S = £X(1+r^n).

Thus if we invest £10,000 now for four years at 10% interest per annum, we will have a total investment worth £10,000 × 1.10^4 = £14,641 at the end of four years (that is, at year 4 if it is now year 0).

 KEY CONCEPT

concept

The basic principle of **discounting** is that if we wish to have a known sum £S in n years' time, we need to know how much to invest *now* (year 0) at an interest rate of r% in order to obtain the required sum of money in the future.

For example, if we wish to have £14,641 in four years' time, how much money would we need to invest now at 10% interest per annum? This is the reverse of the situation described in Paragraph 3 and, fairly obviously, the answer is £10,000. We can prove this.

Using our formula, S = X(1 + r)^n

where	X	=	the original sum invested
	r	=	10%
	n	=	4
	S	=	£14,641

$$£14,641 = X(1 + 0.1)^4$$

$$£14,641 = X \times 1.4641$$

$$\therefore X = \frac{£14,641}{1.4641} = £10,000$$

£10,000 now, with the capacity to earn a return of 10% per annum, is the equivalent in value of £14,641 after four years. The difference between them is the passage of time and the interest earned. We can therefore say that £10,000 is the **present value** of £14,641 at year 4, at an interest rate of 10%.

 KEY CONCEPT

concept

The present value of a future sum is obtained by discounting the future sum at an appropriate discount rate.

The discounting formula is

$$X = S \times \frac{1}{(1+r)^n}$$

where	S	is the sum to be received after n time periods
	X	is the present value (PV) of that sum
	r	is the rate of return, expressed as a proportion
	n	is the number of time periods (usually years).

The rate r is sometimes called a cost of capital.

Example: discounting

(a) Calculate the present value of £60,000 at year 6, if a return of 15% per annum is obtainable.

(b) Calculate the present value of £100,000 at year 5, if a return of 6% per annum is obtainable.

(c) How much would a person need to invest now at 12% to earn £4,000 at year 2 and £4,000 at year 3?

Solution

The discounting formula, $X = S \times \dfrac{1}{(1+r)^n}$ is required.

(a)
S	=	£60,000
n	=	6
r	=	0.15

$$PV = 60,000 \times \frac{1}{1.15^6}$$
$$= 60,000 \times 0.432$$
$$= £25,920$$

(b)
S	=	£100,000
n	=	5
r	=	0.06

$$PV = 100,000 \times \frac{1}{1.06^5}$$
$$= 100,000 \times 0.747$$
$$= £74,700$$

(c)
S	=	£4,000
n	=	2 or 3
r	=	0.12

$$PV = \left(4,000 \times \frac{1}{1.12^2}\right) + \left(4,000 \times \frac{1}{1.12^3}\right)$$
$$= 4,000 \times (0.797 + 0.712)$$
$$= £6,036$$

This calculation can be checked as follows.

	£
Year 0	6,036.00
Interest for the first year (12%)	724.32
	6,760.32
Interest for the second year (12%)	811.24
	7,571.56
Less withdrawal	(4,000.00)
	3,571.56
Interest for the third year (12%)	428.59
	4,000.15
Less withdrawal	(4,000.00)
Rounding error	0.15

Project appraisal

Discounted cash flow techniques can be used to evaluate expenditure proposals such as the purchase of equipment or marketing budgets.

 KEY CONCEPT

concept

Discounted cash flow (DCF) involves the application of discounting arithmetic to the estimated future cash flows (receipts and expenditures) from a project in order to decide whether the project is expected to earn a satisfactory rate of return.

The net present method value (NPV) method

 KEY CONCEPT

concept

The **net present value (NPV) method** works out the present values of all items of income and expenditure related to an investment at a given rate of return, and then works out a net total. If it is positive, the investment is considered to be acceptable. If it is negative, the investment is considered to be unacceptable.

Example: the net present value of a project

Dog Ltd is considering whether to spend £5,000 on an item of equipment. The excess of income over cash expenditure from the project would be £3,000 in the first year and £4,000 in the second year.

The company will not invest in any project unless it offers a return in excess of 15% per annum.

Required

Assess whether the investment is worthwhile.

Solution

In this example, an outlay of £5,000 now promises a return of £3,000 **during** the first year and £4,000 **during** the second year. It is a convention in DCF, however, that cash flows spread over a year are assumed to occur **at the end of the year**, so that the cash flows of the project are as follows.

	£
Year 0 (now)	(5,000)
Year 1 (at the end of the year)	3,000
Year 2 (at the end of the year)	4,000

The NPV method takes the following approach.

(a)   The project offers £3,000 at year 1 and £4,000 at year 2, for an outlay of £5,000 now.

(b)   The company might invest elsewhere to earn a return of 15% per annum.

(c)   If the company did invest at exactly 15% per annum, how much would it need to invest now to earn £3,000 at the end of year 1 plus £4,000 at the end of year 2?

(d)   Is it cheaper to invest £5,000 in the project, or to invest elsewhere at 15%, in order to obtain these future cash flows?

If the company did invest elsewhere at 15% per annum, the amount required to earn £3,000 in year 1 and £4,000 in year 2 would be as follows.

Year	Cash flow £	Discount factor 15%	Present value £
1	3,000	$\dfrac{1}{1.15} = 0.870$	2,610
2	4,000	$\dfrac{1}{1.15^2} = 0.756$	3,024
			5,634

The choice is to invest £5,000 in the project, or £5,634 elsewhere at 15%, in order to obtain these future cash flows. We can therefore reach the following conclusion.

- It is cheaper to invest in the project, by £634.
- The project offers a return of over 15% per annum.

The net present value is the difference between the present value of cash inflows from the project (£5,634) and the present value of future cash outflows (in this example, £5,000 $\times$ $1/1.15^0$ = £5,000).

An NPV statement could be drawn up as follows.

Year	Cash flow £	Discount factor 15%	Present value £
0	(5,000)	1.000	(5,000)
1	3,000	$\dfrac{1}{1.15} = 0.870$	2,610
2	4,000	$\dfrac{1}{1.15^2} = 0.756$	3,024
		Net present value	+634

The project has a positive net present value, so it is acceptable.

Project comparison

The NPV method can also be used to compare two or more investment options. For example, suppose that Daisy Ltd can choose between the investment outlined above *or a* second investment, which also costs £28,000 but which would earn £6,500 in the first year, £7,500 in the second, £8,500 in the third, £9,500 in the fourth and £10,500 in the fifth. Which one should Daisy Ltd choose?

The decision rule is to choose the option with the highest NPV. We therefore need to calculate the NPV of the second option.

Year	Cash flow £	Discount factor 11%	Present value £
0	(28,000)	1.000	(28,000)
1	6,500	0.901	5,857
2	7,500	0.812	6,090
3	8,500	0.731	6,214
4	9,500	0.659	6,261
5	10,500	0.593	6,227
		NPV =	2,649

Daisy Ltd should therefore invest in the second option since it has the higher NPV.

Limitations of using the NPV method

There are a number of problems associated with using the NPV method in practice.

(a) **The future discount factors** (or interest rates) which are used in calculating NPVs can only be **estimated** and are not known with certainty. Discount rates that are estimated for time periods far into the future are therefore less likely to be accurate, thereby leading to less accurate NPV values.

(b) Similarly, NPV calculations make use of estimated **future cash flows**. As with future discount factors, cash flows which are estimated for cash flows several years into the future cannot really be predicted with any real certainty.

(c) When using the NPV method it is common to assume that all cash flows occur **at the end of the year**. However, this assumption is also likely to give rise to less accurate NPV values.

There are a number of computer programs available these days which enable a range of NPVs to be calculated for different circumstances (best-case and worst-case situations and so on). Such programs allow some of the limitations mentioned above to be alleviated.

Chapter 4

Delivering the business case for marketing projects

Topic list

1   Segment validity and attractiveness
2   Target markets
3   Positioning
4   The marketing mix
5   Presenting the business case

Introduction

In the previous chapter we looked at the techniques of market segmentation. In this chapter we will build on this and go on to consider target marketing. It is important to remember that the whole purpose of segmentation is to enable the marketer to choice a target market and serve it with an appropriate market offering. Targeting is closely linked to decisions about the marketing mix, which we discuss after dealing with some modern trends in targeting and positioning.

We conclude this chapter with a substantial section on making oral presentations. There is plenty of good advice here that should help you with your project presentation.

Syllabus-linked learning objectives

By the end of the chapter you will be able to:

Learning objectives	Syllabus link
1 Use market research information to assess and evaluate customer groups relevant to the business case (targeting element)	2.3
2 Evaluate the interaction of target market choice and the marketing mix	2.4
3 Assess resource requirements	2.5
4 Present the business case	2.6

1 Segment validity and attractiveness

1.1 Segment validity

A market segment will only **be valid** if it is worth designing and developing a **unique marketing mix** for it. The following questions are commonly asked to decide whether or not the segment can be used for developing marketing plans.

Criteria	Comment
Can the segment be measured?	It might be possible to conceive of a market segment, but it is not necessarily easy to measure it. For example, for a segment based on people with a conservative outlook to life, can conservatism of outlook be measured by market research?
Is the segment big enough?	There has to be a large enough potential market to be profitable.
Can the segment be reached?	There has to be a way of getting to the potential customers via the organisation's promotion and distribution channels.
Do segments respond differently?	If two or more segments are identified by marketing planners but each segment responds in the same way to a marketing mix, the segments are effectively one and the same and there is no point in distinguishing them from each other.
Can the segment be reached profitably?	Do the identified customer needs cost less to satisfy than the revenue they earn?
Is the segment suitably stable?	The stability of the segment is important, if the organisation is to commit huge production and marketing resources to serve it. The firm does not want the segment to 'disappear' next year. Of course, this may not matter in some industries.

1.2 Segment attractiveness

A segment might be valid and potentially profitable, but is it potentially **attractive**?

(a) A segment which has **high barriers to entry** might cost more to enter but will be less **vulnerable to competitors**.

(b)   For firms involved in **relationship marketing**, the segment should be one in which **viable relationship** between the firm and the customer can be established.

Segments which are most attractive will be those whose needs can be met by building on the company's strengths and where forecasts for demand, sales profitability and **growth** are favourable.

1.2.1 A checklist of factors to consider when evaluating segment attractiveness

Hooley et al (2007) give a comprehensive list of factors for evaluating market attractiveness.

Factors	Characteristics to examine
Market	• Size of the segment
	• Segment growth rate
	• Stage of industry evaluation
	• Predictability
	• Price elasticity and sensitivity
	• Bargaining power of customers
	• Seasonality of demand
Economic and technological	• Barriers to entry
	• Barriers to exit
	• Bargaining power of suppliers
	• Level of technology
	• Investment required
	• Margins available
Competitive	• Competitive intensity
	• Quality of competition
	• Threat of substitution
	• Degree of differentiation
Environmental	• Exposure to economic fluctuations
	• Exposure to political and legal factors
	• Degree of regulation
	• Social acceptability

1.2.2 Marketing resources

When considering a marketing project, the estimation of project time and costs is dependent upon the resources that are to be used. The project manager needs to identify specific skills and materials, equipment and facilities required. The availability, cost, quantities required and possible resource constraints must all be accounted for.

It is important to assess company capability when evaluating attractiveness and targeting a market. This can help determine the appropriate strategy, because once the attractiveness of each identified segment has been assessed it can be considered together with relative strengths to determine the potential advantages the organisation would have. In this way preferred segments can be targeted. Jobber (2009) describes four categories of relevant organisational capability.

Exploitable marketing assets. Current marketing assets, such as brands and distribution networks, should be exploited in order to achieve synergy. However, the impact of the proposed target market on those assets must also be considered. For example, would stretching a successful brand into an unrelated market damage the brand's values?

Cost advantages. A cost advantage relating to any aspect of the business will bring significant commercial benefits. These include the possibility of a high promotional budget, the use of penetration pricing, the ability to survive an economic downturn and the possibility of competing on price.

Technological edge. Technological superiority also confers commercial advantages, especially where it takes the form of legally protected intellectual property.

Managerial capability and commitment. Management's abilities should be assessed against that of competitors, as evidenced by their record in the target segment. Marketing success depends on the existence of significant management capability; similarly, it will not be achieved if there is insufficient commitment.

An assessment of both segment attractiveness and current and potential company strengths will be necessary if potential target markets are to be chosen effectively.

Market segment attractiveness

		Unattractive	Average	Attractive
Current and potential company strengths in serving the segment	Weak	Strongly avoid	Avoid	Possibilities
	Average	Avoid	Possibilities	Secondary targets
	Strong	Possibilities	Secondary targets	Prime targets

2 Target markets

  KEY CONCEPT   concept

A **target market** is a market or segment selected for special attention by an organisation (possibly served with a distinct marketing mix).

If a market segment is both valid and attractive, it may be accepted as a **target market**. This is an important strategic decision and will be taken at a high level. If the decision is taken to target a particular segment, further decisions must then be taken about implementing the strategy. Traditionally, the policy options described below have been available.

Policy	Comment
Undifferentiated marketing	This policy is to produce a single product and hope to get as many customers as possible to buy it; segmentation is ignored entirely. This is sometimes called **mass marketing**.
Concentrated marketing	The company attempts to produce the ideal product for a single segment of the market (for example, *Rolls Royce* cars, *Mothercare* mother and baby shops).
Differentiated marketing	The company attempts to introduce several product versions, each aimed at a different market segment (for example, the manufacture of different styles of the same article of clothing).

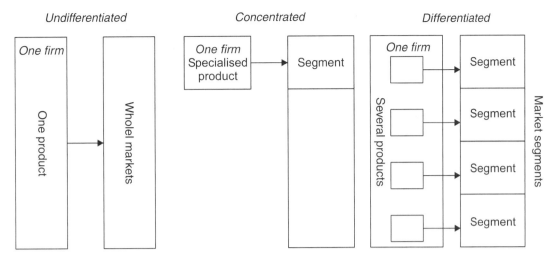

The major **disadvantage of differentiated marketing** is the additional costs of marketing and production (more product design and development costs, the loss of economies of scale in production and storage, additional promotion costs and administrative costs and so on). When the **costs** of differentiation of the market exceed the **benefits** from further segmentation and target marketing, a firm is said to have **over-differentiated**.

The major **disadvantage of concentrated marketing** is the business risk of relying on a single segment of a single market. On the other hand, specialisation in a particular market segment can give a firm a profitable, although perhaps temporary, competitive edge over rival firms.

The choice between undifferentiated, differentiated or concentrated marketing as a marketing strategy will depend on the following factors.

(a) The extent to which the product and/or the market may be considered **homogeneous**. **Mass marketing** may be sufficient if the market is largely homogeneous (for example, for safety matches).

(b) The **company's resources** must not be over extended by differentiated marketing. Small firms may succeed better by concentrating on one segment only.

(c) The product must be sufficiently **advanced in its life cycle** to have attracted a substantial total market; otherwise segmentation and target marketing is unlikely to be profitable, because each segment would be too small in size.

2.1 Micromarketing

Segmentation, as part of target marketing, looks certain to play an even more crucial role in the marketing strategies of consumer organisations in the years ahead. The move from traditional mass marketing to **micro-marketing** is rapidly gaining ground as marketers explore more cost-effective ways to recruit new customers. This has been brought about by a number of trends.

(a) The **ability to create large numbers of product variants without the need for corresponding increases in resources** is causing markets to become overcrowded.

(b) The **growth in minority lifestyles** is creating opportunities for niche brands aimed at consumers with very distinct purchasing habits.

(c) The **fragmentation of the media** to service ever more specialist and local audiences is denying mass media the ability to assure market dominance for major brand advertisers.

(d) The **advance in information technology** is enabling information about individual customers to be organised in ways that enable highly selective and personal communications.

Such trends have promoted the developments in benefit, lifestyle and geodemographic segmentation techniques outlined. Consumer market segmentation has developed so much in the last few years that the vision of multinational marketers accessing a PC to plan retail distribution and supporting promotional activity in cities as far apart as Naples, Nottingham and Nice is now a practical reality.

2.2 Mass customisation

Micro-marketing is made possible by **mass customisation**, which features:

- The huge economies of scale of mass production
- The tailoring of products precisely to the customer's requirements

New manufacturing technology makes this possible. There is less need for a standard product if people's individual preferences can be catered for.

 MARKETING AT WORK   application

Levi Jeans in the US has offered a service whereby customers' measurements are fed through to an automated garment cutting process.

2.3 Postmodern marketing

Postmodernism is principally a term relating to cultural activities such as architecture and literature. However, developments in society and in economic life generally have led to its use as a label for a particular trend in marketing theory. This emphasises the characteristics of individual consumers and suggests that attempts at targeting must acknowledge individual differences. Postmodernism has led to a noticeable quirkiness in branding and advertising, but its major practical impact for our purposes has been its validation of the use of websites and point of sale data capture to tailor marketing activity to **individual characteristics and preferences**. This is summed up in the phrase '**from segmentation to fragmentation**'. The archetypical postmodern marketing development has been *Tesco's* utilisation of the data derived from its store loyalty cards. This has been a major task and it appears that other promoters of loyalty cards, such as *Sainsbury's* have not been as successful as Tesco in organising and mining the huge amounts of data involved.

3 Positioning

 KEY CONCEPT   concept

Positioning is the act of designing the company's offer and image so that it achieves a distinct and valued place in the target customer's mind.

3.1 Problems with positioning

How much do people remember about a product or brand?

(a) **Many products are, in fact, very similar**, and the key issue is to make them **distinct in the customer's mind**.

(b) People remember 'number 1', so the product should be positioned as 'number 1' in relation to a valued attribute.

(c) **Cosmetic changes** can have the effect of repositioning the product in the customer's mind. To be effective, however, this **psychological positioning** has to be **reinforced by real positioning**.

As **positioning is psychological as well as real**, we can now identify **positioning errors**.

Mistake	Consequence
Underpositioning	The brand does not have a clear identity in the eyes of the customer
Overpositioning	Buyers may have too narrow an image of a brand
Confused positioning	Too many claims might be made for a brand
Doubtful positioning	The positioning may not be credible in the eyes of the buyer

3.1.1 Positioning strategy checklist

Positioning variable	Comment
• Attributes	• Size, for example
• Benefit	• What benefits we offer
• Use/application	• Ease of use; accessibility
• User	• The sort of person the product appeals to
• Product category	• Consciously differentiated from competition
• Quality/price	• One should support and validate the other, so that it makes sense to the customer and he understands what he is buying. For example, low quality at a high price is unlikely to sell.

ACTIVITY 1

application

Identify examples of positioning strategies relevant to the positioning variables in the table above.

3.2 Perceptual maps

One simple perceptual map that can be used is to plot brands or competing products in terms of two key characteristics such as price and quality.

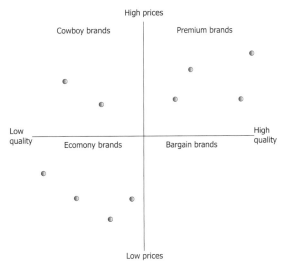

A perceptual map of market positioning can be used to **identify gaps in the market**. The example map we have shown suggests that there could be potential in the market for a low-price high-quality 'bargain brand'.

3.3 Mapping positions

Kotler (1996) identified a 3 × 3 matrix of nine different competitive positioning strategies.

	Product price		
Product quality			
	High price	*Medium price*	*Low price*
High	Premium strategy	Penetration strategy	Superbargain strategy
Medium	Overpricing strategy	Average-quality strategy	Bargain strategy
Low	Hit-and-run strategy	Shoddy goods strategy	Cheap goods strategy

Once selected, the needs of the targeted segment can be identified and the marketing mix strategy developed to provide the benefits package needed to satisfy them. Positioning the product offering then becomes a matter of matching and communicating appropriate benefits.

3.4 Steps in positioning

Step 1   Identify differentiating factors in products or services in relation to competitors

Step 2   Select the most important differences

Step 3   Communicate the position to the target market

The value of positioning is that it enables **tactical marketing mix decisions to be made**.

4   The marketing mix

    KEY CONCEPT   concept

Marketing mix: *is a set of controllable variables that the firm can use to influence the target market.* In its most basic form, the marketing mix has four elements: **product**, **price**, **place** and **promotion**.

The **marketing mix** is a fundamental concept which you are probably already familiar with. It is appropriate to consider it here because, as noted above, it is through the marketing mix that the firm attacks the target market it has chosen. It is absolutely necessary that the marketing mix is properly managed. For example, the elements of the marketing mix must be properly **integrated** so that they are mutually supporting. Also, elements in the marketing mix can, to some extent, act as **substitutes for each other**. For example, a firm can raise the selling price of its products if it also raises product quality or advertising expenditure. Equally, a firm can perhaps reduce its sales promotion expenditure if it is successful in achieving a wider range and larger numbers of sales outlets for its product.

There are four elements in the fundamental marketing mix.

- Product
- Place
- Promotion
- Price

4.1 Product

    KEY CONCEPT    concept

A **product** (goods or services) is anything that satisfies a need or want. It is not a 'thing' with 'features' but a package of benefits.

From the firm's point of view, the product element of the marketing mix is what is being sold, whether it be widgets, power stations, haircuts, holidays or financial advice. From the customer's point of view, a **product is a solution to a problem or a package of benefits**. Many products might satisfy the same customer need. On what basis might a customer choose?

(a)   **Customer value** is the customer's estimate of how far a product or service goes towards satisfying his or her need(s).

(b)   Every product has a price, and so the customer makes a **trade-off** between the **expenditure** and **the value offered**.

(c)   According to Kotler a customer must feel he or she gets a better deal from buying an item than by any of the alternatives.

The nature of the product

(a)   The **core product** is the most basic description of the product – a car is a means of personal transport. The **actual product** is the car itself, with all its physical features such as a powerful engine, comfortable seats and a sun roof. The **augmented product** is the car plus the benefits which come with it, such as delivery, servicing, warranties and credit facilities for buyers.

(b)   The **product range** consists of two dimensions.

  (i)   **Width**. A car maker may have products in all parts, known as segments, of the market: luxury cars, family cars, small cheap cars, and so on.

  (ii)   **Depth**. It may then offer a wide variety of options within each segment – a choice of engines, colours, accessories and so on.

(c)   **Benefits offered to the customer**. Customers differ in their attitudes towards new products and the benefits they offer.

Product issues in the marketing mix will include such factors as:

- Design (size, shape)
- Features
- Quality and reliability
- After-sales service (if necessary)
- Packaging

4.2 Place

Place deals with how the product is distributed, and how it reaches its customers.

(a)   **Channel**. Where are products sold? In supermarkets, corner shops, online? Which sales outlets will be chosen?

(b)   **Logistics**. The location of warehouses and efficiency of the distribution system is also important. A customer might have to wait a long time if the warehouse is far away. Arguably, the **speed of delivery** is an important issue in **place**, and delivery is becoming increasingly important as customers buy more goods online.

A firm can distribute the product itself (direct distribution) or distribute it through intermediary organisations such as retailers. Key issues are:

(a)   **Product push**: the firm directs its efforts to distributors to get them to stock the product.

(b)   **Customer pull**: the firm persuades consumers to demand the product from retailers and distributors, effectively pulling the product through the chain.

4.3 Promotion

Many of the practical activities of the marketing department are related to **promotion**. Promotion is the element of the mix over which the marketing department generally has most control. A useful mnemonic is AIDA which summarises the aims of promotion.

- Arouse **Attention**
- Generate **Interest**
- Inspire **Desire**
- Initiate **Action** (ie buy the product)

Promotion in the marketing mix includes all marketing communications which inform the public of the product or service.

- Advertising (newspapers, billboards, TV, radio, direct mail, internet)
- Sales promotion (discounts, coupons, special displays in particular stores)
- Direct selling by sales personnel.
- Public relations

4.4 Price

The price element of the marketing mix is the only one which brings in revenue. Price is influenced by many factors.

(a) **Economic influences**: supply and demand; price and income elasticities.

(b) **Competitors' prices**. Competitors include other firms selling the same type of product, as well as firms selling substitute products. Generally, firms like to avoid price wars.

(c) **Quality connotations**. High price is often taken as being synonymous with quality, so pricing will reflect the product's image. (Stella Artois lager was once marketed in the UK as being 'reassuringly expensive'.)

(d) **Discounts**. These can make the product attractive to distributors.

(e) **Payment terms** (eg offering a period of interest free credit).

(f) **Trade-in allowances**.

(g) The stage in the **product life cycle**

    (i) **Penetration pricing** is charging a low price to achieve early market share advantages.

    (ii) **Skimming pricing** is charging high prices early on to reap the maximum profits.

4.5 The extended marketing mix

This is also known as the service marketing mix because it is specifically relevant to the marketing of **services** rather than **physical products**. The intangible nature of services makes these extra three Ps particularly important.

4.5.1 People

The importance of employees in the marketing mix is particularly important in **service marketing**, because of the **inseparability** of the service from the service provider: the creation and consumption of the service generally happen at the same moment, at the interface between the server and the served. Front-line staff must be selected, trained and motivated with particular attention to customer care and public relations.

In the case of some services, the **physical presence** of people performing the service is a vital aspect of customer satisfaction. The staff involved are performing or producing a service, selling the service and also liaising with the customer to promote the service, gather information and respond to customer needs.

4.5.2 Processes

Efficient **processes** can become a marketing advantage in their own right. If an airline, for example, develops a sophisticated ticketing system, it can offer shorter waits at check-in or wider choice of flights through allied airlines. Efficient order processing not only increases customer satisfaction, but cuts down on the time it takes the organisation to complete a sale.

Issues to be considered include the following.

- Policies, particularly with regard to ethical dealings (a key issue for many consumers)
- Procedures, for efficiency and standardisation
- Automation and computerisation of processes
- Queuing and waiting times
- Information gathering, processing and communication times
- Capacity management, matching supply to demand in a timely and cost effective way
- Accessibility of facilities, premises, personnel and services

Such issues are particularly important in service marketing; because of the range of factors and people involved, it is difficult to standardise the service offered. Quality in particular specifications will vary with the circumstances and individuals.

Services are also innately **perishable**: their purchase may be put off, but they cannot be stored.

This creates a need for process planning for efficient work.

4.5.3 Physical evidence

Services are **intangible**: there is no physical substance to them. This means that even when money has been spent on them the customer has no **evidence of ownership**. These factors make it difficult for consumers to perceive, evaluate and compare the qualities of service provision, and may therefore dampen the incentive to consume.

Issues of intangibility and ownership can be tackled by making available a physical symbol or representation of the service product or of ownership, and the benefits it confers. For example, tickets and programmes relating to entertainment; and certificates of attainment in training are symbolic of the service received and a history of past positive experiences.

Physical evidence of service may also be incorporated into the design and specification of the service environment by designing premises to reflect the quality and type of service aspired to. Such environmental factors include finishing, decor, colour scheme, noise levels, background music, fragrance and general ambience.

5 Presenting the business case

 WORK BASED PROJECT TIP

format and presentation

Wilson (2006) suggests the following outline structure for an oral presentation.

- Introduction
- Explanation of research methodology
- Key findings
- Conclusions/recommendations
- Questions

This is not unlike the structure of a report, and many of the same points apply.

 ACTIVITY 2

application

What presentations, conferences, or speech-making occasions have you attended recently? For each, note:

- The style of speech (formal/informal etc)
- The length of the speech
- Any visual aids used

How effective was the speaker in targeting each of these elements to:

(a)   The purpose of the speech
(b)   The needs of the audience?

5.1 Audience

The audience's **motivations** and **expectations** in attending a presentation will influence their perceptions of you and your message. Why might they be at your presentation?

(a)   **They need specific information from the presentation**. An audience which is deliberately seeking information, and intending to use it to further their own objectives, is highly motivated. If their objectives match the speaker's (say, in a training seminar, where both trainer and trainees want improved job performance as the outcome), this motivation aids the speaker. It is therefore important to gauge, as far as possible, what this highly-motivated group **want** to hear from you, and **why**.

(b) **They are interested in the topic of the presentation**. The audience may have a general expectation that they will learn something new, interesting, or useful on a topic that they are pre-disposed to gather information about: it is up to the speaker to hold their attention by satisfying the desire for relevant information. They may also have some prior knowledge, on which the speaker can build: there will be a fine line to tread between boring the audience by telling them what they already know, and losing them by assuming more knowledge than they possess.

(c) **They are required to be there**.

    (i) Attendance may be **compulsory**, whether or not those attending are motivated or interested in the subject matter. In this case, you can at least find out the size and composition of your audience, but unless motivation and interest can be stimulated by the presentation, compulsory attendance may simply create resistance to the message.

    (ii) Attendance may be **recommended by a superior**, in which case even if the participants are not interested in the subject matter, they may be motivated to pay attention because they perceive it to be in their own interest to do so.

    This is known as a **captive audience**. Note that it is a double-edged sword: the audience may be compelled to listen to you, but they are actually **less** likely to listen attentively, co-operatively and with positive results, unless you can motivate them to do so once you have them in front of you.

(d) **They expect to be entertained**. The topic of the presentation may be entertaining or the audience may expect the speaker to put information across in an entertaining manner – using humour, illustration and so on. The organisation culture may encourage the idea that attending meetings and conferences is equivalent to rest and recreation: a bit of a 'day out' for the participants, more useful for the networking in the coffee breaks than the technical content of the presentations. As a speaker, you will have to ensure that you do not fulfil such expectations at the expense of your primary objectives – but be aware that the entertainment-seekers are also a potential audience for your message: it may be possible to arouse more motivated interest.

Taking into account any **specific** audience needs and expectations, your message needs to have the following qualities.

(a) **Interest**. It should be lively/entertaining/varied or relevant to the audience's needs and interests, or preferably both.

(b) **Congeniality**. This usually means positive, supportive or helpful in some way (eg in making a difficult decision easier, or satisfying a need).

(c) **Credibility**. It should be **consistent** in itself, and with known **facts**; apparently **objective**; and from a source perceived to be **trustworthy**.

(d) **Accessibility**. This means both:

- **Audible/visible**. (Do you need to be closer to the audience? Do you need a microphone? Enlarged visual aids? Clearer articulation and projection?)

- **Understandable**. (What is the audience's level of knowledge/education/ experience in general? and of the topic at hand? What technical terms or **jargon** will need to be avoided or explained? What concepts or ideas will need to be explained?)

5.2 Physical preparation

At the planning stage, you might also consider physical factors which will affect the audience's concentration: their ability and willingness to *keep* listening attentively and positively to your message. Some of the these may not be in your control, if you are not planning the meeting or conference, arranging the venue and so on, but as far as possible, give attention to the following.

(a) **Listening conditions**. Try and cut out background noise – conversations outside the room, traffic, loud air conditioning or rattling slide projector, say. (There may be a trade-off between peace and quiet, and good ventilation, also required for alertness: be sensible about the need to open a door or window or switch on a fan.)

(b) **Freedom from interruption and distraction**. Do not let the focus shift from the speaker and his message to outside views of people passing by and so on. Arrange not to be disturbed by others entering the room. Announce, if appropriate, that questions and comments will be invited at the end of the session.

(c) **Ventilation, heating and lighting**. A room that is too stuffy, or draughty, too hot or cold, too bright or too dim to see properly, can create physical malaise, and shifts attention from the speaker and his message to the listener and his discomfort.

(d) **Seating and desking**. Excessive comfort can impair alertness – but uncomfortable seating is a distraction. Combined with inadequate arrangements for writing (since many people may wish or need to take notes), it can cause severe strain over a lengthy talk.

(e) **Audibility and visibility**. Inadequate speaking volume or amplification is a distraction and a strain, even if it does not render the message completely inaccessible. Excessive volume and electronic noise is equally irritating. Visibility requires planning not just of effective visual aids (clear projection in suitable light, adequately enlarged etc) but also of seating plans, allowing unobstructed 'sight lines' for each participant.

(f) **Seating layout**. Depending on the purpose and style of your presentation, you may choose formal classroom-like rows of seating, with the speaker in front behind a podium, or informal group seating in a circle or cluster in which the speaker is included. The formal layout enhances the speaker's credibility, and may encourage attention to information, while the informal layout may be more congenial, encouraging involvement and input from the whole group.

(g) **Time**. Listeners get tired over time – however interesting the presentation: their concentration span is limited, and they will not be able to listen effectively for a long period without a break.

    (i) If you have the choice (and a limited volume of information to impart), a ten-minute presentation will be more effective than a one-hour presentation.

    (ii) If the volume of information or time allotted dictate a lengthy talk, you will need to build in reinforcements, breaks and 'breathers' for your listeners, by using repetition, summary, jokes/anecdotes, question-and-answer breaks and so on.

    (iii) Bear in mind, too, that the time of day will affect your listeners' concentration, even if your presentation is a brief one: you will have to work harder if your talk is first thing in the morning, late in the day (or week), or approaching lunch-time.

(h) **The speaker's appearance**. It should already be obvious that the appearance of the speaker may sabotage his efforts if it is uncongenial or unappealing, lacks credibility or the authority expected by the audience, is distracting in some way, and so on.

 ACTIVITY 3   application

In what other research circumstances besides the final presentation might the researcher find it useful to think about physical factors that will affect his or her audience's concentration?

5.3 Content

Armed with your clearly-stated objectives and audience profile, you can plan the **content** of your presentation.

One approach which may help to clarify your thinking is as follows.

Prioritise	Select the **key points** of the subject, and a **storyline** or theme that gives your argument a unified sense of 'direction'. The **fewer** points you make (with the most emphasis) and the clearer the **direction** in which your thoughts are heading, the easier it will be for the audience to grasp and retain your message.
Structure	Make notes for your presentation which **illustrate** simply the **logical order** or **pattern** of the key points of your speech.

Outline	Following your structured notes, **flesh out** your message. • **Introduction** • **Supporting evidence, examples and illustrations** • **Notes** where **visual aids** will be used • **Conclusion**
Practise	Rehearsals should indicate difficult logical leaps, dull patches, unexplained terms and other problems: adjust your outline or style. They will also help you gauge and adjust the **length** of your presentation.
Cue	Your outline may be too detailed to act as a cue or **aide-memoire** for the talk itself. **Small cards**, which fit into the palm of the hand may be used to give you: • **Key words** for each topic, and the logical links between them • Reminders for when to use **visual aids** • The **full text** of any detailed information you need to quote

An effective presentation requires two key structural elements.

(a)   An **introduction** which:

- Establishes your credibility.

- Establishes rapport with the audience.

- Gains the audience's attention and interest (sets up the problem to be solved, uses curiosity or surprise).

- Gives the audience an overview of the **shape** of your presentation, to guide them through it: a bit like the scanning process in reading.

(b)   A **conclusion** which:

- **Clarifies and draws together** the points you have made into one main idea (using an example, anecdote, review, summary).

- **States or implies what you want/expect your audience to do** following your presentation.

- Reinforces the audience's **recall** (using repetition, a joke, quotation or surprising statistic to make your main message **memorable**).

5.4 Clarity

Your structured notes and outline should contain cues which clarify the **logical order**, shape or progression of your information or argument. This will help the audience to **follow you** at each stage of your argument, so that they arrive with you at the conclusion. You can signal these logical links to the audience as follows.

(a)   **Linking words or phrases**

Therefore ...   [conclusion, result or effect, arising from previous point]
As a result ...
However ...   [contradiction or alternative to previous point]
On the other hand ...
Similarly ...   [confirmation or additional example of previous point]
Again ...
Moreover ...   [building on the previous point]

(b)   **Framework**: setting up the structure

'Of course, this isn't a perfect solution: There are advantages and disadvantages to it. It has the advantages of ... . But there are also disadvantages, in that ... '

(c)   You can use more elaborate devices which summarise or repeat the previous point and lead the audience to the next. These also have the advantage of giving you, and the listener, a 'breather' in which to gather your thoughts.

Other ways in which content can be used to clarify the message include the following.

(a)   **Examples and illustrations** – showing how an idea works in practice.

(b) **Anecdotes** – inviting the audience to relate an idea to a real-life situation.

(c) **Questions** – rhetorical, or requiring the audience to answer, raising particular points that may need clarification.

(d) **Explanation** – showing how or why something has happened or is so, to help the audience understand the principles behind your point.

(e) **Description** – helping the audience to visualise the person, object or setting you are describing.

(f) **Definition** – explaining the precise meaning of terms that may not be shared or understood by the audience.

(g) The use of **facts, quotations or statistics** – to 'prove' your point.

Your **vocabulary and style** in general should contribute to the clarity of the message. Remember to use short, simple sentences and non-technical words (unless the audience is sure to know them): avoid jargon, clichés, unexplained acronyms, colloquialisms, double meanings and vague expressions (like 'rather', 'good'). Remember, too, that this is **oral** communication, not written: use words and grammatical forms that you would **normally use in speaking** to someone – bearing in mind the audience's ability to understand you, the formality of the occasion and so on.

Visual aids will also be an important aspect of content used to signal the structure and clarify the meaning of your message. We discuss them specifically later.

5.5 Adding emphasis

Emphasis is the 'weight', importance or impact given to particular words or ideas. This can largely be achieved through delivery – the tone and volume of your voice, strong eye contact, emphatic gestures and so on – but can be reinforced in the content and wording of your speech. Emphasis can be achieved by a number of means.

(a) **Repetition**: 'If value for money is what the market wants, then value for money is what this brand must represent.'

'One in five customers has had a quality complaint. That's right: one in five.'

(b) **Rhetorical questions**: 'Do you know how many of your customers have a quality complaint? One in five. Do you think that's acceptable?'

(c) **Quotation**: '"Product quality is the number one issue in customer care in the new millennium." That's the conclusion of our survey report.'

(d) **Statistical evidence**: 'One in five of your customers this year have had a quality complaint: that's 10% more complaints than last year. If the trend continues, you will have one complaint for every two satisfied customers – next year!'

(e) **Exaggeration**: 'We have to look at our quality control system. Because if the current trend continues, we are going to end up without any customers at all.'

5.6 Adding interest

Simple, clear information often lacks impact, and will only be interesting to those already motivated by the desire for the information. The speaker will has to balance the need for clarity with the need to get the key points across. All the devices discussed so far can be used for impact.

Here are some further suggestions.

(a) **Analogy, metaphor, simile** etc – comparing something to something else which is in itself more colourful or interesting.

(b) **Anecdote or narrative** – as already mentioned, telling a story which illustrates or makes the point, using suspense, humour or a more human context.

(c) **Curiosity or surprise** – from incongruity, anticlimax or controversy. Verbatim quotes from customers can be very useful in this respect.

(d)   **Humour**. This is often used for entertainment value, but also serves as a useful 'breather' for listeners, and may help to get them on the speaker's side. (Humour may not travel well, however: the audience may not be on the speaker's wavelength at all, especially in formal contexts. Use with caution.)

5.7 Controlling nerves

Stage-fright can be experienced before making a phone call, going into an interview or meeting, or even writing a letter, but it is considerably more acute, for most people, before standing up to talk in front of a group or crowd of people. Common fears are to do with **making a fool of oneself**, forgetting one's **lines**, being unable to answer **questions**, or being faced by blank incomprehension or **lack of response**. Fear can make vocal delivery hesitant or stilted and **body language** stiff and unconvincing.

A **controlled amount of fear**, or stress, is actually **good for you**: it stimulates the production of **adrenaline**, which can contribute to alertness and dynamic action. Only at excessive levels is stress harmful, degenerating into **strain**. If you can **manage your stress** or stage-fright, it will help you to be **alert** to feedback from your audience, to think 'on your feet' in response to questions, and to project vitality and enthusiasm.

(a)   **Reduce uncertainty and risk**. This means:

- **Preparing thoroughly** for your talk, including rehearsal, and anticipating questions.

- **Checking** the venue and facilities meet your expectations.

- **Preparing** whatever is necessary for your own confidence and comfort (glass of water, handkerchief, note cards etc).

- **Keeping your notes to hand**, and in order, during your presentation.

(b)   **Have confidence in your message**. Concentrate on the desired outcome: that is why you are there. Believe in what you are saying. It will also make it easier to project enthusiasm and energy.

(c)   **Control physical symptoms**. Breathe deeply and evenly. Control your gestures and body movements. Put down a piece of paper that is visibly shaking in your hand. Pause to collect your thoughts if necessary. Smile, and maintain eye contact with members of the audience. If you **act** as if you are calm, the calm will **follow**.

5.8 Non-verbal messages

Any number of body language factors may contribute to a speaker **looking confident and relaxed**, or nervous, shifty and uncertain. **Cues** which indicate confidence – without arrogance – may be as follows.

(a)   An upright – but not stiff – **posture**: slouching gives an impression of shyness or carelessness.

(b)   **Movement** that is purposeful and dynamic, used sparingly: not constant or aimless pacing, which looks nervous.

(c)   **Gestures** that are relevant, purposeful and flowing: not indecisive, aggressive, incomplete or compulsive. Use gestures **deliberately** to reinforce your message, and if possible keep your hands up so that gestures do not distract the audience from watching your face. In a large venue, gestures will have to be exaggerated – but practise making them look **natural**. Watch out for habitual, irrelevant gestures you may tend to make.

(d)   **Eye-contact** with the audience maintains credibility, maintains the involvement of the audience and allows you to gather audience feedback as to how well you are getting your message across. Eye-contact should be **established immediately,** and **re-established** after periods when you have had to look away, to consult notes or use visual aids.

The most effective technique is to let our gaze wander (purposefully) across the whole audience, **involving** them all, without intimidating anybody: establish eye-contact long enough for it to be registered, to accompany a point you are making, and then move on.

5.9 Visual aids

KEY CONCEPT

concept

The term **visual aids** covers a wide variety of forms which share two characteristics.

(a)   They use a visual image.

(b)   They act as an aid to communication. This may seem obvious, but it is important to remember that visual aids are not supposed to be impressive or clever for their own sake, but to support the message and speaker in achieving their purpose.

A number of media and devices are available for using visual aids. They may be summarised as follows.

Equipment/medium	Advantages	Disadvantages
Slides: photographs, text or diagrams projected onto a screen or other surface	• Allow colour photos: good for mood, impact and realism • Pre-prepared: no speaker 'down time' during talk • Controllable sequence/ timing: pace content/audience needs	• Require a darkened room: may hinder note-taking • Malfunction and/or incompetent use: frustration and distraction
Film/video shown on a screen or TV monitor	• Moving images: realism, impact: can enhance credibility (eye witness effect)	• Less flexible in allowing interruption, pause or speeding-up to pace audience needs
Overheads: films or acetates (hand drawn or printed) projected by light box onto a screen behind/above the presenter	• Versatility of content and presentation • Low cost (for example, if hand written) • Clear sheets: can be used to build-up images as points added	• Require physical handling: can be distracting • Risk of technical breakdown: not readily adaptable to other means of projection
Presentation software: for example, Microsoft PowerPoint. PC-generated slide show (with animation, sound) projected from PC to screen via data projector	• Versatility of multi-media: impact, interest • Professional design and functioning (smooth transitions) • Use of animation to build, link and emphasise as points added	• Requires PC, data projector: expensive, may not be available • Risk of technical breakdown: not readily adaptable to other means of projection • Temptation to over-complexity and over-use: distraction
Flip charts: large paper pad mounted on frame – sheets are 'flipped' to the back when finished with	• Low cost, low-risk • Allows use during session (for example, to 'map' audience views, ideas) • Can be pre-prepared (for example, advertising 'story boards') • Easy to refer back	• Smaller, still, paper-based image: less impact • Hand-prepared: may lack perceived quality (compared to more sophisticated methods)
Handouts: supporting notes handed out for reference during or after the session	• Pre-prepared • Audience doesn't need to take as many notes: reminder provided	• Audience doesn't need to take as many notes: may encourage passive listening.

Equipment/medium	Advantages	Disadvantages
Props and demonstrations: objects or processes referred to are themselves shown to the audience	• Enhances credibility (eye witness effect) • Enhances impact (sensory solidity)	• May not be available • Risk of self-defeating 'hitches'

The following illustrations show two of the media discussed above, demonstrating some of their key features – and showing how a picture can be a helpful 'break' from reading or hearing lots of verbal content!

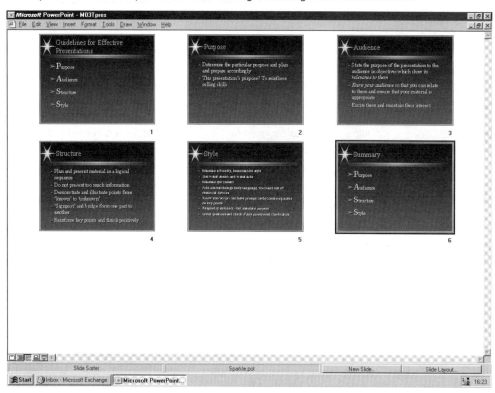

Whatever medium or device you are using, visual aids are **versatile** with regard to **content**: maps, diagrams, flowcharts, verbal notes, drawings, photographs and so on.

When planning and using visual aids, consider the following points.

(a)   Visual aids are **simplified and concrete**: they are easier to grasp than the spoken word, allowing the audience to absorb complex relationships and information.

(b) Visual aids are **stimulating** to the imagination and emotions, and therefore useful in gaining attention and recall.

(c) Visual aids can also be **distracting** for the audience – and for the presenter, who has to draw/write/organise /operate them. They can add complexity and ambiguity to the presentation if not carefully designed for relevance and clarity.

(d) Visual aids impose **practical requirements**.

- The medium you choose must be **suitable** for the needs of your **audience**. Demonstrations, or handing round a small number of samples, is not going to work for a large audience. A flipchart will not be visible at the back of a large room; a slide projector can be overwhelming in a small room. A darkened room, to show video or slides, will not allow the audience to take notes.

- **Skill, time and resources** must be available for any pre-preparation of aids that may be required in advance of the presentation.

- **The equipment, materials and facilities** you require must be available in the venue, and you must **know** how to **use** them. (No good turning up with a slide projector if there is no power source, or film when there is no overhead projector, or without proper pens for a particular type of board.)

The following are some **guidelines** for effective use of visual aids.

(a) Ensure that the aid is:

- **Appropriate** to your message, in content and style or mood
- **Easy to see** and understand
- Only used when there is **support** to be gained from it

(b) Ensure that all **equipment** and materials are **available and working** and that you can (and do) operate them efficiently and confidently. This includes having all your slides/acetates/notes with you, in the right order, the right way up and so on.

(c) Ensure that the aid does not become a **distraction**.

(i) Show each image **long enough** to be absorbed and noted, but not so long as to merge with following idea.

(ii) Maintain **voice and eye contact** with your audience, so they know that it is you who are the communicator, not the machine.

(iii) **Introduce** your aids and what they are for, placing the focus on the verbal presentation.

(iv) Hand out **supporting material** either well before the presentation (to allow reading beforehand) or at the relevant point: if you hand it out just before, it will distract or daunt the audience with information they do not yet understand.

(v) **Write or draw**, if you need to do so during the presentation, as quickly and efficiently as possible (given the need for legibility and neatness).

The look of presentation slides (or other visual aids) is very important. Make sure that they are:

- Simple: not too many points
- Visually appealing: use graphics and type styles to create an effect
- Neat: especially if you are preparing them by hand

5.10 Handling questions

Inviting or accepting questions is usually the final part of a presentation.

(a) In informative presentations, questions offer an **opportunity to clarify any misunderstandings**, or gaps that the audience may have perceived.

(b) In persuasive presentations, questions offer an opportunity to address and overcome specific doubts or resistance that the audience may have, which the speaker may not have been able to anticipate.

The manner in which you 'field' questions may be crucial to your **credibility**. Everyone knows you have prepared your presentation carefully: ignorance, bluster or hesitation in the face of a question may cast doubt on your expertise, or sincerity, or both. Moreover, this is usually the last stage of the presentation, and so leaves a lasting impression.

The only way to tackle questions effectively is to **anticipate** them. Put yourself in your audience's shoes, or, more specifically, in the shoes of an ignorant member of the audience, a hostile member and a member with a particular axe to grind: what questions might *they* ask and why? When questions arise, listen to them carefully, assess the questioner's manner, and draw the questioner out if necessary, in order to ascertain exactly *what* is being asked, and *why*. People might ask questions:

(a)   To **seek additional information** of particular interest to them, or to the group – if you have left it out of your talk

(b)   To seek **clarification** of a point that is not clear

(c)   To **add information** of their own, which may be relevant, helpful and accurate – or not

(d)   To **lead the discussion into another area** (or away from an uncomfortable one)

(e)   To display their **own knowledge or cleverness**

(f)   To **undermine** the speaker's authority or argument, to 'catch him out'

If you have anticipated questions of the first two kinds (a) and (b) in the planning of your talk, they should not arise: incorporate the answers in your outline

The important points about **answering questions** are as follows.

(a)   You may **seek feedback** throughout your talk, as to whether your message is getting across clearly – and it is common to invite the audience to let you know if anything is unclear – but by and large, you should encourage questions only at the *end* of your presentation. That way, disruptive, rambling, hostile and attention-seeking questions will not be allowed to disrupt your message to the audience as a whole.

(b)   You should **add or clarify** information if required to achieve your purpose. An honest query deserves a co-operative answer.

(c)   You need to **maintain your credibility** and authority as the speaker. Strong tactics may be required for you to stay in control, without in any way ridiculing or 'putting down' the questioner.

   (i)   If a question is based on a **false premise** or incorrect information, **correct it**. An answer may, or may not, then be required.

   (ii)   If a question is **rambling**: interrupt, clarify what the question, or main question (if it is a multiple query) is, and answer that. If it is completely irrelevant, say politely that it is outside the scope of the presentation: you may or may not offer to deal with it informally afterwards.

   (iii)   If a question is **hostile or argumentative**, you may wish to show understanding of how the questioner has reached his conclusion, or why he feels as he does. However, you then need to reinforce, repeat or explain your own view.

   (iv)   If a question tries to **pin you down** or 'corner' you on an area in which you do not wish to be specific or to make promises, be straightforward about it.

   (v)   If a question exposes an area in which you do not know the answer, **admit your limitations** with honesty and dignity, and invite help from members of the audience, if appropriate.

   (vi)   Try and answer all questions with **points already made** in your speech, or related to them. This reinforces the impression that your speech was in fact complete and correct.

(d)   **Repeat** any question that you think might not have been **audible** to everyone in the room.

(e)   **Clarify** any question that you think is lengthy, complex, ambiguous or uses jargon not shared by the audience as a whole.

(f)   **Answer briefly**, keeping strictly to the point of the question (while relating it, if possible, to what you have already said). If your answer needs to be lengthy, structure it as you would a small talk: introduce what you are going to say, say it, then confirm what you have said!

(g)   Keep an eye on the **overall time-limit** for your talk or for the question-and-answer session. Move on if a questioner is taking up too much time, and call a halt, courteously, when required. 'I'll take one more question ... ' or 'I'm afraid that's all we have time for' is standard practice which offends few listeners.

Learning objectives		Covered	
1	Use market research information to assess and evaluate customer groups relevant to the business case (targeting element)	☑	Segment validity and attractiveness
		☑	Target markets
		☑	Positioning
2	Evaluate the interaction of target market choice and the marketing mix	☑	Marketing mix explained
3	Assess resource requirements	☑	Marketing resources
4	Present the business case	☑	Audience
		☑	Preparation
		☑	Content and clarity emphasis methods

1   What criteria must be satisfied if a market segment is to be valid?

2   How do barriers to entry affect segment attractiveness?

3   What four categories of organisational capability does Jobber identify as of importance when assessing segment attractiveness?

4   What are the features of mass customisation?

5   What are the three policy options in selecting target markets?

6   What is positioning?

7   What is underpositioning?

8   What did Kotler call a positioning strategy that combines medium price with low quality?

9   What are the three extra Ps present in the extended marketing mix used for services?

10 List five reasons why people might ask questions when attending a presentation.

1.

Positioning strategy	Example
Attributes	Ads for PCs emphasise 'speed', what sort of chip they have (eg Pentium III)
Benefit	Holidays are advertised as offering relaxation or excitement
Use/application	'Easy to use' products (eg hair tints that can be 'washed' in)
User	Reflect user characteristics, to appeal to the target audience and confirm their choice. May use celebrity endorsement, such as David Beckham in Vodafone advertisements
Product category	The Natural History Museum is fundamentally educational, but is moving towards a 'theme park' image for the schools market
Quality/price	'Value for money' advertisements

2. The answer to this depends upon your own experiences.

3. We had in mind a situation when the researcher is conducting qualitative research, particularly focus groups and also when an agency first presents its proposal to a client in a beauty parade.

1 Measurability, size, accessibility, response, profitability, stability

2 Entry might require significant investment, but the barriers then provide some protection against other potential entrants

3 Exploitable marketing assets, cost advantages, technological edge and managerial capability and commitment

4 Economies of scale and tailoring of products to individual requirements

5 Differentiated, undifferentiated and concentrated marketing

6 Designing the offer to achieve a distinct and valued place in the customer's mind

7 Failure to achieve a clear position in the customer's mind

8 Shoddy goods strategy

9 People, processes and physical evidence

10 To seek additional information, to seek clarification, to add information, to lead the discussion into another area, to display their own cleverness, to undermine the speaker.

Hooley, G. et al. (2007) Marketing strategy and competitive positioning, (4th edition), Prentice Hall, Harrow.

Jobber, D. (2009) Principles and Practice of Marketing (6th edition), McGraw-Hill, Maidenhead.

Kotler, P (1996) Marketing Management: Analysis, Planning and Control, 9th revised edition, Pearson, Harlow.

Wilson, A. (2006) Marketing Research: An Integrated Approach, (2nd edition), Financial Times/Prentice Hall, London.

Chapter 5
Understanding risk

Topic list

Introduction

Life is full of risk and it is necessary for us to consider how we will deal with it, both as individuals and in our roles as marketing specialists. We must develop a realistic approach to dealing with risk if we are to take cost-effective precautions where they are warranted and avoid needless concern over unrealistically alarming perceptions of risk. In this chapter we will discuss the nature of risk as it affects organisations generally and businesses in particular. We will also examine the various types and sources of risk we may encounter.

Syllabus-linked learning objectives

By the end of the chapter you will be able to:

Learning objectives	Syllabus link
1 Understand risk in organisations in order to protect the long-term stability of a range of marketing projects	3.1
2 Understand the differences between types of organisational risk	3.2
3 Analyse and assess potential internal and external sources of risk relevant to a specific case and consider the impact of these risks on the organisation	3.3

1 Risk and uncertainty

1.1 Introduction

In the world of business, future events cannot be foretold with certainty. The confidence with which forecasts can be made varies from very high to nil, depending on the matter under consideration. Nevertheless, plans must be made. A consideration of possible future events is thus fundamental to management. Some of the variation in potential outcomes is taken for granted in the normal process of business planning and budgeting. For example, circumstances and business conditions may result in a five or ten per cent difference between actual sales and the budgeted sales without any major consequences for the sales team or the organisation. However, A difference of 60 or 70% would be likely to have major consequences and it would be appropriate for the Sales Director to understand in advance the circumstances that might bring about such a difference, their likely further implications and what, if anything, should be done about them.

1.2 Risk and uncertainty

We may distinguish between **risk** and **uncertainty**.

 KEY CONCEPT concept

(a) **Risk** is measurable by considering the way in which past data varies. For example, records will tell us the number of life assurance policyholders that survive beyond the age of 65.

(b) **Uncertainty** is not quantifiable in this way. For example, we cannot say whether a given policyholder will survive beyond the age of 65, or even until next week.

Thus, if the occurrence of a possible future event is capable of statistical or mathematical evaluation, we may reasonably speak in terms of risk. If no such evaluation is possible, we are dealing with uncertainty.

This definition of risk is clearly most relevant where clear statistical records of past events can be used. Also, it assumes that the future will resemble the past, an idea that should always be treated with caution. In practice, the distinction between risk and uncertainty is not clear. Major insurance losses demonstrate that assessments of risk have been undermined by unexpected events such as floods, and health claims arising from the use of asbestos in the past.

Despite the use of the term 'risk', businesses actually operate under uncertainty. A marketing team that only proposed strategies with precisely quantifiable risk would not launch new products, enter new markets, or develop new technologies.

1.2.1 Probability

Uncertainty is sometimes treated as though it were risk by the use of subjective probabilities.

(a)   **Objective probability** is a statistical measure of likelihood based on data on past occurrences.

(b)   **Subjective probability** is a value for the variability of a factor based on a best guess by management or experts.

Note carefully the use of the word *guess*.

 ACTIVITY 1   application

The records of Palindrome Limited indicate that its fleet of delivery vans has suffered the total loss of 14 vehicles over the last seven years. During that period, turnover has increased by 350%, road vehicle registrations in its region have increased by 84% and annual average mileage per van has increased by 35%.

How many total losses should the transport manager budget for in the coming year?

1.2.2 Classes of uncertainty

Courtney et al (1997) suggest that uncertainty cannot always be quantified into risk. They describe four kinds of uncertainty.

(a)   **Clear enough futures** can be assessed with reasonable accuracy because they continue things much as before, without major change. An example would be the forecasts of milk sales made by a grocer.

(b)   **Alternative futures** depend on an event. An example would be that the value of right to make supporter merchandise for a particular football team depends on whether or not it wins its league.

(c)   A **range of futures** exists when an outcome depends on several variables that interact. For example, hotel operators' sales forecasts depend on resort weather, airline ticket prices, general economic conditions and so on.

(d)   **True ambiguity** exists when the outcome is influenced a large number of unpredictable variables. For example, the outcome of investment in emerging economies will be determined by a wide range of variables such as politics, global economic developments, disasters, cultural change and so on.

The first two of these classes could perhaps be quantified with acceptable accuracy. The other two are much more uncertain. Managers must be prepared to deal with all four.

1.3 Probability and consequences

For business purposes of managing risk, we are concerned with more than the probability of a future event. We must also consider the consequences if it happens. The chance of flipping a coin and getting heads is 50%. Risk only arises if we gamble on the outcome. The larger the amount at stake, the bigger the risk, but the probability stays the same. We must, therefore, always consider both the **probability** and the **potential consequences** of a possible future event.

1.3.1 Defining risk

 KEY CONCEPT   concept

Risk: For the purposes of risk management, risk can be defined as the combination of the likelihood of an event and its consequences.

That is:

Risk = Probability × consequences

Since businesses are mainly interested in financial impact, we may extend this to say:

Risk = Probability × financial consequences

ACTIVITY 2

Flying as a passenger in an airliner is often stated to be safer than crossing the road. However, airliner crashes tend to kill all on board, but road accidents, while deadly for some, merely injure others. Can you make sense of this?

1.4 Upside and downside

When we consider risk, we are usually concerned with negative outcomes: But this is only half the picture. Risk implies **variability**, some of which may work In the favour of the business. We thus have **upside risk** as well as **downside risk**. Risk management is concerned with both the positive and negative aspects of risk.

For example, a home buyer may take out a fixed rate mortgage. This removes the downside risk of possible future mortgage rate increases, but it also removes the upside risk that mortgage rates might fall.

Businesses can use sophisticated financial instruments to manage their downside risk, while at the same time leaving open the potential to share in any upside; generally, this flexibility will come at a price premium. In a house purchase, a capped rate loan would eliminate much of the risk of a mortgage rate rise while retaining the benefit from an interest rate fall. However, such a mortgage would be more expensive from the outset.

When there is only downside risk and no upside potential, this is called **true risk**. An example would be the possibility of a natural disaster.

MARKETING AT WORK

Ford Motor Company

In 2004, the Ford Motor Company identified some of the risks it faced.

(a) Greater price competition resulting from currency fluctuations, industry overcapacity or other factors

(b) A significant decline in industry sales, particularly in the US or Europe, resulting from slowing economic growth, geo-political events or other factors

(c) Lower-than-anticipated market acceptance of new or existing products

(d) Economic distress of suppliers that may require us to provide financial support or take other measures to ensure supplies of materials

(e) Work stoppages at Ford or supplier facilities or other interruptions of supplies

(f) The discovery of defects in vehicles resulting in delays in new model launches, recall campaigns or increased warranty costs

(g) Increased safety, emissions, fuel economy or other regulations resulting in higher costs and/or sales restrictions

(h) Unusual or significant litigation or governmental investigations arising out of alleged defects in our products or otherwise

(i) Worse-than-assumed economic and demographic experience for our post-retirement benefit plans (eg investment returns, interest rates, health care cost trends, benefit improvements)

(j) Currency or commodity price fluctuations, including rising steel prices

(k) Changes in interest rates

Source: Ford Motor Group Annual Report, 2004

How many of these have 'come true' from our vantage point in 2010/2011?

1.5 Risk in the context of project management

Risk is inevitable in projects and needs to be managed in a positive way. There are some specific factors that are commonly associated with high risk.

- Organisational issues (such as attitude to change)
- Management structure (poor communications, undefined responsibilities for example)
- Team composition and level of expertise
- Type of project (R&D and IT projects are particularly risky)
- Projects involving unproven technology
- Inadequate resources
- Fast-tracked projects (timescale involved)
- Complex projects with inherent risks (eg legal, political, safety)

The following diagram illustrates the process of project management and how risk is managed throughout it.

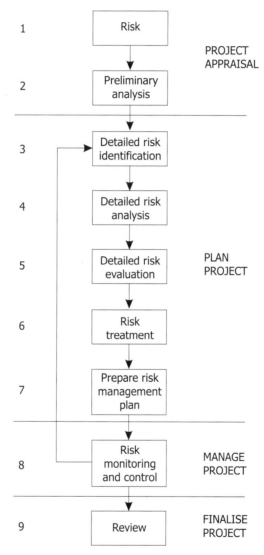

2 Attitudes to risk

2.1 Introduction

People generally have different attitudes to risk and this is as true of them in their management role as it is of them as individuals. Managers must take a measured view of the risk and uncertainty associated with possible future events.

2.2 Risk perspective and risk appetite

It is tempting to try to proceed on the basis that risk and, therefore, undesirable events can be entirely avoided. This is, however, unrealistic: some risk will always be present no matter what precautions may be taken. Also, the avoidance of risk imposes costs and it is a simple principle that costs and benefits should be balanced. Simple precautions will generally have a major impact on risk but the law of diminishing returns is likely to apply: each further reduction in risk is likely to be more expensive to achieve than the previous one. It is important, therefore, that both organisations and individuals should establish a realistic **risk perspective**.

 KEY CONCEPT concept

Risk perspective simply means taking a **measured view** of both the probability of an undesirable future event and its potential impact as already outlined. In broad terms, it is only if both probability and potential impact are of significant magnitude that extensive risk management effort becomes appropriate.

In a business context it is important to remember that risk and reward are usually linked: projects offering higher potential rewards are usually riskier than those offering more modest returns (though high risk linked to low return is not unknown). A company's desire to increase the returns it achieves may thus incline it to take on extra risk. We may thus say that risk appetite or risk tolerance varies.

2.3 Risk and management culture

Miles and Snow (2003) analysed a sample of large corporations. They suggest that superior performance is associated with consistency in mission and values; strategies; and characteristics and behaviour. Attitude to risk is relevant to all of these things. Miles and Snow suggested that there are four types of business, defined by the ways in which their management approach strategic challenges.

- Defenders
- Prospectors
- Analysers
- Reactors

Of the four types identified, the first three may exhibit superior performance. Reactors tend to perform less well.

2.4 Defenders – low risk tolerance

Defenders concentrate on a single core technology and a specific product or service They are often vertically integrated. They tend to have strong finances and a stable structure. The efficiency of their internal processes gives them a competitive advantage, which they maintain by incremental improvements.

Defenders perform best in stable markets with high barriers to entry. They grow cautiously and incrementally. They have a narrow area of operations and tend not to look for business opportunities outside their sphere of expertise, preferring to increase the depth of their skills within their current markets.

The risk tolerance of such businesses is consequently quite low.

2.5 Prospectors – seeking risk

Prospectors are very different from defenders. They are entrepreneurial innovators and pursue new products and markets aggressively. They continually search for potential responses to emerging trends and maintain a flexibility to respond to change. Their innovations cause change and uncertainty to which their competitors must respond.

Prospectors are risk seekers, willing to take on the risks associated with new developments in order to benefit from them.

2.6 Analysers – balancing risk and return

Analysers balance the risk-avoidance attitude of the defenders and the risk-seeking attitude of prospectors. They innovate more deliberately than prospectors, observing market reaction to new developments and analysing the key success factors of any new opportunity before committing themselves. When they launch new products, they aim to achieve a high level of efficiency in order to build and maintain market share. It is these products that tend to be the major revenue generators.

Analysers operate in two product/market areas. In the stable areas, analysers perform as defenders, using efficient structures and processes to achieve high returns. In the changing area they act more like prospectors, adapting to any promising changes.

Analysers cannot be said to be risk-averse, but they minimise risk where they can.

2.7 Reactors – inconsistent attitude to risk

Reactors do not have any consistent or clearly defined strategy or effectively managed supporting technology, structure, and processes. They are inconsistent and ineffective in their responses to environmental developments, seldom making changes until forced to do so.

Reactors generally fail to manage risk sensibly, avoiding the obvious risks, which undermines their strategic development, and failing to detect more fundamental and threatening risks.

2.8 Other influences on risk appetite

Other factors may influence the organisation's risk appetite.

*   **Expectations of shareholders**: a long history of stable performance will attract risk-averse investors.

*   **National origin of the organisation**: the appetite for change and desire for stability vary somewhat from place to place.

*   **Regulatory framework**: many organisations must implement a wide range of regulations designed to minimise various aspects of risk. Airlines are an example: they must minimise the exposure of passengers to risk.

*   **Nature of ownership**: managers of state-owned enterprises gain little from successfully making risky ventures but they will lose heavily if they make unsuccessful ones. Similarly, a family firm may be prevented from risk taking by the influence or dependence of family members.

*   **Personal views**: surveys suggest that managers obtain emotional satisfaction from successful risk-taking. This has been attributed in part to the fact that, unlike shareholders, they will not suffer a loss of wealth if their gambles fail.

3 Risk identification

3.1 Types of risk

Ultimately, all harmful events have financial consequences. For example, the oil leak from the Deepwater Horizon rig in the Gulf of Mexico in 2010 has cost BP dearly, both in terms of financial resources and its reputation. The oil leak was triggered by an explosion at the rig. Before the explosion, senior managers at Transocean (from whom BP leased the rig) had complained BP were taking short cuts in some of their operating routines and in doing so increasing the risk of such a disaster occurring.

It is possible to analyse the risk of potential harmful occurrences into a range of types and for the purpose of managing risk it is helpful to do so.

Business and financial risk

 KEY CONCEPT

concept

Business risk is about the variability of returns traceable to the way a business operates.

Business risk can be analysed into three main areas.

- **Strategic risk** is associated with wider environmental factors that affect the long-term strategic objectives of the business. The business is vulnerable to developments relating to, for instance, competitors, customers, reputation, law, regulation, economic conditions and politics. Strategic risk also encompasses risk relating to knowledge resources, including intellectual property, key personnel and production technology.

- **Operational risk** arises from the effectiveness of day-to-day management and control systems and structures in dealing with such matters as health and safety, consumer protection and data security. **Compliance risk** is the kind of operational risk associated with non-compliance with laws or regulations. This includes breaches by both the company and by a stakeholder, such as a customer or supplier, that have consequences for the company.

- **Hazard risk** arises from the business's exposure to natural and human-induced hazards such as fire, extreme weather, fraud and negligence.

Financial risk arises from the way the business is financed. Its level of **gearing** (the ratio between loan capital and share capital) is particularly important, since interest on loans must be paid even when times are hard, while dividends on shares can be reduced or missed altogether. Also important are exposure to credit risk; interest and exchange rates; and liquidity risks. Financial risk tends to amplify the inherent business risk at low levels of gearing, and at higher levels may directly contribute to the risk of business failure.

Overall risk

The *International Risk Standard* shows these types of risk diagrammatically.

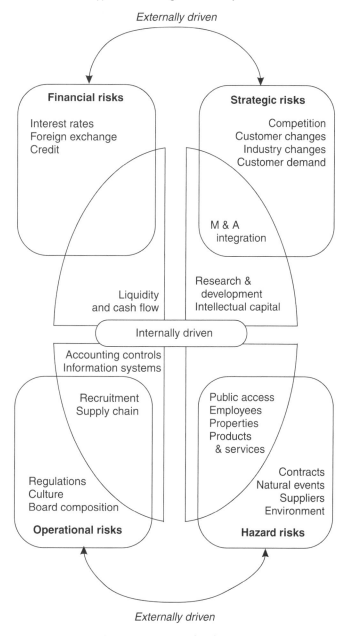

Source: Institute of Risk Management – A Risk Management Standard

4 Sources of risk

4.1 Introduction

The various types of risk discussed above can be traced to a wide variety of sources, both internal to the organisation and external to it (as noted on the risk model diagram above). The external sources of the various types of risk can be analysed using the popular SLEPT classification and its variants (PEST, PESTEL). Organisations cal also use SWOT analysis for analysing risks (weaknesses, threats) they face. In this section we will discuss some important sources of risk, including those affecting companies operating internationally.

4.2 Political risks

Political risk is largely concerned with the possibility of a change of government. Most developed nations offer a reasonably stable political environment, though they may present important risks in relation to such matters as tax rates; building and other development policy and regulation; and labour law. Less developed countries may present enhanced risk of rapid change in government policy. The areas of policy that most commonly present risk are discussed below.

- **Import quotas** limit the quantity of goods that a subsidiary can buy from its parent company and import for resale.

- **Import tariffs** make imports more expensive and domestically produced goods, therefore, become more competitive.

- **Exchange control regulations** can complicate or prevent the remittance of profits.

- **Nationalisation** of foreign-owned companies and their assets, with or without compensation may be a threat.

- **Legal standards** relating to safety or quality can be deliberately used as non-tariff barriers to imports.

- **Laws relating to ownership** could restrict the ability of foreign companies to buy domestic companies, even on a partnership or minority basis. This is especially relevant to companies that operate in politically sensitive industries such as defence contracting, communications, energy supply and so on.

4.3 Business and economic factors

Business operations are heavily influenced by economic fundamentals such as the availability of resources and the operation of market forces. Linked to this is the effect of government attempts at macro-economic management. Several sources of risk can be identified. Developments in any may create sources of risk.

- The **economic cycle** typically varies between benign and difficult trading conditions. Different countries may be at different stages of the cycle at any one time.

- **Monetary**, **fiscal and exchange rate policies** differ both internationally and from time-to-time within a single nation.

- **Labour force** capability, mobility and cost vary widely.

- **Economic infrastructure** such as transport links, training facilities and capital markets may or may not be adequately developed.

4.4 Trading risks

All traders will face trading risks, although those faced by companies trading internationally will generally be greater because of the increased distances and times involved.

- **Physical risk** is the risk of goods being lost or stolen in transit, or of the accompanying documents being lost.

- **Credit risk** is the possibility that the customer will fail to pay.

- **Trade risk is** the risk that the customer may refuse to accept delivery of the goods or cancel the order during transit.

- **Liquidity risk** is the risk of being unable to finance the trade credit required.

4.5 Social and cultural risk

Risks may need to be managed in connection with trends and developments relating to socio-cultural elements such as those listed below.

- Age and sex distribution of the population
- Geographic concentration of the population
- Ethnicity and religion
- Household and family structure: the accepted roles of the sexes may be particularly important.

- Class
- Employment patterns
- Wealth distribution

ACTIVITY 3

application

How might the geographic distribution of the population present risk?

4.6 Legal risk

Companies may be confronted with legislation or legal action that affects its activities. Some important topics are given below.

- The **general legal framework** relating to such matters as tort, agency and contract and product liability

- **Criminal law**, especially relating to such matters as insider trading, deception, product safety and industrial espionage

- **Monopolies, mergers, competition and restraint of trade** legislation

- **Property rights** including law relating to intellectual property

- **Taxation**

- **Marketing communications**, including restrictions on promotional messages, methods and media

Companies may also be at risk from inadequate legislation (or poor enforcement of legislation) that fails to protect them.

Legal penalties and accompanying bad publicity may have severe effects on businesses that fail to comply with the law. Legal standards and costs are particularly significant for companies trading internationally. Companies may relocate to countries with lower legal costs and regulatory burdens.

4.7 Technology

Technological change can present sources of risk affecting commercial organisations. The risks generally are of being too fast or too slow in exploiting the new technology. The most successful companies allow others to take the risks associated with breaking the new ground and move in when a successful launch seems likely. Risk arises from sources such as those shown below.

- **The type of products or services** that are made and sold

- **The way in which products are made** (consider robots, new raw materials)

- **The way in which services are provided**. For example, companies selling easily transportable goods, such as books and CDs can offer much greater consumer choice and are enjoying considerable success over the Internet.

- **The way in which markets are identified**. Database systems make it much easier to analyse the market place.

- **The way in which firms are managed**. IT encourages delayering of organisational hierarchies, home working, and better communication.

- **The means and extent of communications with external clients**. Many services are now provided by telephone and online.

ACTIVITY 4

application

How might risk arise in connection with the way in which products are made?

4.8 Risks from IT systems

IT systems are particularly important sources of risk because of their vulnerability and importance to the organisation.

- **Natural threats** include fire, flood and electrical storms.

- **Human threats**: may be malicious or accidental. Politically inspired cyber-terrorism is a major risk.

- **Data systems integrity** may be compromised by such problems as incorrect entry of data, use of out-of-date files and loss of data through lack of back-ups.

- **Fraud** may be perpetrated by the dishonest use of a computer system.

- **Deliberate sabotage**

- **Viruses** and other malware can spread to all of the organisation's computers through the Internet or through its own internal network. **Hackers** may be able to steal data or damage the system.

- **A denial of service attack** is an attempt by attackers to prevent legitimate users of a service from using it.

- **Non-compliance with regulations**: The use of IT systems, and the data they contain, is subject to close legal supervision in most countries.

 MARKETING AT WORK   application

Cyber attack on Estonia

For a small, hi-tech country such as Estonia, the Internet is vital. But for the past two weeks Estonia's state websites (and some private ones) have been hit by 'denial of service' attacks, in which a target site is bombarded with so many bogus requests for information that it crashes.

The Internet warfare broke out on April 27 [2007], amid a furious row between Estonia and Russia over the removal of a Soviet war monument from the centre of the capital.

The Internet attacks involved defacing Estonian websites, replacing the pages with Russian propaganda or bogus apologies. Most have concentrated on shutting them down. The attacks are intensifying. The number on May 9 – the day when Russia and its allies commemorate Hitler's defeat in Europe – was the biggest yet, says Hillar Aarelaid, who runs Estonia's cyber-warfare defences. At least six sites were all but inaccessible, including those of the foreign and justice ministries. Such stunts happen at the murkier end of Internet commerce: for instance, to extort money from an online casino. But no country has experienced anything on this scale.

Source: Economist Magazine, May 2007

Learning objectives	Covered
1 Understand risk in organisations in order to protect the long-term stability of a range of marketing projects	☑ Probability and consequences
	☑ Attitudes to risk
2 Understand the differences between types of organisational risk	☑ Internal and external

	☑ Int. risk standard
	   – strategic
	   – operational
	   – hazard
	   – financial

3 Analyse and assess potential internal and external sources of risk relevant to a specific case and consider the impact of these risks on the organisation	☑ Political risk
	☑ Business and economic factors
	☑ Trading risks
	☑ Social and cultural risk
	☑ Legal risk
	☑ Technology

Quick quiz

1 Risk = ... × ....

2 Distinguish between and an objective and a subjective probability.

3 What are the main categories of risk identified in the International Risk Standard?

4 Identify the four descriptions of management attitudes to strategic risk identified by *Miles and Snow*.

5 Define a realistic risk perspective.

6 What is credit risk?

7 What is a denial of service attack?

1. This is a very difficult question to answer. There is wealth of statistical information that would permit the calculation of past rates of loss, but they all produce different answers. The most useful pieces of information, which are the number of losses, the average size of the fleet and the average mileage per vehicle in the preceding year are not given. Presumably the transport manager would have these figures available. We do not, so, despite the information given, we can do no more than guess.

2. Accident statistics tend to be computed in terms of 'death or serious injury'. This means that we can make fair comparisons of consequences. On this basis, the much lower probability of accidents per mile travelled mean that flying is much safer.

3. Distribution systems must deal specifically with geography. Where the population is evenly spread over a wide area or perhaps distributed in a linear fashion, distribution costs may be greater than expected where the population is more concentrated.

4. New methods might give competitors a cost saving that would increase their ability to compete on price. However, adoption of new methods might impose unacceptable capital and training costs and interruption to production. There may be hazards associated with new machinery or processes and there may be legal complications involving disputes over intellectual property.

---

1   Risk = probability x consequences

2   Objective probabilities are derived from past data. Subjective probabilities are based on best guesses.

3   Hazard risk
    Strategic risk
    Financial risk
    Operational risk

4   Prospectors
    Defenders
    Analysers
    Reactors

5   Taking a measured view of both the probability of an undesirable future event and its potential impact.

6   The risk that a customer may default on payment

7   An attempt to prevent legitimate users of an Internet service from using it.

Courtney H, Kirkland, J. & Viguerie, P. (1997). "Strategy Under Uncertainty", *Harvard Business Review*, Vol. 75, Nov-Dec., pp67-79.

Ford (2004) *Annual Report*, Ford Motor Company.

Miles, R and Snow, S (2003) *Organisation Strategy, Structure and Process*, Stanford Business Classics.

Chapter 6

Risk management

Topic list

Introduction

Identifying and understanding risk are only the first steps toward dealing with it in an appropriate way. Organisations must also make suitable arrangements to avoid, reduce or transfer risk where possible and appropriate. Normally, only a small proportion of significant risk will be retained.

Risk management is becoming an imperative that ranks alongside the quest for profits and business growth as strategic imperatives. Many business strategies, such as outsourcing, diversification and simplification back to core businesses are aimed as much at risk reduction as they are at cost reduction or revenue enhancement.

Syllabus-linked learning objectives

By the end of the chapter you will be able to:

Learning objectives	Syllabus link
1 Design a risk management programme appropriate to the context of marketing projects	3.4
2 Understand how to undertake risk assessments on marketing projects	3.5
3 Critically evaluate the approaches an organisation can take to mitigate risk	3.6
4 Critically assess the strategic impact of implementing risk control measures as opposed to taking no action	3.7
5 Develop a range of methods for monitoring, reporting and controlling risk on an ongoing basis for project implementation	3.8

1 Risk management

1.1 The role of management

According to the **Turnbull Report** on corporate governance, a company's directors should do two things in the context of risk management. They should acknowledge their responsibility for the company's internal controls and they should explain to stakeholders that they are designed to **manage rather than eliminate** risk. This approach is notable for the following reasons.

(a) It is open, requiring appropriate disclosures to stakeholders about the risk.

(b) It does not seek to eliminate risk, but companies must understand and manage the risks they accept.

(c) It requires regular, integrated review and management of risk throughout all business units and a common terminology of risk.

(d) It is closely related to business objectives and takes a strategic view of, particularly, the need for the company to adapt to its changing business environment.

(e) It requires durable risk management that that can evolve as the business and its environment change.

Risks change and risk management must be a continuous process involving continuous identification, assessment, treatment, monitoring and review. Though it is convenient to discuss risk management as a linear process, it is actually continuous and iterative with the identification, assessment and treatment processes never ceasing and the results of any monitoring and review feeding back into the system so as to refine its response.

 KEY CONCEPT

concept

Effective **risk management** enables a business to:

- Reduce business threats to acceptable levels
- Make informed decisions about potential opportunities

This allows stakeholders to have confidence in the business and its future prospects.

The role of management in dealing with risk is to set an appropriate **risk management policy** and keep it current. This policy should provide effective measure to achieve the following.

(a) **Identify** the risks to which the organisation and its operations are subject.
(b) **Evaluate** the risks identified.
(c) **Address the risks** in an appropriate way.
(d) **Monitor** the risks identified, the risk environment and the success of the methods adopted to deal with them.

1.2 Terminology

The processes of identifying, evaluating, addressing and designing methods of monitoring risk are commonly included in the concept of a **risk assessment**. We will avoid using this term as it is generally understood to be a fairly low-level activity carried out as subsidiary activity in the management of health and safety. Another term commonly used is that of the '**risk audit**', the purpose of a risk audit is to identify where an organisations risks come from; the sources of risk.

1.3 Risk management policy

The organisation's risk management policy describes its approach to and appetite for risk, together with the way it proposes to comply with any legal requirements such as health and safety legislation. Risk appetite may vary according to risk type. For example, it would be unusual for an organisation to have a large appetite for risk in health and safety or other legal compliance matters. More particularly, risk appetite may vary for different aspects of financial, operational and strategic risk. For example, a firm in a poor financial position may be extremely averse to any risk to its ability to satisfy the terms of its bank covenants while it might accept enhanced operational risk (of, say, machine breakdown because it has reduced maintenance spending) in order to stay in business.

An effective system for risk management, reporting and communication is needed in order to implement any risk management strategy. Also, all levels in the business should be involved.

- **The Board of directors** should take an overall business view and should require that approved policies are implemented and enforced.

- **Managers of business units** should assess risks from the perspective of their business units and implement the board's risk management policies.

- **Individuals** must be aware of risks and may be responsible for managing some of them.

Risk management *strategy* should be a top-down process integrated across the entire business. However, it is important that everyone in the organisation should be able to contribute to the *processes* of risk management, so a combination of bottom-up and top-down approaches is valuable, particularly in such areas as risk identification and monitoring. As far as possible, approved processes for dealing with risk should become an integral part of the businesses' culture and systems. Senior management's role is to break down the overall risk management strategy into operational policies; managers and other employees should then be made responsible for implementing them and given the requisite authority to do so.

Risk management policies for a large corporation would include the following.

- **Corporate codes of conduct** regulate how managers and staff deal with each other and with outsiders and will seek to control risks from discrimination, bribery, anti-social behaviour and so on.

- **Environmental policies** deal with issues such as emissions, recycling and waste disposal.

- **Health and safety policies** establish H&S officers at all levels, set up committees, provide for routine risk assessments and lay down fire procedures.

- **Financial controls** include budgetary control of income and spending, authorisation procedures for capital expenditure, credit control procedures, cash management procedures and so on.

- **Information systems controls** include the appointment of information officers at all levels, regulations to control use by staff, password and access controls, requirements for back-ups and stand-by systems, institution of firewalls and other security precautions.

- **Personnel controls** include policies on identity and background checks on new recruits, discipline and grievance procedures, door entry controls and attendance monitoring. Appraisals of staff and management can provide early warnings of stress or potential inability to perform vital tasks.

These policies can mitigate the risk of **financial loss** arising from occurrences such as those below.

- Personal injury litigation.

- Loss of assets to theft or damage.

- Costs arising from internal errors such as those involved in replacing lost data, apologising to injured parties, restoring damaged public image.

- Revenues lost as a result of breakdowns or regulatory action.

ACTIVITY 1

application

Risk management policy of your college

You are probably taking classroom tuition as part of your preparation to pass this exam. Therefore having you on its premises represents one part of the risks being managed by the college or training firm offering you the classes.

Suggest the elements of a risk management policy that your college should adopt to treat the risks of having you in its classrooms.

1.4 Risk identification techniques

Identification of risk is essentially a process of assessing the impact and probability of possible future **events**. There are two main approaches to identifying such events.

(a) **Risk sources**: sources of risk are generally **wide categories** of things, such as people, activities and environmental influences that may throw up risk events. They may be either internal or external to the business. Examples are weather, politics, stakeholders and customers.

(b) **Risk problems**: it may be possible to identify specific threats or even events themselves, such as the threat of incurring excessive costs or the threat of nationalisation.

Example

Print works

A fire officer is conducting a risk assessment of a printing machinery room.

(a) **Risk source approach**: machine operators are smoking as they work and there are piles of scrap paper. Both are risk sources.

(b) **Risk problem approach**: the fire officer knows that machine room fires frequently lead to major loss.

Seeing risks from one end is complementary to seeing them from the other. Use of both approaches is synergistic, giving insights that neither alone could provide.

(c) **Risk source**: More risks arise from smoking than just the possibility of fire. For example, there is the threat to the health of the employee and to non-smoking colleagues and the risk arising from operating machines one-handed. In the UK it is now illegal to smoke in any work place or enclosed public place. Similarly, piles of loose paper create a tripping or sliding hazard, can hide health hazards and may lead to good work being thrown out with scrap during cleaning.

(d) **Risk problem**: Fires are caused by chains of events that extend beyond their immediate physical sources and their effects depend on how they are dealt with. The inspector would check that proper evacuation procedures are in place and have been rehearsed, that extinguishers are regularly maintained and that alarms are satisfactory. Such an assessment would inform management of risks arising from matters other than smoking, such as fires caused by electrical faults and poisonous fumes from chemical spillages.

1.4.1 Specific risk identification technique

The source or problem approaches are rather theoretical; more specific techniques are generally used within the basic framework. The technique used should also identify who should be responsible for managing each risk. Business culture, industry practice and compliance requirements will probably determine the specific technique used to identify risks.

(a) **Objectives-based risk identification** identifies risks as anything that prejudices the attainment of the organisation's objectives.

(b) **Scenario-based risk identification** considers a range of realistic business scenarios. This approach is fundamental to planning for recovery from disaster: it identifies and prioritises potential disasters and enables the design of effective plans for business recovery. This should lead to the best use of resources.

(c) **Taxonomy-based risk identification**: taxonomy is the science of classification. The taxonomy-based approach identifies risks using knowledge of best practices and a questionnaire based on a list of structured risk groupings.

(d) **Common risk checking**: in many industries, history and experience mean that the main risks are well known. Lists of known risks are available and can be used to check for risks likely to be present in a given work environment.

(e) Risk charting effectively combines the risk source and risk problems approaches. A table of the resources at risk is prepared showing the threats to those resources, any factors that may increase or reduce risk and the consequences that a business is seeking to avoid.

ACTIVITY 2

application

Outsourcing

The management of a state-funded hospital is considering outsourcing the cleaning of its premises. This will mean private firms taking over as employers of existing cleaning staff and assuming responsibility for the cleaning of the areas around beds, corridors and communal spaces.

Increases in incidents of infections during hospital stays by patients, some resulting in death, have been widely attributed by the media to poor hospital hygiene. Several legal cases for compensation have been decided against hospitals on the grounds of negligence by management.

What factors should management consider in evaluating the proposal to outsource its cleaning?

1.5 Risk evaluation

KEY CONCEPT

concept

Risk evaluation is the process by which a business determines the significance of any risk and whether those risks need to be addressed.

It utilises the basic concept that the magnitude of a risk is based on the probability of the potential future event concerned and its impact if it does occur. Establishing the potential financial consequences of each risk event is part of risk assessment. However, some risks may involve more serious consequences, such as death and injury.

1.5.1 Quantitative methods of risk evaluation

Quantitative risk evaluation derives numerical values for probabilities and consequences. Some kinds of risk are particularly amenable to this process. For example, insurance companies have detailed statistical records of the occurrence and impact of many risk events. They also have detailed records and current estimates of the cost of insured losses.

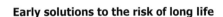
Early solutions to the risk of long life

Longevity risk, the danger that retirees will bleed their pension scheme dry by refusing to die at the rate prescribed by actuaries, is one of the greatest threats to the solvency of pension schemes.

A survey of 76 UK pension schemes by *Aberdeen Asset Management*, released in November 2008, found longevity risk is now perceived as the second largest risk facing schemes – behind investment risk, but a greater danger than interest rate or inflation risk. Four-fifths of respondents said longevity risk was either important or very important.

Yet while techniques for hedging out the other key risks have reached maturity, the market for methods to mitigate against longevity risk has remained in its infancy.

This remains so as ever expanding life expectancy adds to the sense of urgency and the health and well-being of a pension scheme becomes ever more inversely correlated with the health and well-being of its members. *Mercer*, the consultancy, found UK pension funds typically increased member life expectancy assumptions by 11 months in the year to spring 2008.

Steve Johnson, Financial Times, 1 March 2009

1.5.2 Breakeven

Breakeven analysis measures **sensitivity of profit to changes in sales**. It assumes that all units produced are sold immediately. The breakeven point for a product is the volume of sales at which there is neither profit nor loss. That is to say, at the breakeven point, revenue is exactly equal to the sum of fixed costs and variable costs of all kinds.

The calculations require an understanding of **contribution**. The word 'contribution' is an abbreviation of the phrase 'contribution to fixed costs and profit'. The revenue from the sale of one unit can only make such a 'contribution' if it exceeds the variable cost of producing the unit in question. Thus, generally,

> Contribution = revenue – variable cost

This applies whether we are talking about a single unit (contribution per unit) or all the units sold to date (total contribution).

The implication of this is that a profit can only be made when sales volume has grown beyond the point at which total contribution is equal to the total of fixed costs: this is the breakeven point. At higher sales volumes,

Total contribution – Total fixed costs	= Profit
Total contribution	= Contribution per unit × output

Since, at the breakeven point,

Total contribution	= Total fixed costs

Then, at that point

Contribution per unit × output	= Total fixed costs

Therefore:

$$\text{Breakeven level of output in units} = \frac{\text{Total fixed costs}}{\text{Contribution per unit}}$$

To achieve a require level of profit (say £10,000) then:

$$\text{Required unit sales} = \frac{\text{Total fixed costs} + £10,000}{\text{Contribution per unit}}$$

Example

Selling price per unit   £10
Variable cost per unit   £6
Fixed costs   £10,000 per month

Requirements

(a)   Calculate the breakeven volume per month.
(b)   Calculate the volume of output needed to achieve a profit of £2,000 per month.

Solution

Contribution per unit $= £10 - 6 = £4$

(a)   Breakeven output units $= \dfrac{£10,000}{£4}$

                                 $= 2,500 \text{ units}$

(b)   Output for £2,000 profit $= \dfrac{£10,000 + £2,000}{£4}$

                                 $= 3,000 \text{ units}$

If the potential impact of a risk event can be assessed in terms of lost production or lost sales, it can easily be translated into financial impact using this technique.

1.5.3 Event trees

The **event tree** is a useful technique for assessing both probability and impact.

An event tree is a visual representation of all the possible outcomes resulting from an initial event. Event trees are widely used in engineering contexts to analyse possible outcomes from a system failure. The method is based on a binary logic in that events either happen or not.

Possible events and their potential consequences are represented on a diagram, conventionally starting with the initiating event on the left and working towards the right with the illustration of potential consequential events. Both outcomes of each potential event are considered. Since any outcome may lead to further events, the diagrammatic representation fans out like the branches of a tree (albeit one lying on its side).

Example

This event tree shows the possible outcomes of a fire. There are two automated responses to the detection of a fire: a sprinkler system and a call to the fire brigade. If both work as they should, damage will be minimal. If either fails, damage will be significant. If both fail, there will be a total loss.

The event tree would look like this.

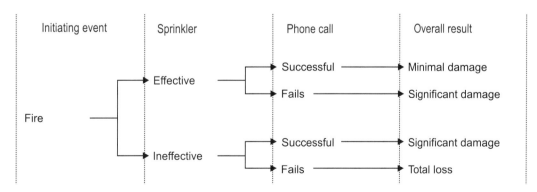

If numerical probabilities can be assigned to the two possible outcomes of each event, a combined probability can be calculated for each possible overall result as shown below. The probabilities are shown in brackets.

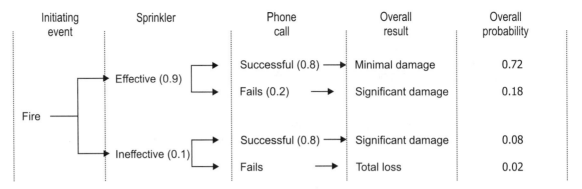

Here we see that in the event of a fire, there is only a 2% chance of total loss, but a 26% chance in total of significant damage. This assessment must, of course, be interpreted in the light of an assessment of the likelihood of a fire's occurring in the first place.

Wider use

The event tree concept may be applied more widely, in order to analyse the potential consequences of any risk element. Here is an event tree dealing with possible outcomes of a serious product contamination event. We assume that there are three elements affecting the ultimate outcome: the effectiveness of the production quality assurance system; the organisation's ability to achieve rapid product recall and the quality of crisis management deployed, including necessary PR communications.

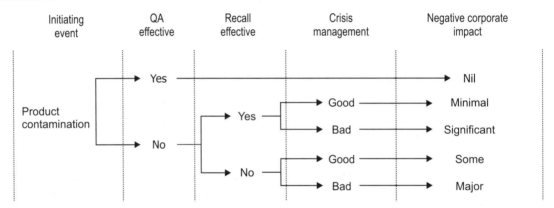

Where quantitative evaluation is possible and valid, the results can be presented in a risk gradient or isorisk contour diagram.

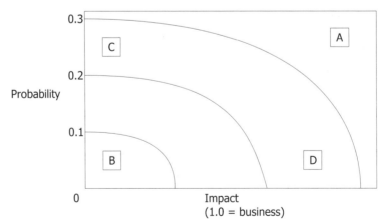

In the diagram above, Risk A is quantified as very significant, scoring high on both probability and consequences, while Risk B is far less significant on both counts. Risk C while relating to a highly likely event, has relatively minor potential consequences, while Risk D has the opposite combination of features.

1.5.4 Quantitative estimates

Some risks are very difficult to evaluate. For example, the impact of an event on the reputation of a business is very hard to quantify, and risk assessment in such a case is inevitably a matter of subjective opinion.

Subjective evaluations of likelihood and impact may be derived in several ways.

(a)   The opinion of a single manager or expert.

(b)   Delphi forecasting technique: essentially a moderated synthesis of the assessments of a panel of experts.

(c)   External sources such as *Dunn and Bradstreet* will provide numerical measures of country risk or default risk based on expert opinions.

Qualitative methods of risk evaluation

A qualitative risk evaluation is a subjective process perhaps using high-medium-low style assessments. The overall risk of an event can, by this system, be recorded on a risk matrix such as the one below. This is essentially a qualitative version of the contour diagram shown above.

| | Likelihood | | | | | |
Consequence	Frequent	Regular	Occasional	Remote	Very rare	Almost impossible
Catastrophic	Huge	Very high	High	Moderate	Low	Negligible
Critical	High	High	Moderate	Low	Low	Negligible
Marginal	Moderate	Moderate	Low	Low	Negligible	Negligible
Negligible	Negligible	Negligible	Negligible	Negligible	Negligible	Negligible

A qualitative assessment has the advantage of being much easier to undertake, though it is highly subjective. However, if it is consistently applied to all risks, it does facilitate identification and prioritisation.

1.6 Semi-quantitative methods of risk evaluation

Semi-quantitative methods use a mixture of qualitative and quantitative data. An experienced team is required to judge risk utilising a numerical rating system that, although arbitrarily chosen, is internally consistent and provides a relative assessment of risk.

1.7 Scenario building

Scenarios are used in two situations.

1   **To develop contingency plans** to cope with the arrival of threats or risks which, although they may arise at any time, are of indeterminable probability. For example, a chemicals company may develop a scenario of a major spillage at one of its plants and then set up emergency routines to cope with it. They cannot assess how likely the spillage is to occur in actual practice.

 MARKETING AT WORK

application

US unemployment

The labour department on Thursday said that initial jobless claims rose by 27,000 to 640,000, in line with economists' predictions. Those making continuing claims rose from a revised 6.04m to 6.14m in the second week of April, the highest total since tracking began in 1967.

Economists had expected that new jobless claims would rise to 640,000 after easing by a revised 613,000 the week before. That decline had surprised consensus estimates that claims would rise, but many attributed it to the Good Friday and Passover holidays.

Unemployment has risen more sharply than US authorities had anticipated and could lead them to consider taking a tougher stance in judging the results of bank stress tests, a development that ultimately could force leading financial groups to hold more capital.

When the stress tests were revealed two months ago, the authorities defined the "adverse" recession scenario as one in which unemployment rose gradually to peak at 10.4% in late 2010.

Earlier this month the labour department said that US unemployment soared to 8.5% last month, its highest level since 1983. Some economists forecast that it will reach 8.9% in April.

Alan Rappeport, Financial Times, 23 April 2009

---

2 **As a prediction technique**: A series of alternative pictures of a future operating environment are developed which are consistent with current trends and consistent within themselves. The impact of each different scenario upon the business is assessed and specific risks highlighted. Contingency plans are drawn up, to be implemented in the event of a given scenario coming true, or to implement now to give protection against the scenario.

Approaches to choosing scenarios as a basis for decisions are as follows.

Assume the most probable: This would seem common sense but places too much faith in the scenario process and guesswork. Also, a less probable scenario may be one whose failure to occur would have the worst consequences for the firm.

Hope for the best: A firm designs a strategy based on the scenario most attractive to the firm. Wishful thinking is usually not the right approach.

Hedge: The firm chooses the strategy that produces satisfactory results under all scenarios. Hedging, however, is not optimal for any scenario. The low risk is paid for by a low reward.

Flexibility: The firm plays a 'wait and see' game. This means that the firm waits to follow others. It is more secure, but sacrifices first-mover advantages.

Influence: A firm will try to influence the future, for example by influencing demand for related products in order that its favoured scenario will be realised in events as they unfold.

2 Addressing risk

2.1 Risk register

Risks that have been identified and assessed should be recorded in a **risk register**. A risk description should include the following detail:

(a) **Name** and **identification number**.

(b) **Risk type** – financial, strategic, operational, hazard and so on.

(c) **Scope** of the risk – a description of the possible future events involved.

(d) **Quantification** of the risk – the probability and scale of any losses or gains, possibly including 'Value at Risk' assessments.

(e) Possible **indicators and symptoms** that may indicate enhanced likelihood that the risk event may occur.

(f) Risk **tolerance/appetite** – level of risk considered acceptable for this matter.

(g) **Parties affected** – both internal and external parties and how they will be influenced.

(h) Risk **treatment and control** – the means by which the risk is managed at present and an assessment of the current risk controls in force.

(i) Potential **action for improvement** – recommendations about further risk reduction options.

(j) Risk **owner** – this person monitors the risk event.

2.2 Addressing risk

Risk is addressed in practical terms by selecting appropriate policies to control and mitigate the effects of potential future events. There are four possible approaches.

- Avoidance
- Reduction
- Transfer
- Retention

2.2.1 Risk avoidance

Avoidance means terminating or not undertaking an activity that incurs risk. An example would be deciding not to invest in the development of a new product. This is an attractively simple approach, but it clearly is not ideal. It eliminates the downside risk involved in the activity, but it also removes any possibility of benefit. Risk avoidance is thus an approach that should be used with caution and a clear understanding of potential costs and benefits.

2.2.2 Risk reduction

Risk reduction is applied when it is appropriate to retain an activity. It requires the undertaking of actions and precautions to reduce the risk to acceptable levels. Methods may be directed at reducing the probability of the risk event or its consequences. Good examples of risk reduction appear in the realm of safety precautions and procedures such as fire alarms and drills.

Risk reduction controls

(a) **Preventative controls** minimise the probability that an undesired event will occur. Many financial procedures such as limits on the authorisation of expenditure are preventative controls. A non-financial example is a no smoking rule, which reduces the chance of fire.

(b) **Corrective controls** deal with the effects of a risk event: an example is a sprinkler system to control fire if it occurs.

(c) **Directive controls** are policies and procedures intended to ensure a particular risk outcome is achieved, especially in the context of security or Health and Safety. For example, a team undertaking an inherently hazardous operation may have to include a nominated first aider.

(d) **Detective controls** identify the occurrence of risk events that did not lead to downside consequences. Various financial audit procedures fall into this category.

2.2.3 Risk transfer

Risk may be transferred to a third party, inevitably at a cost. The obvious form of risk transfer is insurance, which requires the payment of an insurance premium. Outsourcing can also include an element of risk transfer: here the cost will be hidden in the contract fee, but it will exist. Many financial instruments such as futures and options are means of transferring risk. The cost involved in such operations is also usually hidden in the contractual payments involved.

2.2.4 Risk retention

Risk retention means that the loss is accepted and absorbed if it occurs. This is a reasonable way of dealing with minor risks where the cost involved in other approaches would be greater than the total losses they would avoid. Some uninsurable risks such as the effects of war can only be dealt with in this way. Risk retention will normally be supplemented by planning means to deal with the implied contingencies.

Where risk is transferred by means of insurance, it is likely that there will be an 'excess' that represents a retained risk, as would any loss in excess of the sum insured.

Managing risks in a mining company

A large mining company is considering exploiting the mineral reserves in a developing country. The board is concerned that the country's government has in the past effectively expropriated significant foreign assets and profits by adjustments to licensing and ownership regulations.

Suggest strategies that the company could use to manage this area of risk.

3 Developing the risk management process

Like any other aspect of management in a dynamic environment, it would be inappropriate to regard risk management as something that can be done once and for all. Risk management should be understood as a continuing, iterative process. Known risks themselves; measures to address them and detect new ones; and the management process itself must all be subject to attention aimed at improving the organisation's principles and practice. Proper regard must therefore be paid to the matters discussed below.

3.1 Risk monitoring

The organisation's risk profile must be monitored and reported on to establish if is changing. The probability and potential impact of risk events are likely to change and new risks may emerge, just as existing ones may disappear. As a result, the measures taken to address risk must also be reviewed to establish whether they are still appropriate and adequate.

Risk management monitoring and reporting may be embedded in the normal management control reporting system alongside other aspects of routine reporting such as monthly management accounting reports. Also, there should be regular reviews of the overall risk profile and risk management assumptions. A comprehensive review will be particularly important if a risk event, such as a fire or loss of a major customer, does actually occur.

3.2 Examples of risk monitoring processes

(a) Reporting systems, possibly anonymous, should be established for prompt notification of incidents and near misses.

(b) Proper management of projects will include periodic review of projects against targets for progress, cost and quality.

(c) Internal audit is often considered to be an aspect of the financial control system, but it can usefully be expanded to include other aspects of risk, such as health and safety.

(d) Practical measures can be taken to ensure readiness, such as fire drills and rehearsals of moves to alternate sites.

(e) Information can be gathered on occurrences elsewhere, such as frauds, equipment failures, and experience of legal actions.

MARKETING AT WORK

application

Early warnings in the supply chain

When Edscha, a German manufacturer of sun roofs, door hinges and other car parts, filed for insolvency last month, it presented BMW with a crisis. The luxury carmaker was about to introduce its new Z4 convertible - and Edscha supplied its roof. "We had no choice to go to another supplier, as that would have taken six months and we don't have that. We had to help Edscha and try and stabilise it," BMW says.

Today, Edscha is still trading, thanks to the support offered by its leading clients. Nevertheless, BMW remains so worried about disruption to its supply chain that it has increased staff numbers in its risk monitoring department looking only at components-makers.

Richard Milne, Financial Times, 24 March 2009

3.3 Communication and learning

A learning approach is particularly relevant to the development of the risk management process.

Everyone capable of making an input into the risk management process should be familiar with its importance, with the risks they are exposed to and the ways in which the organisation intends to deal with them. This will improve the implementation of the chosen measures and their integration into business systems.

Mangers should be regularly updated on current risk management strategy as it affects their areas of responsibility and should monitor its adequacy and completeness.

Knowledge obtained or created by one area of the business and any lessons learnt from experience should be incorporated into the business-wide risk management strategy and shared with other areas of the business.

Communication with external stakeholders such as suppliers, customers and regulators is also required. This will help to ensure that the organisation is on top of its risk management problems and that it can take its partners' risk management strategies into account. It will also assist in the management of stakeholders' expectations on the subject of risk management.

Learning objectives		Covered
1	Design a risk management programme appropriate to the context of marketing projects	☑ Risk audit
		☑ Risk evaluation
		☑ Risk report
		☑ Risk treatment
		☑ Risk monitoring
2	Understand how to undertake risk assessments on marketing projects	☑ Customer assessment
		☑ Management assessment
		☑ Profit assessment
3	Critically evaluate the approaches an organisation can take to mitigate risk	☑ Risk avoidance
		☑ Risk reduction
		☑ Risk reducing controls
		☑ Risk retention
		☑ Risk transfer
4	Critically assess the strategic impact of implementing risk control measures as opposed to taking no action	☑ Learning approach
		☑ Adjusting risk
5	Develop the use of a range of methods for monitoring, reporting and controlling risk on an ongoing basis for project implementation	☑ Risk audit
		☑ Risk management objectives
		☑ Risk reporting
		☑ Risk awareness
		☑ Risk response
		☑ Industry benchmarking

1 To what extent can risk management be regarded as a project to be completed to specification.

2 Is it likely that an organisation's appetite for risk will vary from risk to risk?

3 What are the two broad approaches to identifying risk?

4 Name two quantitative risk evaluation methods.

5 What methods are used to address risk?

1. Elements of a risk policy for a college offering classroom courses would include the following:

Policies to control admission

The college probably has door entry and identification systems to ensure only those entitled to attend classes can do so. This provides protection for its assets and its revenues. It can also stop undesirables disturbing students and staff.

Health and safety policies

There will be policies to minimise accidents, ensure cleanliness and alleviate occupational stress, among others.

Identity and data security

Course and individual records will be safeguarded and examinations administration standardised.

Course quality

There should be policies in place to make sure that materials you study are appropriate and that tutors are competent both as teachers and in the subjects they present.

2. The list of factors will be very large. It will include:

Costs and benefits from outsourcing

- Fees charged by contractors
- Cost presently incurred by using own staff
- Financial returns from transfer of assets to contractor (floor polishing machines, vacuum cleaners etc)
- Potential redundancy costs of staff not transferred
- Costs of writing and agreeing suitable contracts and service level agreements
- Costs of monitoring compliance of contractors with service agreements

Risks from outsourcing

- Financial stability and robustness of the contractor
- Track record of contractor in delivering suitable service elsewhere
- Availability of controls over performance (eg whether staff will take instructions from hospital managers, performance indicators, regular meetings, legal redress mechanisms)
- Potential staff and media criticism of decision
- Extent of proof of link between hospital cleanliness and acquired infections
- Extent of public hostility to outsourcing as a source of increased infections
- Will legal liability for negligence claim pass to the contractor or stay with the hospital?

Risks from continuing to provide cleaning in-house

- Operational risks from cleaners not being available (eg strike action)
- Employment risks of having own staff (eg claims for industrial injury, discrimination etc)
- Rising wages and other employment costs
- Legal costs of negligence claims resulting from poor cleaning
- Potential fines for inadequate monitoring of staff (work permits, benefit fraud, health and safety)

Risk environment and appetite

- Potential changes in government policy resulting in contract penalties
- Extent of pressure on hospital to cut costs
- Management's previous experience of outsourcing agreements
- Relative risks of other cost-cutting measures under consideration
- Degree of support management enjoys from influential stakeholders (eg media, governors, doctors, nurses)
- Potential personal consequences for management of bad decision (eg personal liability, career impact, stress of dealing with problems)

3.   **Risk avoidance**

Don't invest in the country

Risk reduction

- Obtain public undertakings from the government that they will not expropriate
- Ensure the firm has other sources of earnings
- Undertake political lobbying in order to influence the policy of the government
- Keep as much of the operation as possible outside the country
- Invest small amounts incrementally

Risk transfer

- Set up the venture as a separate company with its own sources of finance, preferably local
- Obtain investment and participation from local minerals firms
- Sell the rights to the minerals to third parties as soon as possible

Risk retention

Accept any residual loss when it occurs

1   Not at all: risks change and the risk management process must be continuous.

2   Highly likely. It will tend to accept risks in the areas it considers to be core activities and seek to eliminate risk elsewhere.

3   The risk source approach and the risk problem approach

4   Breakeven analysis and event trees

5   Avoidance, reduction, transfer and retention

References

Johnson, S. (2009) *'Early Solution to the risk of long life'*, Financial Times, 1 March 2009, London.

Milne, R. (2009) *'Early warnings in the supply chain'*, Financial Times, 24 March 2009, London.

Rappeport, A. (2009) *'US Unemployment'*, Financial Times, 23 April 2009, London.

Chapter 7

Project planning and marketing

Topic list

1 Strategy, marketing and project management
2 The project structured organisation
3 Hard and soft projects

Introduction

Project management is an important aspect of strategic implementation. In the first place, many organisations' business consists largely of projects: civil engineering contractors and film studios are two obvious examples. Second, even where operations are more or less continuous, the need for continuing strategic innovation and improvement in the way things are done brings project management to the forefront of attention. Finally, even relatively low-level, one-off projects must be managed with a view to their potential strategic implications.

Marketing is particularly suited to a project-based management approach. Much of the higher direction of marketing revolves around activities that are, essentially projects.

Syllabus-linked learning objectives

By the end of the chapter you will be able to:

Learning objectives	Syllabus link
1 Develop a culture of project planning within the marketing function and the organisation	4.1
2 Describe and understand the nature of hard and soft projects	4.2

1 Strategy, marketing and project management

1.1 What is a project?

To understand the connection between marketing on the one hand and projects and project management on the other, it is necessary to define what a project is.

KEY CONCEPT

concept

A **project** is an undertaking that has a beginning and an end and is carried out to meet established goals within cost, schedule and quality objectives.

Resources are the money, facilities, supplies, services and people allocated to the project.

In general, the work of organisations involves either **operations** or **projects**. Operations and projects are planned, controlled and executed. So how are projects distinguished from 'ordinary work'?

Projects	Operations
Have a defined beginning and end	On-going
Have resources allocated specifically to them, although often on a shared basis	Resources used 'full-time'
Are intended to be done only once	A mixture of many recurring tasks
Follow a plan towards a clear intended end-result	Goals and deadlines are more general
Often cut across organisational and functional lines	Usually follows the organisation or functional structure

An activity that meets the first four criteria above can be classified as a project, and therefore falls within the **scope of project management**. Whether an activity is classified as a project is important, as projects should be managed using **project management techniques**.

Common examples of projects include:

- Producing a new product, service or object
- Changing the structure of an organisation·

- Developing modifying a new information system
- Implementing a new business procedure process

MARKETING AT WORK

The Carphone Warehouse has appointed creative consultancy Figtree to handle direct and in-store marketing with a focus on encouraging its continental Europe customers to upgrade their phones, BrandRepublic reported. Figtree will work on an ongoing campaign due to launch this spring and summer across seven European countries including France, Germany, and Spain. The communications work is expected to include direct mail, in-store channels, SMS and outbound calling.

Tradingmarkets.com, 6 April 2009

ACTIVITY 1

application

Consider the list of marketing-related activities below. Which do you consider to be of an operations-like nature and which of a project-like nature?

- Buying advertising space
- Dealing with customer complaints
- Summarising marketing research findings
- Procuring sales support material
- Visiting customers
- Responding to media enquiries

1.2 What is project management?

1.2.1 A note on terminology

Unfortunately, the terminology used in project management is not standardised. This is partly because large organisations develop their own methodologies and partly because there are at least two major, widely used methodologies that are taught as professional disciplines. These are **PRINCE2**, developed in the UK and used globally, and the **project management body of knowledge** (PMBOK) approach and terminology developed by the US Project Management Institute (PMI). Your syllabus does not prescribe the use of any specific scheme of terminology, so we will use a selection of technical terms as they become appropriate in the discussion that follows. Where there are equivalents or near-equivalents, we will give them in brackets, together with their provenance, where appropriate, thus: '... project charter (PRINCE2: project initiation document)...'.

1.2.2 The purpose of project management

KEY CONCEPT

concept

Project management is the integration of all aspects of a project, ensuring that the proper knowledge and resources are available when and where needed and, most importantly, that the expected outcome is produced in a timely, cost-effective manner. The primary task of a project manager is to manage the trade-offs between timeliness, cost and performance.

The objective of project management is a successful project. A project will be deemed successful if it achieves the specified **results** and is completed within stated **constraints** of **quality**, **time** and **cost**. The results a project is required to achieve are generally known as its **scope**. A project should have a clear statement of scope. This may be known by several different titles, depending on the organisation concerned, but it should include at least the following elements.

(a) **The overall objective** – for example, to create a website capable of handling e-commerce.

(b) **Specific deliverables** are the expected outputs from each stage of the project's life. These will not be restricted to the requirements at the end of the project but will also include intermediate deliverables such as a full risk management plan or a complete software testing plan.

(c) **Technical requirements** must be clearly specified since they are likely to be at least very important and may be non-negotiable imperatives.

(d) **Limits and exclusions** help to define the boundaries of the project, help to avoid unrealistic expectations and conserve project resources.

The relationship between scope, quality, time and cost is illustrated by Lewis (2008) like this. Project scope is the area of a triangle whose sides are quality, time and cost.

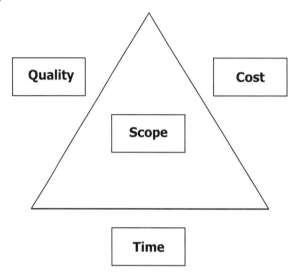

Quality, time and cost effectively define the sum of what can be achieved. If more is required, the length of at least one side will have to be increased: in the nature of things, this will generally be the **cost** dimension.

1.2.3 Projects present some management challenges

Challenge	Comment
Teambuilding	The work is carried out by a team of people often from varied work and social backgrounds. The team must 'gel' quickly and be able to communicate effectively with each other.
Expected problems	Expected problems should be avoided by careful design and planning prior to commencement of work.
Unexpected problems	There should be mechanisms within the project to enable these problems to be resolved quickly and efficiently.
Delayed benefit	There is normally no benefit until the work is finished. The 'lead in' time to this can cause a strain on the eventual recipient who is also faced with increasing expenditure for no immediate benefit.
Specialists	Contributions made by specialists are of differing importance at each stage.
Potential for conflict	Projects often involve several parties with different interests. This may lead to conflict.

1.3 Project success factors

Projects, small or large, are prone to fail unless they are appropriately managed and some effort is applied to ensure that factors that might contribute to success are present. Here are some of the key factors.

* **Clearly defined mission and goals** effectively communicated to and understood by all participants.

* **Top management support** that is visible is important in sending out the right messages regarding the significance of the project.

- **Competent project manager** with the necessary technical and inter-personal skills.

- **Well designed operational process** to ensure that work proceeds efficiently.

- **Competent team members** with the appropriate knowledge, skills and attitudes. A good team spirit helps to smooth the path to completion.

- **Sufficient resources** in terms of finance, materials, people and processes.

- **Excellent communication ethos** to ensure information is shared and there are no misunderstandings.

- **Use of effective project management tools** such as charts, leading edge software and project progress meetings.

- **Clear client focus** so that all work is done bearing in mind the needs of internal and external customers.

Project management ensures responsibilities are clearly defined and that resources are **focused** on specific objectives. The **project management process** also provides a structure for communicating within and across organisational boundaries.

All projects share similar features and follow a similar process. This has led to the development of **project management tools and techniques** that can be applied to all projects, no matter how diverse. For example, with some limitations similar processes and techniques can be applied whether building a major structure (eg Terminal 5 at Heathrow Airport) or implementing a company-wide computer network.

All projects require a person who is ultimately responsible for delivering the required outcome. This person (whether officially given the title or not) is the **project manager**.

1.3.1 Why do projects go wrong?

Project planning is fundamental to project success. **Realistic timescales** and resource requirements must be established, use of **shared resources** must be planned and, most fundamental of all, jobs must be done in a sensible **sequence**.

Common reasons for project failure are also:

- Poor project planning (specifically inadequate risk management and weak project plan)
- A weak business case
- Lack of top management involvement and support.

However, even if all these aspects are satisfactory there are other potential pitfalls that the project planner must avoid or work around. Here are some examples.

(a)　**Unproven technology**

The use of **new technological developments** may be a feature of any project. The range of such developments extends from fairly routine and non-critical improvements, through major innovations capable of transforming working practices, costs and time scales, to revolutionary techniques that make feasible projects that were previously quite impracticable. As the practical potential of a technical change moves from minor to major, so its potential to cause disruption if something goes wrong with it also increases.

(b)　**Changing client specifications**

It is not unusual for clients' notions of what they want to evolve during the lifetime of the project. However, if the work is to come in on time and on budget, they must be **aware** of what is **technically feasible**, **reasonable** in their **aspirations**, **prompt** with their **decisions** and, ultimately, **prepared to freeze the specification** so that it can be delivered.

Note that the term 'client' includes *internal* specifiers.

(c)　**Politics**

This problem area includes politics of all kinds, from those internal to an organisation managing its own projects, to the effect of national (and even international) politics on major undertakings. Identification of a senior figure with a project; public interest and press hysteria; hidden agendas; national prestige; and political dogma can all have disastrous effects on project management. **Lack of senior management support** is an important political problem.

Prisoner tracking system under fire

An 'end-to-end' system intended to manage offenders from sentencing to prison and probation has broken virtually every rule in the book for the introduction of major IT projects, the National Audit Office said on Wednesday.

The original £234m project is now set to cost double that. It is running three years late. And it will now not deliver the single system intended – one designed to cut re-offending and prevent potentially dangerous individuals slipping through the net as they are tracked from sentencing through to re-settlement.

Furthermore, it has failed despite being subjected to three of the government's flagship 'gateway reviews' – regular external reviews of big government projects that are meant to pre-empt failure.

The NAO is so disturbed by the findings that it has called on John Suffolk, the government's chief information officer, to demand an assurance from across government that other major IT projects are not also repeating 'the well known reasons for delivery failure' that the offender management project has demonstrated.

Back in 2002, the Office of Government Commerce listed eight common causes of big project failure. But the offender management system, launched in 2004, suffered from seven of them, four of them entirely and three in part.

The project lacked an experienced 'single responsible owner' for its first three years. It suffered from a consistent shortage of skilled personnel. It was run under an existing framework contract without proper outside competition, despite it being acknowledged as a high risk project, and it had poor financial control and management throughout.

It was subjected to three external 'gateway reviews', two of which classified it as 'red' – meaning immediate action is needed to fix big identified problems and implying the project should not go ahead until they are fixed. Even so, the project ploughed on. In place of the single database intended there will now be three.

The estimated lifetime cost will now be £513m against the original £234m estimate. At least £41m looks to have been wasted, while completion of a project that will still not provide what was originally promised will not happen before 2011 at the earliest – three years late.

The National Audit Office said this failure 'could have been prevented had basic principles and existing good practice been followed'.

Edward Leigh, chairman of the Commons Public Accounts Committee, said the project had proved 'a spectacular failure ... in a class of its own' even compared to other troubled government IT projects.

The project which started life in the Home Office but was transferred to the Ministry of Justice, offered 'a masterclass in sloppy project management'.

Nicholas Timmins, Financial Times, 12 March 2009

1.4 Projects and strategy

1.4.1 Linking projects with strategy

Grundy and Brown (2002) see three links between **strategic thinking** and **project management**.

(a)   Many projects are undertaken as **consequences of the overall strategic planning process**. These projects may change the relationship between the organisation and its environment or they may be aimed at major organisational change.

(b)   Some important projects arise on a bottom-up basis. The need for action may become apparent for operational rather than strategic reasons: such projects must be given careful consideration to ensure that their overall effect is **congruent with the current strategy**.

(c)   Strategic thinking is also required at the level of the **individual project**, in order to avoid the limitations that may be imposed by a narrow view of what is to be done.

1.4.2 Project managing strategy

Project management in its widest sense is fundamental to much strategy. This is because very few organisations are able to do the same things in the same ways year after year. Continuing **environmental change** forces many organisations to include extensive processes of **adaptation** into their strategies. Business circumstances change and new conditions must be met with new responses or initiatives. Each possible new development effectively constitutes a project in the terms we have already discussed.

Gray and Larsen (2008) give examples, some of which have particular relevance to marketing and are noted below.

(a) **Compression of the product life cycle**: product life cycles have fallen to one to three years, on average and it has become necessary to achieve very short time to market with new products if advantage is to be retained.

(b) **Global competition** emphasises cost and quality; project management techniques are used to achieve the new requirements.

(c) **Increased product complexity** requires the integration of diverse technologies.

(d) **Management delayering** has eliminated routine middle-management posts while much work has been outsourced: such organisational change tends to be continuous and project management techniques are required to get things done in a flexible manner.

(e) **Increased customer focus** in the form of customised products and close service relationships is often achieved through a project management approach.

Grundy and Brown (2002) offer an integrative analysis of this trend and suggest three reasons for taking a project management view of strategic management.

(a) Much strategy appears to develop in an incremental or fragmented way; detailed strategic thinking may be best pursued through the medium of a **strategic project** or group of projects. Project management is a way of making *ad hoc* strategy more deliberate and therefore better-considered.

(b) **Strategic implementation** is more complex than strategic analysis and choice; a project management approach, as outlined above, has an important role to play here, but must become capable of handling more complex, ambiguous and political issues if it is to play it effectively. When an apparent need for a project emerges, it should be screened to ensure that it supports the overall strategy.

(c) Even at the smaller, more traditional scale of project management, **wider strategic awareness is vital** if project managers are to deliver what the organisation actually needs

Of course, not all new developments are recognised as worthy of project management. For example, the installation of a new, shared printer in an office would probably be regarded as a matter of routine, though it would no doubt have been authorised by a responsible budget holder and installed and networked by a suitable technician. There would probably have been a small amount of training associated with its use and maintenance and it might have been the subject of a health and safety risk assessment. All these processes taken together look like a project, if a very small one.

In contrast to the multitude of such small events, modern organisations are likely to undergo significant change far less often, but sufficiently frequently and with developments that have sufficiently long lives for project management to be an **important aspect of strategic implementation**. Project management and **change management** are thus intimately linked.

An atmosphere of change and continuing development will be particularly evident in relation to marketing; information systems and technology; organisation structure; and organisation culture.

1.4.3 Marketing projects

Marketing as a business activity is, of course, closely linked to strategy and much of what has been said about the relevance of project management to strategy also applies to marketing. A moment's thought will produce many illustrations of this: here are some examples of marketing activities that require a major element of skilled project management.

- Test marketing
- Marketing research
- Creation of a customer database
- New product development

- Promotional campaigns
- Introduction of the various aspects of e-commerce

This is not to imply that all marketing management is project management, for that is simply not the case: there are many aspects of marketing that can be managed as continuing operations. However, the extensive applicability of project management to strategic implementation in general, and to marketing in particular, means that project management skills are a core competence for many organisations and for many marketing managers.

1.5 Project management as a core competence

Project management can be a **core strategic competence** for many companies. This is particularly true for companies working in such industries as consulting and construction, but it is also true of organisations of all kinds that can benefit from Grundy and Brown's (2002) approach outlined above. Such companies must ensure that they maintain and improve their project management abilities if they are to continue to be commercially successful.

Kerzner describes a five-level **project management maturity model** of continuous organisational improvement in the methodology of project management. Organisations should aspire to progress to the highest level, which is a state of **continuous improvement**. The five levels need not necessarily follow one another in a linear fashion: they may overlap, but the degree of overlap allowed is reflected in the risk associated with the overall process.

Level 1 **Common knowledge**

The importance of project management to the organisation is understood and training in the basic techniques and terminology is provided.

Level 2 **Common processes**

The processes employed successfully are standardised and developed so that they can be used more widely, both for future projects and in concert with other method such as total quality management.

Level 3 **Singular methodology**

Project management is placed at the centre of a single corporate methodology, achieving wide synergy and improving process control in particular. A separate methodology may be retained for IS matters.

Level 4 **Benchmarking**

Competitive advantage is recognised as being based on process improvement and a continuing programme of benchmarking is undertaken.

Level 5 **Continuous improvement**

Benchmarking information is critically appraised for its potential contribution to the improvement of the singular methodology.

Models such as Kerzner's are a guide to progress; in particular they indicate corporate training needs and career development routes for project managers.

1.6 Strategic project management

It is possible to move from the slightly *ad hoc* approach outlined above, where project management is essentially an implementation method, to a more all-embracing theory of strategic development (which will inevitably involve marketing management activities). Grundy and Brown (2002) suggest that it is often appropriate for organisations to combine project management and strategic management into a process that they call **strategic project management**. This envisages strategy as a **stream of projects**.

Strategic project management is the process of managing complex projects by combining business strategy and project management techniques in order to implement the business strategy and deliver organisational breakthroughs.

Grundy and Brown (2002)

The link between strategy and project is most clearly seen in the concept of the **breakthrough project**.

A **breakthrough project** is a project that will have a material impact on either the business's external competitive edge, its internal capabilities or its financial performance. *Grundy and Brown (2002)*

Breakthrough projects are a feature of the Japanese technique of *hoshin* or 'breakthrough management'. *Hoshin* requires that there should be not more than three concurrent breakthrough projects. This has distinct advantages.

- Resources are concentrated where they will do the most good.
- Projects of marginal value are avoided.
- Managerial attention remains focused.

The link from strategy to project management is a process influenced by both **internal** and **external change**. Vision gives rise to ideas for **strategic breakthroughs**. These lead to the establishment of **strategic programmes** and these, in turn generate **strategic projects**.

2 The project-structured organisation

Globalisation, other aspects of rapid environmental change and, above all, the need to **exploit knowledge** make the **structures**, **processes** and **relationships** that compose configurations vital for strategic success.

Johnson, Scholes and Whittington (2008) identify three major groups of challenges for twenty-first century organisation structures.

(a)   The rapid pace of **environmental change** and increased levels of **environmental uncertainty** demand flexibility of organisational design.

(b)   The creation and exploitation of **knowledge** requires effective systems to link the people who have knowledge with the applications that need it.

(c)   **Globalisation** creates new types and a new scale of technological complexity in communication and information systems; at the same time, diversity of culture, practices and approaches to personal relationships bring their own new problems of organisational form.

Of these three sets of issues, the need to capture, organise and exploit knowledge is probably the most pressing for most organisations. An important element of response to this need is therefore an emphasis on the importance of facilitating effective **processes** and **relationships** when designing **structures**. Johnson, Scholes and Whittington (2008) use the term **configuration** to encompass these three elements.

(a)   **Structure** has its conventional meaning of organisation structure.

(b)   **Processes** drive and support people: they define how strategies are made and controlled; and how the organisation's people interact and implement strategy. They are fundamental to systems of control.

(c)   **Relationships** are the connections between people within the organisation and between those internally and those externally.

Effective processes and relationships can have varying degrees of formality and informality and it is important that formal relationships and processes are aligned with the relevant informal ones.

It is very important to be aware that structures, processes and relationships are **highly interdependent**: they have to work together intimately and consistently if the organisation is to be successful. Here we will be concerned with structures and processes: relationships in this model are not really relevant to project management.

 MARKETING AT WORK application

Knowledge management

In 1988 Peter Drucker wrote:

The typical business [of the future] will be knowledge-based, an organisation composed largely of specialists who direct and discipline their own performance through feedback from colleagues, customers and headquarters. For this reason it will be what I call an information-based organisation.

In such an organisation, the management of knowledge and information becomes a key to gaining competitive advantage.

'*Business today*', echoed Charles Handy in 1992, '*depends largely on intellectual property, which resides inalienably in the hearts and heads of individuals*.' Both writers were reflecting a growing awareness that companies had moved far from Victorian times, when they were (as Handy put it) '*properties with tangible assets worked by hands whose time owners bought*'. They had become properties whose most valuable asset was intangible—the knowledge which exists in the heads and hearts of employees or in formal databases, patents, copyrights and so on.

Knowledge was seen as the key to the creation not only of business wealth but also of national wealth. In the British government's 1998 White Paper on the competitiveness of the nation, it said:

'*Our success depends on how well we exploit our most valuable assets: our knowledge, skills and creativity … they are at the heart of a modern knowledge-driven economy.*'

Lester Thurow, an American management professor, went so far as to suggest in a 1997 article in *Harvard Business Review* that intellectual property rights had become more important than manufacturing products or dealing in commodities. Once companies realised this they became aware of the need to find out how to manage that knowledge, how best to use it to create extra value. This was not an issue they had addressed systematically in the past.

Information technology helped in their efforts to introduce good knowledge-management practices. Developments in it advanced the science immeasurably. Data warehousing (the centralising of information in vast electronic databases) enabled companies to be more sophisticated and customer-oriented in their business. At last the left hand knew what the right hand was doing; the marketing department knew who was already a customer of the company, and for what product or service.

Knowledge management has been considered as four separate activities:

- **Capturing information**. Companies need to ensure that they are not suddenly bereft of vital information when an important individual moves to another employer.

- **Generating ideas**. All employees should be encouraged to come up with new ideas, through ideas boxes or by being rewarded for ideas that make or save money for the company.

- **Storing information**. Data warehouses have to be structured so that the information in them can be accessed by everybody who needs it.

- **Distributing information**. Organisations must encourage the spread of information to others. The hoarding of information has historically been seen as a source of power.

Economist, 19 January 2009

A **Project-oriented Organisation** ("POO")is an organisation, which

- Defines "Management by Projects" as an organisational strategy,
- Applies temporary organisations for the performance of complex processes,
- Manages a project portfolio of different project types,
- Has specific permanent organisations to provide integrative functions,
- Applies a "New Management Paradigm",
- Has an explicit project management culture, and
- Perceives itself as project-oriented

A **Project-oriented culture** ("POC") is characterised by the existence of an explicit culture of project management. In the POC, project management is considered as a business process, for which there exist specific procedures and a common understanding of the performance of this process.

2.1 Structure

An organisation's formal structure reveals much about it.

(a)   It shows who is **responsible** for what.

(b)   It shows who **communicates** with whom, both in procedural practice and, to a great extent, in less formal ways.

(c)   The upper levels of the structure reveal the **skills the organisation values** and, by extension, the **role of knowledge and skill** within it.

We are concerned here with the project-structured organisation, but we will approach it via some other forms that are relevant to it.

2.1.1 The functional structure

In a functional organisation structure, departments are defined by their **functions,** that is, the work that they do. It is a traditional, commonsense approach and many organisations are structured like this. Primary functions in a manufacturing company might be production, sales, finance, and general administration. Sub-departments of marketing might be selling, advertising, distribution and warehousing.

Functionally structured organisations can undertake projects successfully, partly, because they are able to provide in-depth expertise to project managers by allocating expert staff from appropriate functions. However, such staff can suffer from lack of focus if they still have a major functional role to play and it can be difficult to integrate their efforts properly.

Functional structures are simple and almost intuitive in their operation. However, they tend to promote insularity of thought and even distrust between functions. Achieving full co-ordination of the work of the various departments can be very difficult. This sort of problem leads to the matrix structure.

2.1.2 The matrix structure

The matrix structure imposes an extra layer of cross-functional management on top of the functional structure in order to improve co-operation and integration of effort by granting authority to project managers. Typically, the superimposed structure will be concerned with individual products or product groups. Product or brand managers may be responsible for budgeting, sales, pricing, marketing, distribution, quality and costs for their product or product line, but have to liaise with the R&D, production, finance, distribution, and sales departments in order to bring the product to the market and achieve sales targets.

The product managers may each have their own marketing team; in which case the marketing department itself would be small or non-existent. The authority of product managers may vary from organisation to organisation. The division of authority between product managers and functional managers must be carefully defined. Many decisions and plans will require careful negotiation if there is to be proper co-operation. This can result in stress, conflict and slow progress.

The matrix structure is now regarded as rather old-fashioned, since it is essentially a complex way of retaining the basic functional structure by adding extra resources to overcome its disadvantages. More modern approaches seek fundamental improvements and tend to focus on processes and projects.

2.1.3 The team-based structure

Both team-and project-based structures use cross-functional teams. The difference is that projects naturally come to an end and so project teams disperse.

A team-based structure extends the matrix structures' use of both vertical functional links and horizontal, activity-based ones by utilising **cross-functional teams**. Business processes are often used as the basis of organisation, with each team being responsible for the processes relating to an aspect of the business. Thus, a purchasing team might contain procurement specialists, design and production engineers and marketing specialists, to ensure that outsourced sub-assemblies are properly specified and contribute to brand values as well as being promptly delivered at the right price.

2.1.4 The project-based structure

The project-based structure is similar to the team-based structure except that projects, by definition, have a **finite life** and so, therefore, do the project teams dealing with them. Staff are allocated to a project team as needed to deliver the project end state. This approach has been used for many years by such organisations as civil engineers and business consultants.

A high level of motivation is common and the integration of specialist work is eased by commitment to project delivery. Staff may work on several projects at the same time and thus have responsibilities to several project managers.

This approach is very flexible and easy to use; it tends to complete projects quickly if the discipline of project management is well-understood. In particular, it requires clear project definition if control is to be effective and comprehensive project review if longer-term learning is to take place.

There is a downside to project-based organisation, however.

- It can be expensive in staff and loss of economies of scale.
- Project teams can become insular, rivalrous and unwilling to import expertise when necessary.

In the project-based organisation, specialist functional departments still exist, but their role is to support the project teams. Since the project teams are staffed from a pool of experts, the functional structure remains intact and is not weakened by secondments to project work.

2.2 Processes

Control processes determine how organisations function. They may be analysed according to whether they deal with inputs or outputs and whether they involve direct management action or more indirect effects. Balanced scorecards are direct output-based processes.

Here, we are concerned with control processes. Such processes are an important part of how organisations work. Johnson, Scholes and Whittington (2008) analyse them into four categories according to whether they deal with inputs or outputs and whether they operate by direct contact or through more indirect means. We will describe only those parts of their analysis that are directly relevant to project management.

2.2.1 Supervision

Direct supervision is often used for overall control in small organisations and in larger ones displaying little complexity. This technique requires that the managers thoroughly understand all aspects of the business. Direct personal control is also used in a crisis when firm and rapid action is vital.

2.2.2 Budgetary control

Despite having suffered many attacks on its relevance and usefulness, budgetary control is still fundamental to many organisations. It is certainly basic to project management. A budget is established at the outset, probably by a process of negotiation between stakeholders and expenditure is carefully monitored against the plan and actual achievement. Further negotiation may lead to the provision of supplementary funds, or to budget cuts. In any event, the project manager is generally held responsible for controlling expenditure without compromising either quality or time constraints.

2.2.3 Self-control

Control can be exercised indirectly by promoting a high degree of **employee motivation**. When combined with autonomy, this can lead to both the exploitation of knowledge and effective co-ordination of activities by individuals interacting with one another. The role of management is then not to supervise but to provide appropriate channels for interaction and for knowledge creation and information use. **Leadership** is of fundamental importance to this technique, and depends particularly on providing role models, supporting autonomous processes and providing resources. This approach is highly relevant to project work undertaken by responsible professionals and may be an appropriate method to incorporate into the overall control of marketing projects.

2.2.4 Cultural processes

Cultural control processes are **indirect** and **internalised by employees** as they absorb the prevailing organisational culture and its norms of behaviour and performance. Culturally conditioned behaviour can provide effective response to environments that are both dynamic and complex; it can be just as effective in a bureaucracy as in an informal, innovative, project-based organisation, for example. Training and development systems are an important aspect of the cultural control system.

Cultural processes also form important **links between organisations**, especially those that are highly dependent on the talent and knowledge of the people working in them; such people need an element of discussion, debate and cross-fertilisation in order for them to work effectively.

Cultural processes can be very valuable in all forms of management. However, they do have a negative aspect, in that they can create **rigidities** of thought and behaviour, fossilising what was successful once, but may come to form an obstacle to progress.

2.3 Performance targets

Performance can be judged against pre-set targets or **key performance indicators** (KPIs). This system is objective and permits the establishment of a hierarchy of supporting objectives that cascades down through the managerial structure. Managers are then free to organise their work and staff as they think best, so long as they achieve the targets set for them.

The extensive autonomy of method permitted by this system makes it useful in **large organisations** where the centre cannot possibly control everything in detail.

A problem with performance targets is that it can be difficult to identify appropriate KPIs. High-level financial KPIs, such as **return on investment** (ROI), are well-established and present no difficulty. However, even where data is easily expressed in quantitative form, non-financial targets that are actually useful can be difficult to define. The problem is even greater with aspects of performance that are **largely qualitative**, such as customer satisfaction. As a result, attention tends to be directed towards the easily measured financial aspects of performance.

2.4 The balanced scorecard

The **balanced scorecard** approach emphasises the need for a broad range of KPIs and builds a rational structure that reflects longer-term prospects as well as immediate performance.

The balanced scorecard focuses on **four different perspectives**.

Perspective	Question	Explanation
Customer	What do existing and new customers value from us?	Gives rise to targets that matter to customers: cost, quality, delivery, inspection, handling and so on.
Internal business	What processes must we excel at to achieve our financial and customer objectives?	Aims to improve internal processes and decision-making.

Perspective	Question	Explanation
Innovation and learning	Can we continue to improve and create future value?	Considers the business's capacity to maintain its competitive position through the acquisition of new skills and the development of new products.
Financial	How do we create value for our shareholders?	Covers traditional measures such as growth, profitability and shareholder value but set through talking to the shareholder or shareholders direct.

Performance targets are set once the key areas for improvement have been identified, and the balanced scorecard is the **main monthly report**.

The scorecard is **balanced** in the sense that managers are required to think in terms of all four perspectives, to **prevent improvements being made in one area at the expense of another**.

Kaplan and Norton (1992), who first described the balanced scorecard, recognise that the four perspectives they suggest may not be perfect for all organisations: it may be necessary, for example, to add further perspectives related to the environment or to employment.

3 Hard and soft projects

Project management, as a management discipline, has largely been developed in a context of engineering, where there have been **well-defined, tangible objectives** to be achieved. Examples abound in the civil engineering and aircraft industries. Even where objectives have been events rather than things, such as mounting the Olympic games, it has been fairly clear what the desired outcomes were and what was involved in achieving them. There is, however, a wide category of projects for which **clear-cut scope does not exist** and it is difficult to see quite how to proceed. The project sponsors are aware that something must be done, but they are not quite sure what, precisely, it is, nor how to achieve it. The public sector could provide many illustrations, such as, for example, a perceived need to improve secondary education. Such a mission would be subject to extensive debate: first as to what was to be understood by 'improve'; and, second, how to go about the 'improving'.

3.1 Hard and soft labels

This apparent dichotomy represented by clearly defined, engineering-oriented programmes on the one hand and, vaguer areas of aspiration on the other has led to the use of the terms **hard** and **soft** to label the two types of project. This usage is not confined to the sphere of project management. For example, on his unofficial home page (http://www.lancs.ac.uk/staff/smamp/MPSystMod.html), Mike Pidd, a specialist in operations research (OR) says:

'Unfortunate though these terms are, they have crept into common usage in recent years. They are really extreme points on a spectrum ...

- In hard OR, the question of problem definition is seen as relatively straightforward, and is more a question of finding out what is going on so that some appropriate analysis can be conducted ... The key assumption is that this real world can be understood and (sic) a taken-for-granted way.

- By contrast, in soft OR, problem definition is seem as problematic and the process of problem structuring is regarded as crucial to the success of any soft OR. This relates to *John Dewey's* maxim that, 'a problem well put is a problem half solved'. The world is seen as multi-faceted, and the approaches adopted to try to understand it are interpretive or pluralistic. Thus, problem definition is seen as something which must be negotiated between parties who may have different interests and interpretations. '

Professor Pidd's remarks about problem definition are as applicable to project management as to OR. The other insight he offers us here is the idea of hard and soft as extreme points on a spectrum: an awareness that an apparently hard project has some soft aspects will be very useful to the project manager, as will be an awareness of the opposite case.

3.2 Hard and soft projects

Crawford and Pollack (2004) offer further description of what is meant by the terms hard and soft in the context of project management and offer a **seven element analysis** of the practical differences. They say:

Generally, objectivist, scientific approaches are hard, while subjectivist, social approaches are soft.

'Hard' approaches are about seeking and deploying objective knowledge, while soft approaches depend on the construction and subjective interpretation of knowledge.

3.2.1 Seven dimensions for analysis

Just as the overall classifications of hard and soft should be seen as ends of a spectrum, so Crawford and Pollacks's factors have degrees of presence in a project; they are not qualities that are present or absent. Most of these factors are both visible in the project and in the methods used in its management, though some are more relevant to one or the other.

(a) **Goal/objective clarity**. The degree of definition of the goal or objectives is the first dimension of analysis. Clear and specific desired outcomes are typical of engineering projects, while projects relating to research or organisational change, for example, tend to have less well-defined objectives.

(b) **Goal/objective tangibility**. The clarity and tangibility of project goals and objectives are often linked and the link may be very strong indeed, as with many engineering projects, where the objective is the construction of a physical object. However, this is not always the case: very clear goals can relate to intangible outcomes, such as individual exam success, while some very tangible construction objectives, for example, may be approached *via* ambiguous specifications.

(c) **Success measures**. Generally, it is easier to measure the degree of success of hard projects than of soft ones, partly as a result of their higher degree of goal tangibility and clarity. Quantitative performance measures are associated with hard projects and qualitative with soft. It should not be assumed that quantitative measures are superior to qualitative ones: each has its place. Quantitative measures are generally confined to a few variables considered significant in order to minimise the cost of data capture; this does not give a full picture. Nor are quantitative measures adequate when projects deal with qualitative matters such as attitude, learning and morale.

(d) **Project permeability**. The permeability of a project is the extent to which its objectives and processes are subject to influences outside the control of the project manager. The extent of these influences might be very limited in a short, simple project of a well-understood type. However, larger, less well-defined projects in less well-understood environments are likely to display considerable permeability. A good example of a factor increasing project permeability is the use of sub-contractors: their competence and diligence are far less subject to the control of the project manager than are those of in-house teams.

(e) **Number of solution options**. Hard projects will normally have one or more clearly defined outcomes, possibly handed down by authority. Softer projects will tend to have a range of possible outcomes that require consideration.

(f) **Degree of participation and practitioner role**. This dimension relates specifically to the nature of the appropriate project management practice and is dealt with below under implementation.

(g) **Stakeholder expectations**. Clear and logical stakeholder relationships are typical in hard projects, where the emphasis is on efficiency and predictability. Soft projects, because of their indeterminate nature, require a greater degree of interaction between stakeholders in order to overcome differences of style, language, assumptions and competence. The credibility of project staff in the eyes of stakeholders may become an issue.

3.3 Implementation considerations

The chances of making a project a success are enhanced if project management methods are tailored to the degree of its hardness or softness. Hard and soft approaches are not mutually exclusive and can be combined in ways that reflect the project's position on the various dimensions.

(a) **Goal/objective clarity**. The extent of clarity in the definition of a project's goals and objectives affects the methods that are used to move the project forward. Well-defined goals permit the application of techniques designed to achieve them efficiently. Where there is goal ambiguity, effort must be deployed on consultation, learning and negotiation in order to reach an adequate degree of goal definition. These processes will almost certainly have to be continued throughout the life of the project as new ambiguities arise and have to be dealt with. The management of the project thus entails as much consideration of **what** is to be done as of **how** to do it.

(b) **Project permeability**. Where project permeability is low, hard management methods that concentrate on clear objectives and techniques are appropriate. However, where permeability is high, a softer approach is needed. It may be necessary to deal with, for example, bureaucratic, organisational, cultural and political influences that are capable of affecting both objectives and methods. These influences will probably have to be dealt with sympathetically and diplomatically. They will require a **learning approach** to management and a degree of adjustment to project processes and intended outcomes as understanding of the environment grows.

(c) **Number of solution options**. Hard projects tend to be managed to achieve efficient delivery of clearly defined outcomes. Softer project management methods will tend to explore a range of methods and solutions to problems. This will be appropriate when there is potential benefit in questioning assumptions and exploring a range of options. Crawford and Pollack (2004) say 'the soft paradigm emphasises learning, debate, participation, exploration and questioning'.

(d) **Degree of participation and practitioner role**. A soft approach to project management is participative and collaborative, with expertise in facilitating the efforts of others being a major competence for the project manager. By contrast, the hard project management style tends to be based on individuals' technical expertise in their areas of concern. Project staff will have clearly defined roles and boundaries. This hard approach can achieve faster project delivery, but at a potential cost in lost innovation and learning.

(e) **Stakeholder expectations**. The implementation aspects of this dimension follow on from the previous one. A hard management approach will tend towards command and control, whereas a soft approach 'has culture, meaning and value as central concerns'. Organisations are seen as cultural systems and project success will depend on the perceptions of the stakeholders involved.

Learning objectives	Covered
1 Develop a culture of project planning within the marketing function and the organisation	☑ Definition of project
	☑ Management challenges
	☑ Structure
	☑ Processes
	☑ Relationship
2 Describe and understand the nature of hard and soft projects	☑ Hard = Straightforward Objective
	☑ Soft = Problematic Subjective
	☑ Crawford & Pollack – 7 Dimensions for Analysis

Learning objectives review

1   What are the two main project management methods in the UK and the US?

2   What is the relationship between project quality, cost, scope and time?

3   What is a breakthrough project?

4   What are the three components of an organisation's configuration?

5   What are the disadvantages of the project-based structure?

6   What are the perspectives of the standard balanced scorecard and how do they fit together?

7   A project has clear and tangible goals, but they are subject to amendment by a range of stakeholders; several external contractors are involved and the project manager has doubts about their competence. Should the project manager tend towards hard or soft approaches in managing this project?

1.   Did you realise that each of these activities could form part of a project or, equally, could be part of continuing operations? The point of this exercise is to demonstrate that neither projects nor operations are *necessarily* defined by the activities involved. You must look beyond the individual activities and discern the wider nature of what is happening.

1   PRINCE2 and PMBOK

2   Project scope is the totality of what is to be done during the life of the project and what is to be achieved at the end of it. *Lewis* describes it as the area of a triangle whose sides are quality, time and cost.

3   One that will have a material effect on either the business's external competitive edge, its internal capabilities or its financial performance

4   Structures, processes and relationships

5   It can be expensive in staff and loss of economies of scale; and project teams can become insular, prone to rivalry and unwilling to import expertise when necessary.

6   The **innovation** perspective's measures of skills and processes should support the **internal business** perspective's measures of quality, efficiency and timeliness, which support the **customer perspective's** measures of relationships and loyalty, which support the overall **financial** perspective measure, ROCE.

7   It seems likely that the project manager will have to make use of a participative, exploratory style in order to achieve the best outcome. The project seems to lie towards the soft end of the hard-soft spectrum.

References

Crawford, L and Pollack, J. (2004) *Hard and soft projects: a framework for analysis*, International Journal of Project Management, Volume 22, Issue 8, November pp 645-653.

Grundy, T. and Brown, L. (2002) Strategic Project Management, Thompson Learning, London.

Gray, C. F. and Larson, W. L. (2008) Project Management: the Managerial *Process*, McGraw-Hill, London.

Johnson, G. Scholes, K. and Whittington, R. (2008) Exploring Corporate Strategy, (8th edition), Prentice Hall, Harlow.

Kaplan, R. S. and Norton, D. P. (1992) *'The balanced scorecard: measures that drive performance'*, Harvard Business Review, January – February pp. 71-80.

Lewis, J. P. (2008) Mastering Project Management , (2nd edition), McGraw-Hill, Harlow.

Timmons, N. (2009) *'Prisoner Tracking System under Fire'*, Financial Times, 12th March 2009, London.

Chapter 8

The marketing project plan

Topic list

Introduction

Having considered the nature of a project in the previous chapter, we are now in a position to look at project management in more detail and we will focus on managing marketing projects in particular. We will look at a simple model of how projects can be expected to progress and then examine in detail the important ideas affecting how a project is initiated. Determining project scope is a very important aspect of this process and is unlikely to be an easy task.

Project stakeholders are likely to be a major concern for project managers and skill in dealing with them is an essential quality for such managers. Finally we will look at the problem of providing adequate and appropriate resources for the project.

Syllabus-linked learning objectives

By the end of the chapter you will be able to:

Learning objectives	Syllabus link
1 Describe the main stages of a marketing project plan	4.3
2 Establish a marketing project's scope	4.4
3 Describe the management of project stakeholders	4.4
4 Identify the skills needed to complete a marketing project	4.3

1 The project lifecycle

Projects may be thought of as having a **lifecycle**. This concept is useful for understanding the processes involved in project management and control, since the resources required and the focus of management attention vary as projects move from one stage to the next.

1.1 A typical four stage project lifecycle

Typically, four stages exist within a project lifecycle. It may help you to remember the four stages if you think of them as the **four Ds** (definition, design, delivery, development).

1.1.1 Project definition

Project definition is the first stage. Its essential element is the definition of the purpose and objectives of the project. This stage may include abstract processes of conceptualisation, more rigorous analysis of requirements and methods, feasibility studies and, perhaps most important, a **definition of scope**. As discussed in the previous chapter, the scope of a project is, effectively, what is included and what is not, both in terms of what it is intended to achieve and the extent of its impact on other parts of the organisation, both during its execution and subsequently. An important initial consideration will always be **projected cost**, even if this cannot be estimated very accurately at this stage.

The project definition stage may also include the procedures required for **project selection**. We will discuss this further below, but for now we may simply point out that an organisation may be aware of a larger number of worthwhile projects than it has resources to undertake. Some rational process for deciding just which projects will proceed is therefore required.

1.1.2 Project design

The project design phase will include detailed planning for **activity**, **cost**, **quality**, **time** and **risk**. Final project authorisation may be delayed until this stage to ensure that the decision is taken in the light of more detailed information about planned costs and benefits.

1.1.3 Project delivery

The project delivery phase includes all the work required to deliver the planned project outcomes. Planning will continue, but the emphasis is on getting the work done. Sub-phases can be identified.

(a) The people and other resources needed initially are assembled at **start up**.

(b) Planned project activities are carried out during **execution**.

(c) **Completion** consists of success or, sometimes, abandonment.

(d) The delivery phase comes to an end with **handover**. This is likely to include **project closure** procedures that ensure that all documentation, quality and accounting activities are complete and that the customer has accepted the delivery as satisfactory.

1.1.4 Project development

Handover brings the delivery phase to an end but the project continues through a further stage of management largely aimed at **improving the organisation's overall ability to manage projects**.

(a) There should be an **immediate review** to provide rapid staff feedback and to identify short-term needs such as staff training or remedial action for procedure failures.

(b) **Longer-term review** will examine the project outcomes after the passage of time to establish its overall degree of success. **Lifetime costs** are an important measure of success. There should also be longer-term review of all aspects of the project and its management, perhaps on a functional basis.

It is tempting to ignore the need for project review, especially since, done properly, it imposes significant costs in terms of management time and effort. It is, however, essential if the organisation is to improve the effectiveness of its project management in the future.

 ACTIVITY 1 application

Reflect on any project of which you have personal experience. This could be something you have been involved in at work, something you have read about in a newspaper or something as simple as going away on holiday.

Prepare notes for a presentation in which you explain the project in terms of the four Ds: definition, design, delivery and development.

Note also that some commentators regard '**Project Termination**' as a stage of the project lifecycle. See Chapter 10 for more on this.

2 Defining the project

Limits to resource availability mean that not all potential projects will be undertaken; rational methods are used to select them.

Project initiation tasks include the appointment of project manager and sponsor; stakeholder analysis and the definition of project scope. The business case explains why the project is needed, while the project charter gives authorisation for it to be undertaken.

2.1 Project selection

As already mentioned, it is likely that an organisation will be aware of a greater number of potentially advantageous projects than it has resources to undertake. It is, therefore, necessary to **select projects carefully** in order to make the best use of those limited resources. Project assessment and selection is analogous to strategic choice, not least because many projects are of strategic significance. The techniques used for making strategic choices are, therefore, also applicable. The criteria of **suitability**, **acceptability** and **feasibility** are applicable to many project choice problems, perhaps reinforced by the use of more detailed assessment techniques such as those below.

(a) **Risk/return analysis** using **discounted cash flow** techniques, expected values and estimates of attractiveness and difficulty of implementation. Discounting was outlined in the Annex to Chapter 3.

(b)   **Weighted scoring** of project characteristics.

(c)   Assessment of **organisational priority**.

(d)   **Feasibility studies** addressing technical, environmental, social and financial feasibility; such studies are costly and time-consuming and are likely to be restricted to front-running project proposals.

(e)   **SWOT analysis**, assessing the strengths and weaknesses of individual projects against the opportunities and threats facing the organisation.

2.2 Project initiation

When a project has been approved in general terms, it should be the subject of a number of management processes and tasks in order to initiate it and move into the execution phase. The exact nature of these processes may well vary from project to project and according to the particular project management methodology adopted. Schwalbe lists **pre-initiating tasks** and **initiating tasks**. The pre-initiating tasks follow on directly from the formal project selection process.

2.2.1 Pre-initiating tasks

Pre-initiating tasks are the responsibility of the senior managers who decide that the project should be undertaken.

(a)   Determination of **project scope** and quality, time and cost targets.

(b)   Identification of the **project sponsor** (a senior manager who is accountable for the resources used by the project manager).

(c)   Selection of the **project manager**.

        Note: The roles and responsibilities of the project manager are discussed later in this chapter.

(d)   **Senior management meeting** with project manager to review the process and expectations for managing the project.

(e)   Decision whether the project actually needs to be divided into two or more smaller projects.

2.2.2 Initiating tasks

Initiating tasks are carried out by the **project manager**,

(a)   Identification of **project stakeholders** and their characteristics.
(b)   Preparation of a **business case** for the project.
(c)   Drafting of a **project charter** (PRINCE2: project initiation document).
(d)   Drafting an initial statement of **project scope.**
(e)   Holding a **project initiation meeting** (PMBOK: 'kick-off' meeting).

2.3 More on project definition

It will be common with 'hard' projects, managed in a top-down fashion, to proceed directly from project selection to project initiation. However, many projects, especially 'soft' ones, will require an extensive project definition stage. This will help to increase the clarity with which overall objectives are understood, increase motivation and reduce **mission creep**, which is the tendency for expectations to increase as time passes.

2.3.1 Developing vision and shared understanding

It is important to spend time at the earliest stage of project planning on reaching a shared understanding of what the project is about. This applies to all projects but is particularly vital to the kind of 'soft' project that will be common in marketing. Lewis (2008) recommends a process of brainstorming, discussion and group activity in order to create a sense of ownership and an agreed vision and understanding of what the project is to achieve. Lewis also recommends the use of mindmaps as an aid to this process and suggests that the outcome should effectively be a list of desired features to be provided at the culmination of the project. These features or attributes should be prioritised into three groups.

- Musts
- Wants
- Nice to haves

When this stage is complete, it is appropriate to move on to more detailed consideration of consideration of **project scope and strategy**.

2.4 Developing an understanding of project scope

As we have already indicated, the word '**scope**' is used in project management to mean both the outcomes that are required and the work that is to be done to achieve them. It is obviously of great importance that everyone involved in a project should have a common understanding of these matters. If this common understanding is not reached, sooner or later there will be acrimonious disputes. A **careful specification of project scope** is, therefore, of great importance and the project management methodology in use may require that this be a separate document, known as a **project scoping document.** Equally, it may be that the business case and the project charter between them provide a clear statement of agreed scope. Under the **PRINCE2** method, the **business case** performs the role of a statement of project scope.

Gray and Larson (2008) say that the document defining scope should be developed under the direction of the project manager and customer (or project owner). It will be an essential foundation for project planning and measuring the extent of project success, and needs to be developed in conjunction with key project stakeholders.

The following diagram shows the process of scope definition.

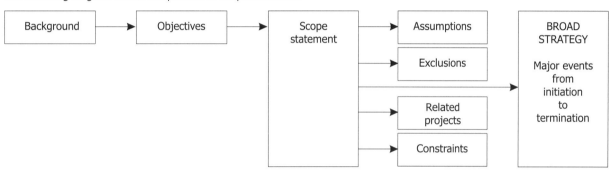

Scope statements identify all of the elements of work in the project. A scope statement must be linked directly to meeting the defined project requirements. For example, a marketing project may be to investigate and recommend a low cost communication strategy for improving awareness of a new brand of high fibre bread and thereby increasing sales by 15%.

The project scoping document would specify factors to be considered:

- Ways to achieve the sales target
- Likely audience / stakeholders
- Costings
- Timeframes
- Resource considerations
- Effect on sales of other products

It is likely that in larger projects it will become necessary to **adjust the project scope**. This might occur, for example, if resources are unavoidably reduced or it becomes clear that a feasibility study was too optimistic or too pessimistic. When a change to project scope becomes apparent, it is important that it is **clearly stated** and that the revision is **approved by the interested stakeholders**.

Grundy and Brown (2002) summarise the process of **project definition** as the preparation of answers to a series of questions.

- What **opportunities and threats** does the project present?
- What are its **objectives**?
- What are its potential **benefits, costs** and **risks**?
- What is its overall **implementation difficulty**?
- Who are the **key stakeholders**?

A number of techniques that aid analytical thinking may be used when addressing these questions.

2.4.1 Defining the key issues – fishbone analysis

Fishbone analysis (root-cause, cause and effect or *Ishikawa* diagram analysis) is useful for establishing and analysing key issues. It can be used both on existing problems, opportunities and behavioural issues, and on those that may be anticipated, perhaps as a result of the construction of a scenario.

The essence of fishbone analysis is to break down a perceived issue into its smallest underlying causes and components, so that each may be tackled in a proper fashion. It is called fishbone analysis because the overall issue and its components are traditionally analysed and presented on a diagram such as the one below.

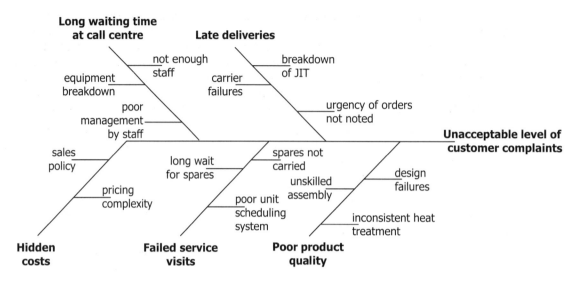

Fishbone analysis

The major issue or problem is shown at the right-hand side of the page and the perceived causes and influences are shown, in no particular order, on the 'bones' radiating from the central spine. Each 'bone' can be further analysed if appropriate. It is common to use familiar models such as the Ms list of resources (men, money, machines and so on) to give structure to the investigation, though not necessarily to the diagram. The fish bone diagram itself is not, of course, essential to the process of analysis, but it forms a good medium for brainstorming a problem and for presenting the eventual results.

2.4.2 Determining performance drivers

Many projects are aimed at or include improving some aspect of the performance of a department, activity or function: this is true at the strategic level and is likely to be true of projects at lower levels, such as marketing projects. **Performance driver analysis** is useful in such cases; essentially it is another brainstorming and presentation technique. It has a lot in common with the **force field analysis** we will deal with in more detail later in this chapter. The essential difference between the two is that force field analysis is concerned with factors affecting future change activity, while performance driver analysis is used to identify the factors that account for past (and current) performance.

The essence of the technique is to identify two groups of performance-related influences: those that **enable good performance** and those that **hinder or prevent it**. The factors in these two groups are drawn as arrows against a baseline, the length of each arrow representing the perceived strength of the influence it represents.

Product design

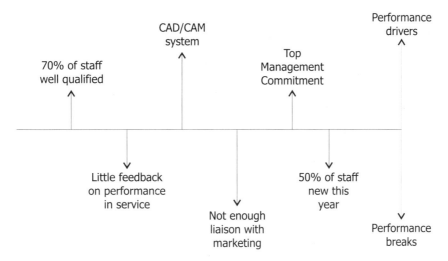

Performance driver analysis

2.4.3 Gap analysis

Gap analysis is widely used in business strategy to focus attention on the **anticipated gap** between **desired** future strategic performance and **likely** future performance if there is no intervention. It is not limited to strategic management use and we discussed it in the context of marketing and management information systems in an earlier chapter. It can be used in a similar way in project selection and definition as a route to establishing both what projects should be undertaken and what their scope should be. Projects are selected for their potential to fill a perceived gap in some aspect of customer-oriented performance.

MARKETING AT WORK

application

Citigroup and KorAm Bank

Since Citigroup bought KorAm Bank in February 2004, it has worked on merging two widely differing cultures, systems and people.

'At stake is more than just Citibank Korea, the enlarged group that will be the sixth-largest lender in one of Asia's most promising banking markets, with $57.4bn in assets, around 250 branches and some 5m customers. Senior executives at Citigroup regard the KorAm integration as the acid test for future expansion in higher-growth, higher-risk markets. KorAm's purchase could be a template for future acquisitions because it gives Citigroup what it lacks in many other countries: a large branch network and a significant exposure to small and medium-sized enterprises (SMEs).'

One of Citigroup's 'Pillars of performance' was described like this:

'Integrating cultures and systems: Citigroup and KorAm to use 'gap analysis' going through the business units, spotting the differences between the practices employed by the two banks and choosing the best of the two. Citigroup will not always prevail.'

Francesco Guerrera and Andrew Ward, Financial Times, 17 October 2004

2.4.4 From – to analysis

From – to analysis is appropriate for establishing the scope of projects concerned with **organisational change** or **operational improvement**. The essence of the technique is to both define the **current state** ('from this') and the **desired state** ('to this') of relevant issues such as management style, control methods, power structures, communications practices, working methods, cost base and customer service. Deciding which issues are relevant is as important as deciding what should be done about them, so **fishbone analysis** might lead in to this technique. From–to analysis would supplement **gap analysis** by looking at the gap from a different perspective.

2.5 Force field analysis

Grundy and Brown (2002) suggest that force field analysis can be useful in project planning. This is an important example of the **close relationship between project management and strategic management** that appears in their analysis.

The emphasis of force field analysis is an assessment of the **degree of difficulty** that implementing a project is likely to encounter. A wide range of problems, attitudes and conditions will affect the degree of difficulty encountered and this will be particularly the case with projects of a strategic nature. It is important that such matters are carefully considered as part of the planning process, and force field analysis is one way of doing this.

The essence of force field analysis is the identification and assessment of the underlying forces tending to promote successful implementation or to hold it back. These forces may be referred to as **enablers** and **constraints**. The overall potential of each force must be estimated. As in the performance driver analysis already discussed, it is usual to show enablers and constraints as arrows against a baseline in a visual presentation.

A degree of objectivity can be brought into this analysis by seeking to **expose implicit assumptions** about these factors and the overall situation. This process can be moved forward by asking three questions.

- What is it about each force that allows it to be identified as an enabler or a constraint?
- How great is its potential influence on the change process?
- What other, less obvious factors does it depend on?

A further important part of the overall analysis is the identification of potential **showstoppers**. These are constraints that can make implementation so difficult as to cause overall project failure. These factors must be continuously monitored.

Management of constraints includes two important possibilities.

(a)   It may be possible to turn one of the constraints around and turn it into a driver. Changing the mind of an unsympathetic stakeholder would be a good example.

(b)   Careful examination of the context of the project may reveal **latent enablers** that could be called into play. For example, there may be sympathetic stakeholder groups whose driver potential has been ignored.

2.6 Preparation of a business case

When the project selection process is complete and a project selected for action, there is likely to be a great deal of information available to justify the decision to proceed. However, it is unlikely that a full account of the project has been prepared.

We have dealt with the nature, preparation and presentation of the business case earlier in this text. It will suffice to provide a brief summary here. A **business case** is a reasoned account of **why** the project is needed, **what** it will achieve and **how** it will proceed. The business case is a fundamental component of the PRINCE2 methodology, which is built on the assumption that a project is, in fact, **driven by its business case**. An important use of the business case in any project is to maintain **focus** and prevent **mission creep** by regular reference back to it. It is possible that final approval for a large project will depend upon the preparation of a satisfactory business case.

A business case is not, of course, something that is confined to commercial organisations: the principles are equally applicable to any organisation undertaking a project.

2.7 Typical content of a business case

- Background to the project and reasoning behind it
- Overall objectives and success criteria
- Important assumptions and constraints
- Project scope
- Summary budget
- Time estimate
- Summary risk analysis

2.8 The project charter

The **project charter** (PRINCE2: project initiation document) complements the business case: while the business case explains the **need** for work on the project to start, the charter gives **authorisation** for work to be done and resources used. The charter also has an important role in internal communication, since it can be given wide distribution to keep staff informed of what is happening. The exact content of a charter will vary from organisation to organisation and from project to project, but some elements are likely to be present in all charters.

- Project title
- Project scope: ie purpose and objectives
- Project start date and expected finish date
- Details of the project sponsor and project manager
- Authorisation by the main stakeholders

Other elements of information may be included.

- Outline schedule of work
- Budget information
- Outline of project scope and work sequence
- Further details of roles and responsibilities

3 Stakeholders

 KEY CONCEPT

 concept

Project stakeholders are the individuals and organisations that are involved in, or may be affected by, project activities and outcomes.

3.1 Stakeholder interests

It is important to understand who has an interest in a project, because part of the responsibility of the project manager is **communication** and the **management of expectations**. An initial assessment of stakeholders should be made early in the project's life, taking care not to ignore those who might not approve of the project, either as a whole, or because of some aspect such as its cost, its use of scarce talent or its side-effects. The nature and extent of each stakeholder's interest in and support for (or opposition to) the project should be established as thoroughly as possible and recorded in a stakeholder register. This will make it possible to draw on support where available and, probably more important, anticipate and deal with stakeholder-related problems. The project manager should be aware of the following matters for each stakeholder or stakeholder group.

(a)   Goals
(b)   Past attitude and behaviour
(c)   Expected future behaviour
(d)   Reaction to possible future developments

3.2 Managing stakeholders

It is important to be thorough in assessing stakeholders: a failure to identify and consider a stakeholder group is likely to lead to problems. Here is a list of individuals and groups that might be expected to have a stake in a project.

(a)   **The project manager** – reputation and even employment are at stake.

(b)   **The project team** – they have to work on the project but may have other roles and higher personal priorities.

(c)   **The project sponsor/ budget holder** – this senior figure will demand high standards but may be reluctant to fund all the desirable resources.

(d) **The customers** – may be external or internal and may break down into several groups, such as an internal user group and an external group who should receive improved service as a result of the enhanced capability the user group should acquire on successful completion of the project.

(e) **Managers and staff in supporting functions** such as finance and HR can have extensive influence on the project and its chances of success.

(f) **Line managers of seconded staff** – their own work and prospects may be disrupted.

(g) **Other project managers, teams and sponsors** – rivalry for resources may cause conflict.

(h) **Regulators and auditors** of all kinds, both internal and external, are likely to take an interest in a project.

Project stakeholders may be divided into two main groups.

(a) **Process stakeholders** have an interest in how the project process is conducted. This group includes those involved in it, those who want a say in it, and those who need to evaluate and learn from it.

(b) **Outcome stakeholders** have an interest in the outcomes, results or deliverables of the project. This group includes not only the customer groups described above, but also, typically, some regulators and compliance staff.

The project manager must manage a broad range of complex relationships if the project is to succeed. This amounts to achieving co-operation through influence rather than authority. Gray and Larson (2008) speak of creating a social network to manage the relationships with those the project depends on. The project manager should know whose co-operation, agreement or approval is required for the project to succeed and whose opposition could prevent success. It is particularly important to enlist the support of top management. This not only brings an adequate budget, it signals the project's importance to the organisation and enhances the motivation of the project team.

3.3 Managing stakeholder disputes

Unfortunately, even the most skilled and diplomatic project manager is likely to encounter disputes among project stakeholders. All project managers should be aware of the potential for disputes around their projects and be prepared to act to resolve them.

 MARKETING AT WORK   application

GM bondholders call for new terms

General Motors bondholders, frustrated with the restructuring process for the troubled US carmarker, are calling on the company and the government to actively negotiate new terms …

Bondholders feel they are being asked to disproportionately shoulder concessions in GM's turnround plan …

The terms of federal aid set last year require the carmaker to cut unsecured debt by two-thirds with a debt-for-equity swap …

An administration official said: 'We expect all of the stakeholders to make significant sacrifices in this process and that includes the bondholders.'

Nicole Bullock and Julie MacIntosh, Financial Times, 20 March 2009

The first step is to establish a **framework** to predict the potential for disputes. This involves **risk management**, since an unforeseen event (a risk) has the potential to create conflict, and **dispute management**: the managing of dispute procedures to minimise impacts on costs, goodwill and progress.

Conflict between project stakeholders may be resolved by:

(a) **Negotiation**: the parties discuss the issue with a view to finding mutually acceptable solutions.

(b) **Mediation** (or assisted negotiation): a third party facilitates the negotiation process.

(c)   **Partnering**: creating communication links between project participants with the intention of directing them to a common goal – the project outcome – ahead of their own self-interest.

(d)   **Arbitration**: a third party may be asked to intervene to impose a solution.

On very large projects a **Disputes Review Board** (DRB) may be formed. This may comprise persons directly involved in the project engaged to maintain a 'watching brief' to identify and attend upon disputes as they arise. Usually there is a procedure in place which provides for the DRB to make an 'on the spot' decision before a formal dispute is notified so that the project work can proceed, and that may be followed by various rights of review at increasingly higher levels.

4   Project resources – skills and people

4.1 The project manager

All projects require a person who is ultimately responsible for delivering the required outcome. This person (whether officially given the title or not) is the **project manager**. The duties of a project manager are summarised below.

Duty	Comment
Outline planning	• Project planning (eg targets, sequencing)
	• Developing project targets such as overall costs or timescale needed (eg project should take 20 weeks).
	• Dividing the project into activities and placing these activities into the right sequence.
	• Developing a framework for procedures and structures, manage the project (eg decide, in principle, to have weekly team meetings, performance reviews etc).
Detailed planning	Work breakdown structure, resource requirements, network analysis for scheduling.
Teambuilding	Build cohesion and team spirit.
Communication	The project manager must keep supervisors informed about progress as well as problems, and ensure that members of the project team are properly briefed.
Co-ordinating project activities	Between the project team and users, and other external parties (eg suppliers of hardware and software).
Monitoring and control	The project manager should estimate the causes for each departure from the standard, and take corrective measures.
Problem-resolution	Even with the best planning, unforeseen problems may arise.
Quality control	There is often a short-sighted trade-off between getting the project out on time and the project's quality.
Risk management	A key consideration is project failure and hence project risks and potential risk areas must be identified and monitored.

Project management as a discipline developed because of a need to co-ordinate resources to obtain desired results within a set timeframe. Common project management tasks include establishing goals and objectives, developing a work-plan, scheduling, budgeting, co-ordinating a team and communicating.

The project management process helps project managers maintain control of projects and meet their responsibilities.

4.2 The responsibilities of a project manager

A project manager may be regarded as having responsibilities both to management and to the project team.

Responsibilities to management

(a)   Ensure resources are used efficiently – strike a balance between cost, time and results.

(b)   Keep management informed with timely and accurate communications about progress and problems.

(c)   Manage the project competently and take action to keep it on schedule for successful completion.

(d)   Behave ethically, and adhere to the organisation's policies.

(e)   Maintain a customer orientation (whether the project is geared towards an internal or external customer) – customer satisfaction is a key indicator of project success.

Responsibilities to the project team

(a)   Ensure the project team has the resources required to perform tasks assigned.

(b)   Provide new team members with a proper briefing and help them integrate into the team.

(c)   Provide any support required when members leave the team either during the project or on completion.

(d)   Listen properly to team members so that potential problems are identified and can be dealt with as soon as possible.

4.3 The skills required of a project manager

To meet these responsibilities a project manager requires a broad range of skills. The skills needed are similar to those necessary when managing a wider range of responsibilities. A project manager requires excellent technical and personal capabilities. Some of the skills required are described in the following table.

Type of skill	How the project manager should display the type of skill
Leadership and team building	• Be **enthusiastic** about what the project will achieve. • Be **positive** (but realistic) about all aspects of the project. • Understand where the project fits into the **'big picture'**. • **Delegate** tasks appropriately – and not take on too much personally. • Build team spirit through encouraging **co-operation** and sharing of information. • Do not be restrained by organisational structures; a high tolerance for ambiguity (lack of clear-cut authority) will help the project manager. • Be prepared to motivate team members and give due praise and encouragement.
Project administration	• Ensure all project **documentation** is clear and distributed to all who require it. • Use project **management tools** to analyse and monitor project progress.
Communication	• **Listen** to project team members. Exploit good ideas whatever the source. • Use **persuasion** to win over reluctant team members or stakeholders to support the project. • Ensure management is kept **informed** and is never surprised. • Encourage team members to share their knowledge and support each other.
Technical	• By providing (or at least access to) the **technical expertise** and experience needed to manage the project.
Personal	• Be **flexible**. Circumstances may develop that require a change in plan. • Show **resilience**. Even successful projects will encounter difficulties that require repeated efforts to overcome. • Be **creative**. If one method of completing a task proves impractical a new approach may be required. • **Patience** is required even in the face of tight deadlines. The 'quick-fix' may eventually cost further time than a more thorough but initially more time-consuming solution. • **Keep in touch** with team members as their performance is key to the success of the project.

You should note carefully the difference between the skills required and the responsibilities of the project manager.

4.4 Building a project team

The **project team** comprises the people who report directly or indirectly to the project manager.

Project success depends to a large extent on the team members selected. The ideal project team achieves project completion on time, within budget and to the required specifications – with the minimum amount of direct supervision from the project manager.

The team will comprise individuals with **differing skills and personalities**. The project manager should choose a balanced team that takes advantage of each team member's skills and compensates elsewhere for their weaknesses.

The project team will normally be drawn from existing staff, but highly recommended **outsiders with special skills** may be recruited. When building a team the project manager should ask the following questions.

(a)   **What skills** are required to complete each task of the project? This list will be based on the project goals established previously. (This process is explained in the next chapter.)

(b)   **Who** has the talent and skills to complete the required tasks, whether inside or outside the organisation?

(c)   Are the people identified **available**, **affordable**, and able to join the project team?

(d)   What level of **supervision** will be required?

This information should be **summarised in worksheet format**, as shown in the following example.

Project Skill Requirements		
Project Name: _____	Date worksheet completed: _____	
Project Manager: _____		
Task	*Skill needed*	*Responsibility*

The completed worksheet provides a document showing the skills required of the project team. Deciding who has the skills required for each task and if possible seconding those identified to the project team, should be done **as early as possible**. Team members should then be able to **participate** in the planning of schedules and budgets. This should encourage the acceptance of agreed deadlines, and a greater commitment to achieve project success.

The individuals selected to join the team should be told **why they have been selected**, referring both to their technical skills and personal qualities. This should provide members with guidance as to the role they are expected to play.

Although the composition of the project team is critical, project managers often find it is not possible to assemble the ideal team, and have to do the best they can with the personnel available. If the project manager feels the best available team does not possess the skills and talent required, the project should be **abandoned or delayed.**

Once the team has been selected each member should be given a (probably verbal) project briefing, outlining the overall aims of the project, and detailing the role they are expected to play.

4.5 Developing the project team

Group cohesiveness is an important factor for project success. It is hoped that team members will **develop and learn from each other**, and solve problems by drawing on different resources and expertise.

The performance of the project team will be enhanced by the following.

(a)   Effective communication

(b)   All members being aware of the team's purpose and the role of each team member

(c)   Collaboration and creativity among team members

(d)   Trusting, supportive atmosphere in the group

(e)   A commitment to meeting the agreed schedule

(f)   Innovative/creative behaviour

(g)   Team members highly interdependent, interface effectively

(h)   Capacity for conflict resolution

(i)   Results orientation

(j)   High energy levels and enthusiasm

(k)   An acceptance of change

Collaboration and interaction will help ensure the skills of all team members are utilised, and should result in 'synergistic' solutions. Formal (eg meetings) and informal channels (eg e-mail links, a bulletin board) of **communication** should be set up to ensure this interaction takes place.

Learning objectives		Covered
1 Describe the main stages of a marketing project plan	☑	Project lifecycle
		– Definition
		– Design
		– Delivery
		– Development
2 Establish a marketing project's scope	☑	Project definition
	☑	Initiation analysis
	☑	Performance drivers
	☑	Business case
	☑	Project charter
3 Describe the management of project stakeholders	☑	Stakeholder analysis
	☑	Managing disputes
4 Identify the skills needed to complete a marketing project	☑	Project manager's roles and responsibilities
	☑	Project team responsibilities
	☑	Developing the project team

1   What are four phases of a typical project lifecycle?

2   What is the purpose of the project development phase?

3   What is the aim of fishbone or Ishikawa analysis?

4   What document does the PRINCE2 methodology assume drives the project?

5   What are the four techniques for resolving stakeholder disputes?

6   What are the project manager's responsibilities to the project team?

---

1.   Let us take the very simple example of going on holiday. We might make the following notes:

Project definition

Purpose of holiday: rest, recreation, broadening of mental horizons or merely spend some time in the sun?

Scope: how many involved? How to travel? Where to stay? Package deal? Activity holiday?

Estimated overall budget? Allow for extra living expenses but note reduced normal expenses – heat, light, travel.

Project design

(Let us assume we have selected a summer activity package holiday)

Project: White water rafting, Colorado, 6-13 June 2009, for 4 people. Outline budget: £6,780 + pocket money.

Travel Agent: Crazee Travel, Shepherds Bush; project liaison staff: Juanita.

Flight itinerary: outbound – depart Heathrow 6 June 14.30hrs Whiteknuckle Airways flight 13, arrive Denver 23.30hrs (local time); inbound – depart Denver 12 June 11.50hrs, Bugle-air flight 69, arrive Heathrow 13 June 07.45hrs.

Local arrangements: stay night 6 June at Denver Holiday Inn – hotel shuttle bus from airport. Collected 7 June 10.00hrs for transfer to Rancho Jornada del Muerto. 7 – 11 June – at ranch, bunkhouse accommodation, full board. Liaison, Randy Q Scott III.

Finance: £500 pocket money per person is advised as there will be several opportunities to visit local townships. Deposit £850 each to be paid to travel agent by 1 May 2009. Copy invoices available.

Risk management: full travel health insurance is advised for travel to the USA – available online from Flybenite.com for £55 per person.

Project delivery

Delivery involves assembling the party at Heathrow, with luggage and all travel documentation, locating the Holiday Inn shuttle bus at Denver, dealing with misunderstandings and failures of communication at hotel check-in, assisting Rancho staff with transfer bus breakdown, giving EAR and CPR to tourists after river raft overturns, preserving patience and equanimity when return flight delayed for 17 hours with no explanation, accommodation or even a cup of tea and dispersing party for own arrangements return home from Manchester, where eventual return flight actually lands.

Project development

Immediate review: never travel with Crazee Travel again.

Longer-term review: actually it was all quite exciting, apart from being held at gun point on arrival in the US, which was a bit OTT.

---

1   Definition, design, delivery, development

2   To provide rapid staff feedback and to identify short-term needs such as staff training or remedial action for procedure failures

3   To break a perceived issue down into its smallest underlying causes and components

4   The business case

5   Negotiation, mediation, partnering and arbitration

6   Provide resources, brief new members, support departing team members and listen carefully

References

Bullen, N. and MacIntosh, J. (2009) *'GM bond holders call for new terms'*, Financial Times, 20 March 2009.

Guerra, F. and Ward, A. (2004) *'City Group and KorAm Bank'*, Financial Times, 17 October 2004.

Gray, C. F. and Larson, W. L. (2008) <u>Project Management: the Managerial Process</u>, McGraw-Hill, London.

Grundy, T. and Brown, L. (2002) <u>Strategic Project Management</u>, Thompson Learning, London.

Johnson, G., Scholes, K. and Whittington, R. (2008) <u>Exploring Corporate Strategy</u>, (8th edition), Prentice Hall, London.

Lewis, J. (2008) <u>Mastering Project Management</u>, (2nd edition), McGraw-Hill, London.

Chapter 9

Project management tools and techniques

Topic list

1   Management tools and techniques
2   Project management software

Introduction

Managing a project can be very demanding. Effective project management requires thorough planning, monitoring and control.

We start this chapter by studying some of the **management tools and techniques** available to help the project management process. These tools and techniques are likely to be relevant to your project, so it is essential that you understand and are able to apply the techniques covered.

As with many tasks, project management activities are now usually carried out using computers. **Project management software** packages are covered in Section 2 of this chapter.

Syllabus-linked learning objective

By the end of the chapter you will be able to:

Learning objectives	Syllabus link
1 Utilise a range of tools and techniques to support project planning, scheduling, resourcing and control	4.5

1   Management tools and techniques

The techniques we discuss in this section are concerned with the fundamentals of planning projects and controlling their progress. As with most activities, it is difficult to separate the process of planning a project from that of controlling it: planning is likely to continue throughout the life of the project. A **baseline plan** will show the following.

(a)   Start and end dates for the project and its major phases or activities
(b)   The resources needed and when they are required
(c)   Estimates of cost for the project and the major phases or activities

1.1 Project management plan

The project manager should also develop a **project management plan**. (In some organisations what is described here as the project management plan would simply be called the project plan. In other organisations the project plan refers only to the project schedule, usually in the form of a network diagram.)

KEY CONCEPT

concept

The **project management plan** is used as a reference tool for managing the project. The plan is used to guide both project execution and project control. It outlines how the project will be planned, monitored and implemented.

The **project management plan** should include:

(a)   Project objectives and how they will be achieved and verified.
(b)   How any **changes** to these procedures are to be **controlled**.
(c)   The **management and technical procedures**, and **standards**, to be used.
(d)   The **budget** and **time-scale.**
(e)   **Safety**, health and environmental policies.
(f)   Inherent **risks** and how they will be managed.

An example of a simple **project management plan** is shown below. This plan was produced by the American Project Management Institute (PMI) – to manage a project to produce formal project management principles.

The project management plan **evolves** over time. A high-level plan for the whole project and a detailed plan for the current and following stage is usually produced soon after project start-up. At each subsequent stage a detailed plan is produced for the following stage and, if required, the overall project plan is revised.

Project management plan	
Project name	The full name of this project is 'Project Management Principles.'
Project manager	The project manager is Joe Bloggs. The project manager is authorised to (1) initiate the project, (2) form the project team and (3) prepare and execute plans and manage the project as necessary for successful project completion.
Purpose/ Business need	This project addresses a need for high-level guidelines for the project management profession through the identification and presentation of project management principles. The project sponsor and accepting agent is the Project Management Institute (PMI) Standards Program Team (SPT). The principal and beneficial customer is the membership of PMI. Principles are needed to provide high-level context and guidance for the profession of project management. These Principles will provide benefit from the perspectives of practice, evaluation, and development.
Product description and deliverables	The final deliverable of this project is a document containing a statement of project management Principles. The text is to be fully developed and ready for publication. As a research and development project, it is to be approached flexibly in schedule and resource requirements, with an initially proposed publication date of June 20XX.
Project management	The project team will use project methodology consistent with PMI Standards. The project is to be managed with definitive scope and acceptance criteria fully established as the project progresses and the product is developed.
Assumptions, constraints and risks	The project faces some increased risk that without a clearly prescribed definition of a Principle, standards for product quality will be more difficult to establish and apply. To mitigate this risk, ongoing communication between the project team and the project sponsor on this matter will be required.
Resources	The PMI SPT is to provide the project team with the following.
	Financial. SPT will provide financial resources as available. The initial amount for the current year is $5,000. The project manager must not exceed the allocated amount, and notify the SPT when 75% of the allocation has been spent.
	Explanation of Standards Program. SPT will provide guidance at the outset of the project, updates as changes occur, and clarifications as needed.
	Personnel/Volunteers. SPT will recruit volunteer team members from within the membership of PMI through various media and liaisons. The project team is to consist of no less than ten members, including the project manager. General qualifications to be sought by SPT in recruiting will be:
	Mandatory
	• Acceptance of project plan
	• Demonstrated capability for strategic, generalised or intuitive thinking
	• Capability to write clearly on technical subject matter for general audiences
	• Capability to work co-operatively with well-developed interpersonal skills
	• Be conversant in English and be able to use telephone and Internet e-mail telecommunications
	As possible
	• Time availability (Team members may contribute at different levels. An average of approximately five to ten hours per month is desired.)
	• Diversity (Team members collectively may represent diverse nationalities, types of organisations or corporate structure, business sectors, academic disciplines, and personal experience.)
	• Travel (As determined mutually by the project sponsor and manager, some travel for face-to-face meetings may be requested.)

Approach	The project will progress through the following phases.

Phase 1: Team formation – Recruit and orient volunteer team members. Establish procedures and ground rules for group process and decision-making.

Phase 2: Subject matter clarification – Identify and clarify initial scope and definitions of project subject matter.

Phase 3a: Exploration – Begin brainstorming (through gathering, sharing, and discussion) of data and views in unrestricted, non-judgemental process.

Phase 3b: Selection – Conclude brainstorming (through evaluation and acceptance or rejection) of collected data and views. As the conclusion to this phase, the SPT will review as an interim deliverable the selection made by the project team.

Phase 4: Development – Conduct further research and discussion to develop accepted subject matter.

Phase 5: Articulation – Write a series of drafts to state the accepted and developed subject matter as appropriate for the project business need and product description.

Phase 6: Adoption – Submit product to SPT for the official PMI standards approval and adoption process. Revise product as needed.

Phase 7: Closeout – Perform closure for team and administrative matters. Deliver project files to SPT.

Communication and reporting	The project manager and team will communicate with and report to the PMI Standards Program Team as follows.

Monthly status reports – Written monthly status and progress reports are to include:

- Work accomplished since the last report
- Work planned to be performed during the next reporting period
- Deliverables submitted since the last report
- Deliverables planned to be submitted during the next reporting period
- Work tasks in progress and currently outside of expectations for scope, quality, schedule or cost
- Risks identified and actions taken or proposed to mitigate
- Lessons learned
- Summary statement for posting on PMI website

Monthly resource reports – Written monthly resource reports are to include:

Financial resources

- Total funds allocated
- Total funds expended to date
- Estimated expenditures for the next reporting period
- Estimated expenditures for entire project to completion

Human resources

- List of all volunteer team members categorised by current involvement (i.e., active, new (pre-active), inactive, resigned)
- Current number of new and active volunteer team members
- Estimated number of volunteer team members needed for project completion

Milestone and critical status reports – Additional status reports are to be submitted as mutually agreed upon by SPT and the project manager and are to include at least the following items.

- Milestone status reports are to include the same items as the monthly status reports, summarised to cover an entire project phase period since the last milestone report, or entire project to date.
- Critical status reports are to focus on work tasks outside of expectations and other information as requested by SPT or stipulated by the project manager.

Project management plan	
Acceptance	The project manager will submit the final product and any interim deliverables to the Standards Program Team (SPT) for formal acceptance. The SPT may (1) accept the product as delivered by the project team, or (2) return the product to the team with a statement of specific requirements to make the product fully acceptable. The acceptance decision of the SPT is to be provided to the project manager in writing.
Change management	Requests for change to this plan may be initiated by either the project sponsor or the project manager. All change requests will be reviewed and approved or rejected by a formal proceeding of the Standards Program Team (SPT) with input and interaction with the project manager. Decisions of the SPT will be documented and provided to the project manager in writing. All changes will be incorporated into this document, reflected by a new version number and date.

Plan acceptance	*Signature and Date*	
By PMI Standards Program Team	_____	12 July 20XX
	Fred Jones – PMI Technical Research & Standards Manager	
By Project Manager	_____	20 July 20XX
	Joe Bloggs – PMI Member	

The format and contents of a project management plan will **vary** depending on the organisation involved and the complexity of the project. The contents page and introduction from a detailed project management plan relating to a software implementation project at a call centre follow.

 MARKETING AT WORK application

Call centre software implementation - Project Management Plan

CONTENTS	Page
1 INTRODUCTION	
2 PROJECT ROLES	
3 COMMUNICATIONS PLAN	
4 TRAINING PLAN	
5 CHANGE MANAGEMENT PLAN	
6 QUALITY MANAGEMENT	
7 PROJECT DOCUMENTATION	
8 FINANCIAL MANAGEMENT	
9 PROGRAMME MANAGEMENT	

SECTION 1

INTRODUCTION

1.1   Purpose of the Project Management Plan

The purpose of this Plan is to define the working relationship between Project Team (PT) and the Manager, Customer Centres Group (MCCG). It details the level of service to be provided by Project Team to the client and the associated cost. If the nature of the project changes, or if situations develop which indicate a need for modification, then this plan will be altered accordingly in consultation with the Client. This Plan details key milestones, the methods for delivering these milestones, and responsibilities of the project manager, project owner and the project team representatives.

Project Objective

To develop and fully support a call centre environment that promotes the achievement of '80% of all incoming calls resolved at the first point of contact.'

1.3 **Project Deliverable**

To deliver to the MCCG, fully commissioned and operational system upgrades as defined within this project plan, including an appropriately skilled call centre team, by 15 April 20XX at an estimated Project Team cost of £123,975.

Note: Only the contents page and introduction of this comprehensive plan are reproduced here.

1.2 Work breakdown structure

Work breakdown structure (WBS) is fundamental to project planning and control. Its essence is the **analysis** of the work required to complete the project into **manageable components**. These are also known as **work packages** which have defined outcomes and responsibilities.

A good way to approach WBS is to consider the outputs (or 'deliverables') the project is required to produce. This can then be analysed into physical and intangible components, which can in turn be further analysed down to whatever level of simplicity is required. Working backwards in this way helps to avoid preconceived ideas of the work the project will involve and the processes that must be undertaken. (This is the basis of the PRINCE2 approach.)

For example, a simple domestic project might be to create a vegetable plot in a garden. The output would be a plot of cultivated, well-drained soil that was free of weeds, of a suitable level of fertility and with suitable exposure to sun and rain, together with protection from strong winds. This has obvious implications for what must be done. A plot must be selected; existing vegetation must be cleared; weeds must be dug out; the soil must be improved if necessary, by liming and composting; and a physical boundary or kerb must be provided to prevent invasion by creeping weeds such as grass.

The WBS can allow for several levels of analysis, starting with major project phases and gradually breaking them down into major activities, more detailed sub-activities and individual tasks that will last only a very short time. There is no standardised terminology for the various levels of disaggregation, though an activity is sometimes regarded as being composed of **tasks**.

The delivery phase of many projects will break down into significant stages or sub-phases. These are very useful for control purposes, as the completion of each stage is an obvious point for reviewing the whole plan before starting the next one.

1.2.1 Dependencies and interactions

A very important aspect of project planning is the determination of **dependencies** and **interactions**. At any level of WBS analysis, some tasks will be dependent on others; that is to say, **a dependent task cannot commence** until the task upon which it depends is completed. In our vegetable plot example, it is quite obvious that thought must be given to selecting the site of the plot in order to achieve the necessary sun, rain and shelter *before* seizing a spade and starting to dig. Similarly, it would be physically impossible to apply fertiliser if it had not already been positioned at the site. Careful analysis of dependencies is a major step towards a workable project plan, since it provides an **order in which things must be tackled**. Sometimes, of course, the dependencies are limited and it is possible to proceed with tasks in almost any order, but this is unusual. The more complex a project, the greater the need for analysis of dependencies.

Interactions are slightly different; they occur when tasks are linked but not dependent. This can arise for a variety of reasons: a good example is a requirement to share the use of a scarce resource. If there were two of us working on our vegetable plot but we only possessed one spade, we could not use it simultaneously both to cultivate the plot itself and to dig the trench in which we wish to place the kerbstones. We could choose to do either of these activities first, but we could not do them both at the same time.

The output from the WBS process is a list of tasks, probably arranged hierarchically to reflect the disaggregation of activities. This then becomes the input into the planning and control processes described in the rest of this section.

1.2.2 PRINCE2 – product breakdown

Rather than using **work breakdown structure**, PRINCE2 uses a **product-based** approach to planning. This has the advantage of directing management attention to *what* is to be achieved rather than *how* to do it, thus providing an automatic focus on achieving the product goals. Also, it can be helpful in complex projects, where the processes involved may be initially unclear.

Under this approach, work breakdown is preceded by **product breakdown**. PRINCE2 starts this analysis by dividing the **project products** into three groups.

(a)   **Technical products** are the things the project has been set up to provide to the users. For an IT system, for example, these would include the hardware, software, manuals and training.

(b)   **Quality products** define both the quality controls that are applied to the project and the quality standards the technical products must achieve.

(c)   **Management products** are the artefacts used to manage the project. They include the project management organisation structure, planning documentation, reports and so on.

Each of these groups of products is then broken down into manageable components as part of the planning process, using the traditional work breakdown structure approach if the complexity of the project requires it. Project and stage plans may make use of the normal planning tools such as CPA, Gantt charts and resource histograms.

1.3 The project budget

KEY CONCEPT   concept

Project budget. The amount and distribution of resources allocated to a project.

Building a project budget should be an orderly process that attempts to establish a realistic estimate of the cost of the project. There are two main methods for establishing the project budget; **top-down** and **bottom-up**.

Top-down budgeting describes the situation where the budget is imposed 'from above'. Project managers are allocated a budget for the project based on an estimate made by senior management. The figure may prove realistic, especially if similar projects have been recently undertaken. However, the technique is often used simply because it is quick, or because only a certain level of funding is available.

In **bottom-up budgeting** the project manager consults the project team, and others, to calculate a budget based on the tasks that make up the project. Detailed analysis of the deliverables and work to be done to achieve them will be necessary in order to produce an accurate and detailed budget.

It is useful to collate information on a **budgeting worksheet**.

Budgeting worksheet				
Project Name: _____ Date worksheet completed: _____				
Project Manager: _____				
Task (code)	Responsible staff member or external supplier	Estimated material costs	Estimated labour costs	Total cost of task

Estimates (and therefore budgets) cannot be expected to be 100% accurate. Business **conditions may change**, the project plan may be amended or estimates may simply prove to be incorrect.

Any **estimate** must be accompanied by some **indication of expected accuracy**.

Estimates can be **improved** by:

(a) **Learning** from past mistakes.
(b) Ensuring sufficient design **information**.
(c) Ensuring as **detailed a specification as possible** from the customer.
(d) Properly **analysing the job** into its constituent units.

The overall level of cost estimates will be influenced by:

(a) **Project goals**. If a high level of quality is expected costs will be higher.

(b) **External vendors**. Some costs may need to be estimated by outside vendors. To be realistic, these people must understand exactly what would be expected of them.

(c) **Staff availability**. If staff are unavailable, potentially expensive contractors may be required.

(d) **Time schedules**. The quicker a task is required to be done the higher the cost is likely to be – particularly with external suppliers.

The budget may express all resources in monetary amounts, or may show money and other resources – such as staff hours.

Budgets should be presented for approval and **sign-off** to the stakeholder who has responsibility for the funds being used.

Before presenting a budget for approval it may have to be revised a number of times. The 'first draft' may be overly reliant on rough estimates, as insufficient time was available to obtain more accurate figures.

On presentation, the project manager may be asked to find ways to cut the budget. If he or she agrees that cuts can be made, the consequences of the cuts should be pointed out – eg a reduction in quality.

It may be decided that a project costs more than it is worth. If so, scrapping the project is a perfectly valid option. In such cases the budgeting process has highlighted the situation before too much time and effort has been spent on an unprofitable venture.

1.4 Gantt charts

Gantt charts are a **visual** planning tool useful for projects but are limited in their use as they do not recognise the interrelations between tasks.

A **Gantt chart**, named after the engineer Henry Gantt who pioneered the procedure in the early 1900s, is a horizontal bar chart used to plan the **time scale** for a project and to estimate the **resources** required.

The Gantt chart displays the time relationships between tasks in a project. Two lines are usually used to show the time allocated for each task, and the actual time taken.

A simple Gantt chart, illustrating some of the activities involved in a network server installation project, follows.

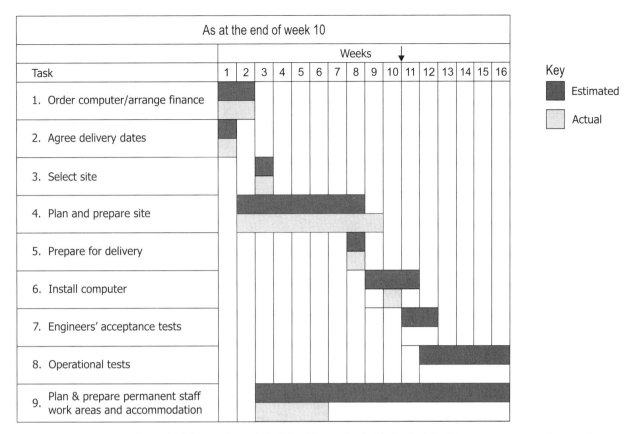

The chart shows that at the end of the tenth week Activity 9 is running behind schedule. More resources may have to be allocated to this activity if the staff accommodation is to be ready in time for the changeover to the new system.

Activity 4 has not been completed on time, and this has resulted in some disruption to the computer installation (Activity 6), which may mean further delays in the commencement of Activities 7 and 8.

A Gantt chart does not show the interrelationship between the various activities in the project as clearly as a **network diagram** (see below). A combination of Gantt charts and network analysis will often be used for project planning and resource allocation.

1.5 Network analysis

Network analysis illustrates interactions and dependencies. It is used to plan the sequence of tasks making up project scope and to determine the **critical path**. **PERT** (Project Evaluation and Renew Technique), a method for analysing tasks involved in completing a firm's project, uses probabilities to make estimates of likely completion and milestone dates.

Network analysis, also known as **critical path analysis** (CPA), is a useful technique to help with planning and controlling large projects, such as construction projects, research and development projects and the computerisation of systems.

 KEY CONCEPT

concept

Network analysis requires breaking down the project into tasks, arranging them into a logical sequence and estimating the duration of each.

This enables the series of tasks that determines the minimum possible duration of the project to be found. These are the activities on the **critical path**.

CPA aims to ensure the progress of a project, so the project is completed in the **minimum amount of time**. It pinpoints the tasks which are **on the critical path**; those tasks which, if delayed beyond the allotted time, would **delay the**

completion of the project as a whole. The technique can also be used to assist in **allocating resources** such as labour and equipment.

Critical path analysis is quite a simple technique. The events and activities making up the whole project are represented in the form of a **diagram**. Drawing the diagram or chart involves the following steps.

Step 1   Estimating the time needed to complete each individual activity or task that makes up a part of the project.

Step 2   Sorting out what activities must be done one after another, and which can be done at the same time, if required.

Step 3   Representing these in a network diagram.

Step 4   Estimating the critical path, which is the longest sequence of consecutive activities through the network.

The duration of the whole project will be fixed by the time taken to complete the longest path through the network. This path is called the **critical path** and activities on it are known as **critical activities**. Activities on the critical path **must be started and completed on time**, otherwise the total project time will be extended. The method of finding the critical path is illustrated in the example below.

Network analysis shows the **sequence** of tasks and how long they are going to take. The diagrams are drawn from left to right. To construct a network diagram you need to know the activities involved in a project, the expected duration of each and the order (or precedences, or dependencies) of the activities. For example:

Activity	Expected duration (days)	Preceding activity
A	3	-
B	5	-
C	2	B
D	1	A
E	6	A
F	3	D
G	3	C, E

1.5.1 Activity on arrow presentation

Here is a network diagram showing our example in the form known as **activity on arrow**.

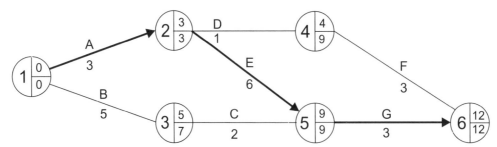

(a)   The network is made up of events and activities, represented by circles and arrows respectively. The diagram is laid out to show the dependencies that exist between the activities, working from left to right. The first event is the start of the overall sequence of activities (or the project). Each subsequent event marks the beginning of at least one activity and, therefore, the end of any activities upon which it is dependent. In the network diagram above, for example, event 5 marks the completion of activities E and C and the start of activity G.

(b)   Events are numbered, working from left to right and the numbers are entered in the left-hand halves of the event circles. Also by convention, the events are numbered so that the event at the end of any activity has a higher number than the one at its start.

(c)   Activities are lettered, again working from left to right. The duration of each activity is shown by a number entered against its identifying letter.

(d)   When the basic information has been entered on to the network, it becomes possible to determine the **critical path** through it: this is the sequence of activities that takes the longest time and which therefore determines the overall expected duration of the project.

(e)   A **forward pass** is made through the network and the **earliest event time** (EET) is entered in the upper right quadrant of each event circle. This time depends on the duration of any sequence of activities leading to the event in question and therefore reflects the dependencies involved. In the diagram, event 5, for example, cannot occur (and activity G therefore cannot begin) until the sequences A-E and B-C are both complete. B-C takes (5 + 2) days, while A-E takes (3 + 6) days. The *earliest* event time for event 5 is therefore 9 days. This is a general rule: the EET for any event shows the **longest duration sequence of activities leading to it**.

(f)   When the forward pass is complete, a **rearward pass** is made, starting at the final event and working back to establish the **latest event time** (LET) for each event. The LET for an event is entered in the lower right quadrant of its symbol. Like the EET, the LET depends on the longest sequence of activities involved, but this time it is the sequences of events that follow the event in question that are relevant rather than the ones that precede it. In the example network diagram, event 2 is followed by sequences D-F and E-G with durations (1 + 3) days and (6 + 3) days respectively. If there is to be time to complete the longer sequence E-G, the LET for event 2 must be 3 days.

(g)   When both forward and rearward passes are complete, the **critical path** is identifiable as the route through the network that links all the events that have LET equal to EET: there is no **float** on this path. We discuss float times later in this section. The critical path activities are highlighted on the diagram in some way, such as by using double lines or hash marks.

The **critical path** in the diagram above is AEG. Note the **float time** of five days for activity F. Activity F can begin any time between days 4 and 9, thus giving the project manager a degree of flexibility.

(h)   Sometimes it is necessary to use a **dummy activity** in a network diagram. Dummies indicate dependency, but they take no time. The need for them arises from the convention that activity arrows are always straight. Thus, if an activity, C, depends on both activity A and activity B, the presentation below is not used:

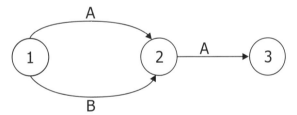

Instead, an extra event and a dummy are inserted:

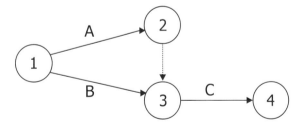

The dummy activity is shown as a broken line. Note also how the dummy starts at an event with a lower number than the one it ends at. Sometimes it is necessary to use a dummy activity not just to comply with the convention, but to **preserve the basic logic** of the network.

In our initial example in this section, if activity G had depended on activity D as well as on activities C and E, this would have been shown as a dummy running from event 4 to event 5.

Dummy activities are not required when the **activity on node** technique (discussed below) is used for drawing the network.

Consider the following example of a project to install a new office telephone system.

Activity	Preceding activity
A: buy equipment	–
B: allocate extension numbers	–
C: install switchboard	A
D: install wiring	B, C
E: print office directory	B

The project is finished when both D and E are complete.

Identify why there may be a need for a dummy activity, and draw the basic network showing it.

1.5.2 Activity on node presentation

Network diagrams may also be drawn using **activity on node** presentation which is similar in style to that used by the **Microsoft Project** software package.

1.6 Example: Activity on node

Suppose that a project includes three activities, C, D and E. Neither activity D nor E can start until activity C is completed, but D and E could be done simultaneously if required.

This would be represented as follows.

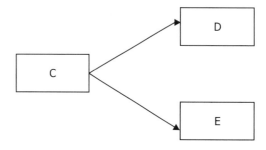

Note the following.

(a)   An **activity** within a network is represented by a rectangular box. (Each box is a **node**.)
(b)   The **flow** of activities in the diagram should be from **left to right**.
(c)   The diagram clearly shows that **D and E must follow C**.

A second possibility is that an activity cannot start until two or more activities have been completed. If activity H cannot start until activities G and F are both complete, then we would represent the situation like this.

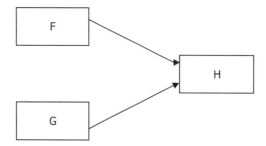

In some conventions an extra node is introduced at the start and end of a network. This serves absolutely no purpose (other than to ensure that all the nodes are joined up), so we recommend that you do not do it. Just in case you ever see a network presented in this way, both styles are shown in the next example.

1.7 Example: starts and ends

Draw a diagram for the following project. The project is finished when both D and E are complete.

Activity	Preceding activity
A	–
B	–
C	A
D	B & C
E	B

Solution

Microsoft Project style

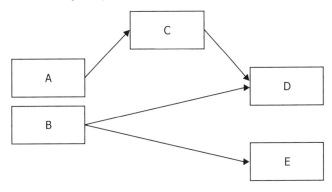

With start and end nodes

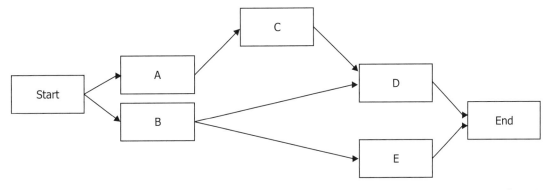

Any network can be analysed into a number of different paths or routes. A path is simply a sequence of activities which can take you from the start to the end of the network. In the example above, there are just three routes or paths.

(a)   A C D.
(b)   B D.
(c)   B E.

The time needed to complete each individual activity in a project must be estimated. This duration is shown within the node as follows. The reason for and meaning of the other boxes will be explained in a moment.

Task A	
6	

1.8 Example: the critical path

Activity	Immediately preceding activity	Duration (weeks)
A	–	5
B	–	4
C	A	2
D	B	1
E	B	5
F	B	5
G	C, D	4
H	F	3
I	F	2

(a)   What are the paths through the network?

(b)   What is the critical path and its duration?

Solution

The first step in the solution is to draw the network diagram, with the time for each activity shown.

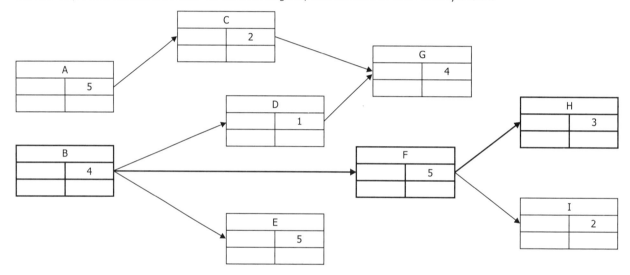

We could list the paths through the network and their overall completion times as follows.

Path		Duration (weeks)	
A C G	(5 + 2 + 4)	11
B D G	(4 + 1 + 4)	9
B E	(4 + 5)	9
B F H	(4 + 5 + 3)	12
B F I	(4 + 5 + 2)	11

The critical path is the longest, BFH, with a duration of 12 weeks. This is the minimum time needed to complete the project.

The critical path is indicated on the diagram by drawing thick (or double-line) arrows, as shown above. In Microsoft Project the arrows and the nodes are highlighted in red.

Listing paths through the network in this way should be easy enough for small networks, but it becomes a long and tedious task for bigger and more complex networks. This is why software packages are used in real life.

Project management software packages offer a much larger variety of techniques than can easily be done by hand. Microsoft Project allows each activity to be assigned to any one of a variety of types: 'start as late as possible', 'start as soon as possible', 'finish no earlier than a particular date', 'finish no later than a particular date', and so on.

In real life, too, activity times can be shortened by working weekends and overtime, or they may be constrained by non-availability of essential personnel. In other words with any more than a few activities the possibilities are mind-boggling, which is why software is used.

Nevertheless, a simple technique is illustrated in the following example.

1.9 Find the critical path

The procedure for finding the critical path is essentially the same as we used with the activity on arrow example earlier.

One way of showing earliest and latest **start** times for activities is to divide each event node into sections. This is similar to the style used in **Microsoft Project** except that Project uses real dates, which is far more useful, and the bottom two sections can mean a variety of things, depending what constraints have been set.

These sections record the following things.

(a)   The **name** of the activity, for example Task A. This helps humans to understand the diagram.

(b)   An **ID number** which is unique to that activity. This helps computer packages to understand the diagram, because it is possible that two or more activities could have the same name. For instance two pieces of research done at different project stages might both be called 'Research'.

(c)   The **duration** of the activity.

(d)   The **earliest start time**. Conventionally for the first node in the network, this is time 0.

(e)   The **latest start time**.

(*Note*. Don't confuse start times with the **'event'** times that are calculated when using the **activity-on-arrow** method, even though the approach is the same.)

Task D	
ID number: 4	Duration: 6 days
Earliest start: Day 4	Latest start: Day 11

1.9.1 Earliest start times

To find the earliest start times, always start with activities that have no predecessors and give them an earliest starting time of 0. In the example we have been looking at, this is week 0.

Then work along each path from **left to right** through the diagram calculating the earliest time that the next activity can start, just as with activity on arrow.

For example, the earliest time for activity C is week 0 + 5 = 5. The earliest time activities D, E and F can start is week 0 + 4 = 4.

To calculate an activity's earliest time, simply look at the box for the *preceding* activity and add the bottom left figure to the top right figure.

If *two or more* activities precede an activity take the *highest* figure as the later activity's earliest start time: it cannot start before all the others are finished!

1.9.2 Latest start times

The latest start times are the latest times at which each activity can start **if the project as a whole is to be completed in the earliest possible time**, in other words in 12 weeks in our example.

Work backwards from **right to left** through the diagram calculating the latest time at which the activity can start, if it is to be completed at the latest finishing time. For example, the latest start time for activity H is 12 - 3 = week 9 and for activity E is 12 - 5 = week 7.

Activity F might cause difficulties as two activities, H and I, lead back to it.

(a)   Activity H must be completed by week 12, and so must start at week 9.
(b)   Activity I must also be completed by week 12, and so must start at week 10.

Activity F takes 5 weeks so its latest start time is either 9 − 5 = week 4 or 10 − 5 = week 5. However, if it starts in week 5 it will not be possible to start activity H on time and the whole project will be delayed. We therefore take the *lower* figure.

The final diagram is now as follows.

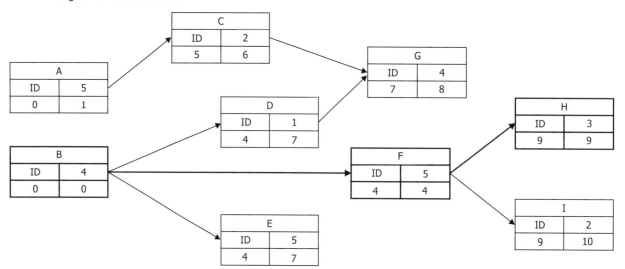

Critical activities are those activities which must be started on time, otherwise the total project time will be increased. It follows that each event on the critical path must have the same earliest and latest start times. The critical path for the above network is therefore B F H.

1.10 Float times

Float time is the time available for unforeseen circumstances.

(a)   **Total float** on an activity is the time available (earliest start date to latest finish date) *less* time needed for the job. If, for example, job A's earliest start time was day 7 and its latest end time was day 17, and the job needed four days, total float would be:

(17 − 7) − 4 = 6 days

(b)   **Free float** is the delay possible in an activity on the assumption that all preceding activities start as early as possible and all subsequent activities also start at the earliest time.

(c)   **Independent float** is the delay possible if all preceding jobs have finished as late as possible, and all succeeding jobs are to start as early as possible.

By definition there is no float time on the critical path.

1.11 Delays on the critical path

A delay on the critical path will delay the whole project. Project time overrun can often be avoided by deploying extra resources on the critical activity suffering delay. This is called 'crashing'. Sometimes, the extra resources can be found by transferring them from non-critical activities, thus exploiting their inherent float.. However, it will often be necessary to use extra resources. Crashing will generally increase **time** and **risk**.

1.12 Criticisms of critical path/network analysis

(a)   It is not always possible to devise an effective WBS for a project.

(b)   It assumes a **sequential relationship** between activities. It assumes that activity B starts after activity A has finished. It is not very good at coping with the possibility that an activity 'later' in the sequence may be relevant to an earlier activity.

(c)   There are **problems in estimation**. Where the project is completely new, the planning process may be conducted in conditions of relative ignorance.

(d)   Although network analysis plans the use of resources of labour and finance, it does not appear to develop plans for **contingencies**, other than crashing time.

(e)   CPA **assumes a trade-off between time and cost**. This may not be the case where a substantial portion of the cost is **indirect overheads** or where the direct labour proportion of the total cost is limited.

1.13 Resource histogram

KEY CONCEPT

concept

A **resource histogram** shows a view of project data in which resource requirements, usage, and availability are shown against a time scale.

A simple resource histogram showing programmer time required on a software development program is shown below.

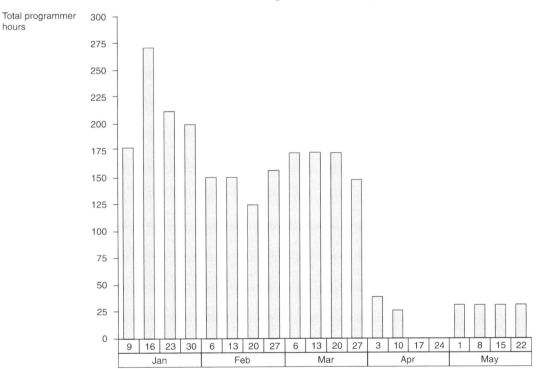

Programmer time required

Week ending

Some organisations add another bar (or a separate line) to the chart showing resource availability. The chart then shows any instances when the required resource hours exceed the available hours. Plans should then be made to either obtain further resource for these peak times, or to reschedule the work plan. Alternately the chart may show times when the available resource is excessive, and should be redeployed elsewhere. An example follows.

No. of workers

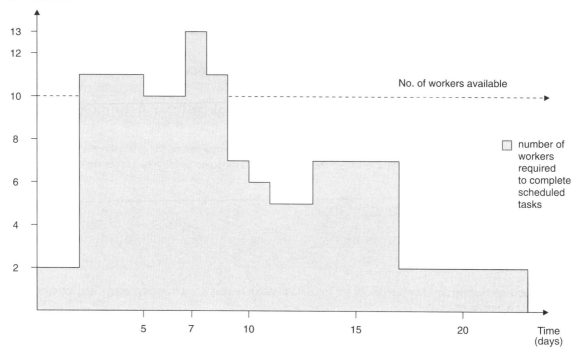

The number of workers required on the seventh day is 13. Can we reschedule the non-critical activities to reduce the requirement to the available level of 10? We might be able to rearrange activities so that we can make use of the workers available from day 9 onwards.

2 Project management software

Project management techniques are ideal candidates for computerisation. Inexpensive project management software packages have been available for a number of years. *Microsoft Project* and *Micro Planner X-Pert* are two popular packages.

Software might be used for a number of purposes.

(a) **Planning and scheduling**
Calendars, **network diagrams** (showing the critical path) and Gantt charts (showing resource use) can be produced automatically once the relevant data is entered. Packages also allow a sort of 'what if?' analysis for initial planning, trying out different levels of resources, changing deadlines and so on to find the best combination.

(b) **Estimating and controlling costs**
As a project progresses, actual data will become known and can be entered into the package and collected for future reference. Since many projects involve basically similar tasks (interviewing users and so on), actual data from one project can be used to provide more accurate estimates for the next project. The software also facilitates and encourages the use of more sophisticated estimation techniques than managers might be prepared to use if working manually.

(c) **Monitoring**
Actual data can also be entered and used to facilitate monitoring of progress and automatically updating the plan for the critical path and the use of resources as circumstances dictate.

(d) **Reporting**
Software packages allow standard and tailored progress reports to be produced, printed out and circulated to participants and senior managers at any time, usually at the touch of a button. This helps with co-ordination of activities and project review.

Most project management packages feature a process of identifying the main steps in a project, and breaking these down further into specific tasks. A typical project management package requires four **inputs**.

(a)   The length of **time** and the resources required for each activity of the project.

(b)   The **logical relationships** between each activity.

(c)   The **resources** available.

(d)   **When** the resources are available.

The package is able to analyse and present this information in a number of ways. The views available within Microsoft Project are shown in the following illustration – on the drop down menu.

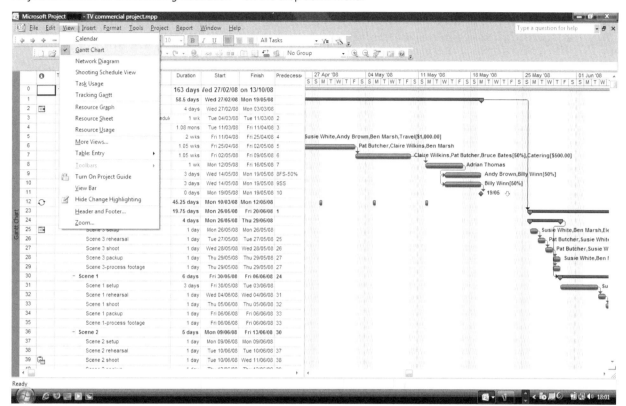

The advantages of using project management software are summarised in the following table.

Advantage	Comment
Enables quick re-planning	Estimates can be **changed many times** and a new schedule produced almost instantly. Changes to the plan can be reflected immediately.
Document quality	Outputs are accurate, well presented and easy to understand.
Encourages constant progress tracking	Actual times can be captured, enabling the project manager is able to compare **actual** progress against **planned** progress and investigate problem areas promptly.
What if? analysis	Software enables the effect of various scenarios to be calculated quickly and easily. Many project managers conduct this type of analysis using **copies** of the plan in separate computer files – leaving the actual plan untouched.
Complexity	Software can handle projects of size and complexity that would be very difficult to handle using manual methods.

The software also has several **disadvantages**, some of which also apply to manual methods.

(a)   **Focus**. Some project managers become so interested in software that they spend too much time producing documents and not enough time managing the project. Entering actual data and producing reports should be delegated to an administrator.

(b)   **Work practices**. The assumptions behind work breakdown structure are not always applicable: people tend to work in a more flexible way rather than completing discrete tasks one by one.

(c)   **Estimates**. Estimation is as much an art as a science and estimates can be wildly wrong. They are subject to the **experience** level of the estimator; influenced by the **need to impress clients**; and based on **assumptions** that can easily change.

(d)   **Human factors**. Skill levels, staff turnover and level of motivation can have profound effects on performance achieved. Also, human variation makes rescheduling difficult since employing more people on an activity that is running late may actually slow it down at first, while the newcomers are briefed and even retrained.

Learning objectives	Covered
1 Utilise a range of tools and techniques to support project planning, scheduling, resourcing and control	☑ Work breakdown structures
	☑ Project budget
	☑ Gantt charts
	☑ Network analysis
	☑ Critical path
	☑ Resource histogram
	☑ Project management software

Learning objective review

Quick quiz

1   What is the purpose of work breakdown structure?

2   What is the probable effect on the project budget of introducing a requirement for higher quality than originally anticipated?

3   What are some of the main purposes of using project management software?

4   What is the critical path?

5   How much float is available for critical activities?

6   What is a resource histogram?

1. The problem arises because D can only start when both B and C have been finished, whereas E is only required to follow B. The only way to draw the network is to use a dummy activity.

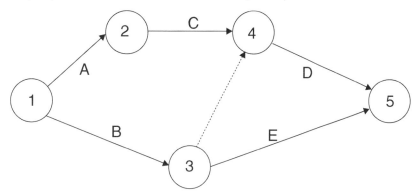

1   To analyse the work required to complete the project into manageable components

2   Budgeted cost will almost inevitably rise.

3   Planning and scheduling; estimating and controlling costs; monitoring and reporting

4   The series of tasks that determines the minimum possible duration of the project

5   By definition, there is no float on the critical path.

6   A resource histogram shows a view of project data in which resource requirements, usage, and availability are shown against a time scale.

Chapter 10

Controlling and evaluating projects

Topic list

Introduction

With this chapter we conclude our coverage of project management. There are two main elements here. The first is the project control process. No project will run itself and all project managers must expend effort on constant review of progress and the taking of control action where necessary. A number of techniques have been developed to aid in the process of project control.

The other main topic is the extensive work that is required when the project seems to be at an end. There is first the problem of closing it down in an effective and tidy fashion so that no loose ends are left to unravel. Second, there must be a process of review so that the lessons learned during the project are not immediately forgotten. This review process can take a considerable time to complete.

Syllabus linked learning objectives

By the end of the chapter you will be able to:

Learning objectives	Syllabus link
1 Utilise a variety of techniques to control project progress	4.6
2 Explain the main techniques for reviewing and evaluating project success and failure	4.7

1   Control reports

WORK BASED PROJECT TIP

format and presentation

Project managers (including you, in your project) will be required to produce reports dealing with the progress of their projects. The names allocated to documents will vary across different organisations. What is constant is the need for clear and relevant documentation that helps monitor and control the project.

Remember that reports are not a substitute for **face-to-face communication**. Too many (or too lengthy) reports will result in **information overload**.

When outlining possible content of documents some duplication of items occurs. This does not mean that information should be repeated, but that the information may appear in one or other of the documents depending on the format adopted by the organisation.

1.1 Progress report

KEY CONCEPT

concept

A **progress report** shows the current status of the project, usually in relation to the planned status.

The frequency and contents of progress reports will vary depending on the length of, and the progress being made on, a project.

The report is a **control tool** intended to show the discrepancies between where the project is, and where the plan says it should be. Major considerations will be time and cost and reports will highlight comparisons of planned and actual progress.

Any additional content will depend on the format adopted. Some organisations include only the 'raw facts' in the report, and use these as a basis for discussion regarding reasons for variances and action to be taken, at a project review meeting.

Other organisations (particularly those involved in long, complex projects) produce more comprehensive progress reports, with more explanation and comment.

Gray and Larson (2008) suggest the following basic format for a control report.

1   Progress since last report

2   Current project status
    Time schedule
    Cost
    Scope

3   Cumulative trends

4   Problems and issues since last report
    Actions and resolution of earlier problems
    New variances and problems identified

5   Corrective action planned

1.1.1 Control charts

Several different types of chart may be used to display project progress. The **Gantt chart**, described in the previous chapter, is inherently suited to use as a control chart, displaying planned and actual usage of resources, as is, to some extent, the **resource histogram**. Gray and Larson (2008) illustrate a 'project schedule control chart' that displays overall progress against plan.

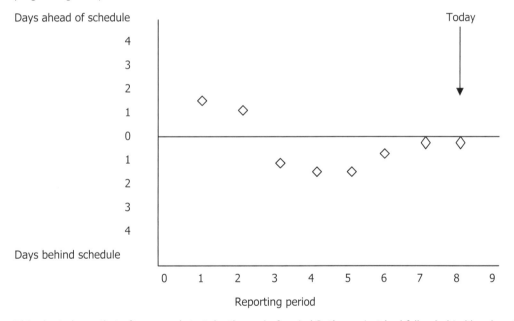

This chart shows that after a good start, by the end of period 3, the project had fallen behind by almost two days. Efforts were obviously made to recover the lost time, because the latest report, at the end of period 8, shows the project only about half a day behind.

ACTIVITY 1

application

Draw a control chart of the type illustrated above showing a project that was:

*   3 days behind schedule when it started
*   Gradually recovered 2 days by the end of reporting period 4
*   Lost a day during reporting period 6
*   Gained 3 days by the end of reporting period 8

1.1.2 Milestones

Milestones should be definite, easily identifiable events that all stakeholders can understand. Monitoring progress towards key milestones can be done on a control chart of the type described above, or on a **milestone slip chart** such as that shown below. This chart compares planned and actual progress towards project milestones. Planned progress is shown on the X-axis and actual progress on the Y-axis. Where actual progress is slower than planned progress **slippage** has occurred.

Milestone slip chart

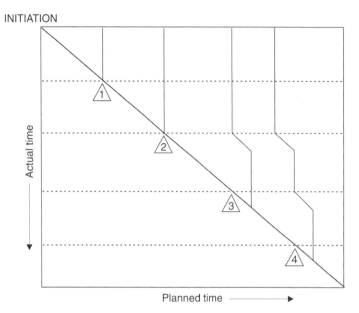

On the chart above milestones are indicated by a triangle on the diagonal planned progress line. The vertical lines that meet milestones 1 and 2 are straight – showing that these milestones were achieved on time.

At milestone 3 some slippage has occurred. The chart shows that no further slippage is expected as the progress line for milestone 4 is the same distance to the right as occurred at milestone 3.

We look at ways of dealing with slippage later in this chapter.

 MARKETING AT WORK

application

Qatar: Thursday, February 21 - 2008 at 08:51

Qatargas second new wellhead platform topsides installed

Qatargas recently achieved another major project milestone with the installation of the second of three new wellhead platform topsides in the North Field, 80 kilometres offshore of Qatar.

The QW4 platform topsides was installed safely and without incident on February 9th in a multi-hour operation which involved the use of a special heavy lift crane , NPCC's HLS 2000, that is capable of lifting up to 2,500 tonnes.

The topsides, which weighed approximately 2,200 tonnes, were carefully positioned above the legs of the previously installed jacket structure and successfully lowered over the ten pre-drilled wells onto the jacket.

Mr Faisal M. Al Suwaidi, Chairman and Chief Executive Officer of Qatargas said;

'Qatargas 2 is a project made up of many large projects within a project. This milestone takes the project one step closer to completion. I would like to thank all the parties involved - our staff, and contractors NPCC and Technip - for their dedication to seeing this job completed safely.'

www.ameinfo.com

1.1.3 Budget reports – earned value

The progress report should include cost information: the **earned value** approach is widely used, especially when projects are managed using the US Project Management Institute methodology. The essence of monitoring using earned value is the computation of **variances for cost and schedule** (schedule here means time progress). Three cost figures are required for the computations.

(a)   **Actual cost of work completed** (**AC**). This is the amount spent to date on the project.

(b)   **Planned value of the work scheduled to date** (**PV**). The amount that was budgeted to be spent to this point on scheduled activities.

(c)   **Earned value** (**EV**). This figure is calculated by pricing the work that has actually been done – using the same basis as the scheduled work.

EV – AC = The **cost variance** for the project.

EV – PV = The **schedule variance** for the project.

It should be noted that the schedule variance, while a useful overall indicator, is not the best indicator of time progress: the project network is far more accurate and informative.

 ACTIVITY 2    application

At day 30, the earned value of project 23/076 is £3.46 million, the planned value of work scheduled is £4.04 million and the actual cost of work completed is 3.95 million. What are the cost and schedule variances?

1.1.4 Traffic light reports

Traffic light control can also provide a higher level visual summary of progress.

In the traffic light approach, project members estimate the likelihood of various aspects of a project meeting its planned target date. Each aspect is then colour-coded.

Green   means 'on target': the work is on target and is expected to meet stakeholder expectations.

Yellow   signified the work is behind target, but the slippage is recoverable. Yellow indicates that some problem areas have been identified, but corrective actions can be taken to deal with them.

Red   signifies the work is behind is behind target and will be difficult to recover. A 'red' traffic light suggests there are major problems: for example, if a major component of the project is behind target could significantly affect the progress of the project as a whole.

Traffic light control can also be applied to cost and quality aspects of a project as well as time.

Equally, traffic light control could be applied to the three elements of time, cost and quality together. If a project is on course to substantially meet its objectives in all three elements, it will be indicated by a green traffic light. If two out of the three are likely to be substantially met, the traffic light will be yellow, but if less than two objectives are substantially met, the traffic light will be red.

1.2 Project meetings

Project progress reports will often be presented at meetings of stakeholders. However, the presentation of such reports is not the only purpose for which meetings may be convened. The multi-disciplinary nature of most larger projects makes frequent meetings unavoidable: they are essential for the proper management of project progress. There will be both scheduled, regular meetings and occasional meetings as required. The meeting will be concerned with three main areas of project management.

(a)   **Project design review meetings** are held to air technical problems and possible solutions and to gain approval for design features and changes.

(b) **Project status review meetings** are held regularly to monitor progress and gain approval for schedule changes.

(c) **Problem-solving meetings** are held as required to investigate, define and solve (and gain approval for the solutions to) problems as they arise.

2 Corrective action

Measuring progress is only the first stage of control. Where a significant discrepancy from plan is detected, some form of control action is likely to be required. A **feedback loop** thus exists, in that unsatisfactory performance is fed back to control and improve performance in the next period.

Consideration should also be given to the possibility that the plan itself might need modification. The process of using performance information to drive modifications to the plan is called **double loop feedback control**. The diagram below shows the two feedback loops.

Control system

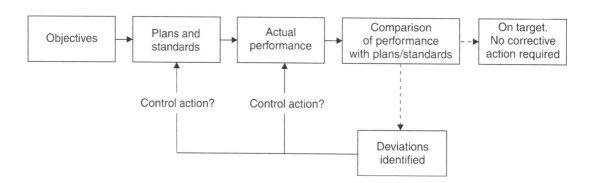

2.1 Project management problems

Project managers are often appointed from the ranks of technical experts. Technical ability is no guarantee of management skill - an individual might be highly proficient technically, but not a good manager.

The project manager has a number of **conflicting requirements**.

(a) The project sponsor wants the project **delivered on time**, to specification and within budget.

(b) **User** expectations may be misunderstood, ignored or unrealistic.

(c) The project manager has to plan and supervise the work of experts in fields about which he may have little knowledge.

(d) The project manager needs to develop an **appropriate management style**. What he or she should realise is the extent to which the project will fail if users are not consulted, or if the project team is unhappy. As the project manager needs to encourage participation from users, an excessively authoritarian style is not suitable.

(e) The project manager may accept **an unrealistic deadline** - the timescale is fixed early in the planning process. User demands may be accepted as deadlines before sufficient consideration is given to the realism of this.

(f) **Poor or non-existent planning** is a recipe for disaster. Unrealistic deadlines would be identified much earlier if a proper planning process was undertaken.

(g) A lack of **monitoring** and **control**.

(h) Users **change their requirements**, resulting in costly changes to the system as it is being developed.

2.2 Trade-offs in project objectives

The relationship between key project objectives of quality, cost and time (QCT) can be shown as a triangle.

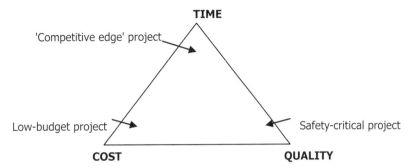

The Time/Cost/Quality Triangle

All three objectives are important: we would like our projects to finish on time, within budget *and* to the level of quality/performance required. However:

(a)   The **relative importance** of each objective may depend partly on the type of project. Where a project is aiming to beat a competitor to market, or has a non-negotiable deadline (eg organising an event that has been advertised for a particular date) time will be a priority. In a low-budget or fixed-grant project, cost is a priority: once resources run out, the project ceases – complete or not! In a safety-critical project (such as building or aircraft construction) quality is a priority.

(b)   This inevitably requires **trade offs** between the three objectives. Schedule slippage could be brought back on track by extra expenditure, for example, or cost slippage could be brought back on track by 'cutting corners' on quality. Ideally, such decisions should be taken within a framework of stakeholder expectations and consultation.

The balance of time, cost and quality will influence decision making throughout the project – for example whether to spend an extra £5,000 to fix a problem completely or only spend £1,000 on a quick fix and implement a user work-around?

2.3 Dealing with slippage

When a project has slipped behind schedule there are a range of options open to the project manager. Some of these options are summarised in the following table.

Action	Comment
Do nothing	After considering all options it may be decided that things should be allowed to continue as they are.
Add resources	If capable staff are available and it is practicable to add more people to certain tasks it may be possible to recover some lost ground. Could some work be subcontracted?
Work smarter	Consider whether the methods currently being used are the most suitable – for example could prototyping be used.
Replan	If the assumptions the original plan was based on have been proved invalid a more realistic plan should be devised.
Reschedule	A complete replan may not be necessary – it may be possible to recover some time by changing the phasing of certain deliverables.
Introduce incentives	If the main problem is team performance, incentives such as bonus payments could be linked to work deadlines and quality.
Change the specification	If the original objectives of the project are unrealistic given the time and money available it may be necessary to negotiate a change in the specification.

2.4 Controlling project changes

Some of the reactions to slippage discussed above would involve changes that would significantly affect the overall project. Other possible causes of changes to the original project plan include:

(a) The availability of new technology
(b) Changes in personnel
(c) A realisation that user requirements were misunderstood
(d) Changes in the business environment
(e) New legislation eg Data protection

The **earlier** a change is made the **less expensive** it should prove. However, changes will cost time and money and should not be undertaken lightly.

When considering a change **an investigation** should be conducted to discover:

(a) The consequences of **not** implementing the proposed change
(b) The impact of the change on **time, cost** and **quality**
(c) The expected costs and benefits of the change
(d) The risks associated with the change, and with the *status quo*

The process of ensuring that proper consideration is given to the impact of proposed changes is known as **change control.**

Changes will need to be implemented into the project plan and communicated to all stakeholders. Both the PRINCE2 and PMBOK systems treat change control as being of major importance. A very important feature is the absolute necessity of ensuring that approved changes to plans are **fully communicated** to all concerned and **properly recorded** in all copies of relevant documentation, such as the project plan, the project risk plan and the project quality plan.

 MARKETING AT WORK

application

Project Deadlines Put Pressure On Security

Few professionals would dispute the difficulties putting in new corporate systems. They are all large, complex, challenging projects. Within the past month, several Chief Information Security Officers (CISOs) have discussed the pressure that project managers, most of them from consulting companies, have exerted to try to gain full access to the production environment so they can make 'changes, updates, and modification' to the production systems.

Case Example: An organization decided to replace their ERP systems with a hybrid mainframe, server, and Web model. The project was late and over budget. Towards the end of the project, change controls and security processes were all but completely dropped. About three months after cut-over, the system began having problems. An investigation began and the 'new' consultants found that in forty days, there were over 10 thousand system abends (abnormal ending to executing applications) and over 20 million pieces of bad data were found in the production database. While this is perhaps the worst I have ever experienced, it really illustrates the need to keep control of the production environment and follow accepted standards for change control.

NOTE: The term 'abend' is derived from a mainframe error message on the IBM (News – Alert) 360, and used jokingly by hackers.

Kevin G Coleman, tmcnet.com, 27 April 2009

3 Project completion and review

When a project appears to be coming to an end, it is very important that appropriate measures are taken to ensure that it is brought to completion in an orderly fashion, with no loose ends left dangling. It is very easy to overlook important matters at this stage, especially if there is any move to cut back on the availability of project resources such as staffing.

Equally, after the project has been satisfactorily concluded, it is important that a detailed process of review should be undertaken in order to develop the organisation's project management capability. **Project termination** is in itself a key stage of any project.

MARKETING AT WORK

application

Successful Project Review for Sochi 2014

The International Paralympic Committee (IPC) today completed its first Project Review of the Sochi 2014 Paralympic Winter Games, which took place from 27-29 April in Moscow, Russia.

During a series of high-level meetings, five representatives from the IPC, including IPC CEO Xavier Gonzalez, received an overview about Sochi 2014's functional areas that will ensure the delivery of an accessible first Paralympic Winter Games in Russia. Key areas of discussion included venue development, transport, marketing and communications, education, technology and the Sochi 2014 Paralympic legacy.

www.paralympic.org/release/Main_Sections_Menu/News/Current_Affairs/2009_04_29

3.1 Project termination

Project termination is generally the most neglected stage of project management, and the temptation is always for finished projects to simply 'fade away'. Yet in order for the organisation to learn from past mistakes and issues, the project termination stage must include the following:

- Completion of all project management tasks

- Assessing whether or not it was well managed

- Looking at what can be learnt for the future (What went right? What went wrong? Would we use that agency again, for example?). Such questions should start to be asked throughout the project, not just at the end.

The following diagram illustrates features of the project termination process.

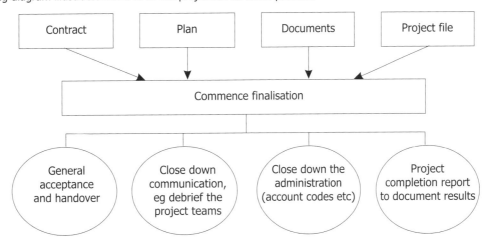

The project is complete when its intended deliverables have been realised. There will normally be a **project completion meeting** at which relevant stakeholders will agree completion. However, project scope will normally extend beyond customer deliverables: archiving project records, for example is an important aspect of completion, as is making appropriate arrangements for the dispersal of project staff. This may include performance assessment. Financial matters are particularly important: recording of project expenses is unlikely to be complete at the completion date and supplier invoices may continue to arrive for a considerable time after it.

Provision must also be made for any **continuing issues** that will need to be addressed after completion. Such issues would be related to the project, but are not part of it. (If they are part of the project the project is not yet complete). An example of such of an issue would be a procedure for dealing with any bugs that become apparent after a new software program has been tested and approved.

KEY CONCEPT

concept

The **completion report** summarises the results of the project, and includes client sign-off.

On project completion, the project manager will produce a **completion report**. The main purpose of the completion report is to document (and gain client sign-off for) the end of the project.

The report should include a summary of the project outcome.

(a)   Project objectives and the outcomes achieved.

(b)   The final project budget report showing expected and actual expenditure (If an external client is involved this information may be sensitive – the report may exclude or amend the budget report).

(c)   A brief outline of time taken compared with the original schedule.

Responsibilities and procedures relating to any such issues should be laid down in the report.

3.1.1 The outcome matrix

A matrix approach may be taken to the presentation of various aspects of the completion report. The simplest kind of matrix will simply list project deliverables in the left hand column of cells and show an objective assessment of achievement in the right hand column. The matrix can be made more informative by incorporating further columns to summarise outcomes in terms of , for example, time, cost and stakeholder satisfaction. An example is given below.

New product development project outcomes

Deliverable	Schedule	Cost	Production engineering	Sales	Finance
Product design	3 weeks late	£10,900 under budget	Complexity considered marginally acceptable	Good market performance anticipated	Breakeven unlikely below 14,600 units per month
Packaging	On time	£2,700 over budget	Satisfactory	Satisfactory	Considered expensive
Service requirements specification	6 weeks late	£4,900 over budget	Satisfactory	Over-complex	Satisfactory

A more complex type of outcome matrix can be used to analyse performance against two interacting criteria. This is the very common two-axis type of matrix that you are probably already familiar with through ideas such as Ansoff's product/market matrix. An example of an outcome matrix would be one that analysed technical aspects of a project deliverable in terms of quality of design and quality of execution.

3.1.2 Other forms of analysis

Various other forms of analysis are possible.

Profit/loss analysis is appropriate where a project is essentially an identifiable, separate trading operation, such as the establishment of a new product in an existing market. **Breakeven analysis**, **cashflow analysis** and consideration of **liquidity** are also relevant to such projects, as are normal financial reporting methods such as the computation of **payback** and **return on investment**.

Asset utilisation analysis will indicate if assets of all types have been employed in an appropriate fashion and at an appropriate rate during the life of the project. Asset utilisation should be planned and monitored during the life of the project in order to detect both overuse and underuse.

3.1.3 The preliminary report

The manager may find it useful to distribute a **provisional report** and request feedback. This should ensure the version presented for client sign-off at the completion meeting is acceptable to all parties.

A more detailed review of the project follows a few months after completion, the post-completion audit.

3.2 The post-completion audit

Any project is an **opportunity to learn** how to manage future projects more effectively.

 KEY CONCEPT  concept

The **post-completion audit** is a formal review of the project that examines the lessons that may be learned and used for the benefit of future projects.

The audit looks at all aspects of the project with regard to two questions.

(a)   Did the end result of the project meet the client's expectations?

    (i)   The actual design and construction of the end product
    (ii)   Was the project achieved on time?
    (iii)   Was the project completed within budget?

(b)   Was the management of the project as successful as it might have been, or were there bottlenecks or problems? This review covers:

    (i)   Problems that might occur on future projects with similar characteristics.
    (ii)   The performance of the team individually and as a group.

The post-completion audit should involve input from the project team. A simple questionnaire could be developed for all team members to complete, and a reasonably informal meeting held to obtain feedback, on what went well (and why), and what didn't (and why).

This information should be formalised in a report. The post-completion audit report should contain the following.

(a)   A **summary** should be provided, emphasising any areas where the structures and tools used to manage the project have been found to be unsatisfactory.

(b)   A **review of the end result** of the project should be provided, and compared against the **results expected**. Reasons for any **significant discrepancies** between the two should be provided, preferably with suggestions of how any future projects could prevent these problems recurring.

(c)   A **cost-benefit review** should be included, comparing the forecast costs and benefits identified at the time of the feasibility study with actual costs and benefits.

(d)   **Recommendations** should be made as to any steps which should be taken to improve the project management procedures used.

Lessons learnt that relate to the way the project was managed should contribute to the smooth running of future projects.

A starting point for any new project should be a review of the documentation of any similar projects undertaken in the past.

3.2.1 The balanced scorecard for project review

The **balanced scorecard** has already been described in this Workbook. Here it will suffice to give a brief reminder of that coverage. Kaplan and Norton (1992) suggested a performance measurement approach that looks at the business in four perspectives; performance in all must be satisfactory if the business is to prosper.

(a)   The **financial perspective**, or 'how do we look to shareholders?'
(b)   The **customer perspective**, or 'how do customers see us?'
(c)   The **internal business perspective**, or 'what must we excel at?'
(d)   The **innovation and learning perspective**, or 'can we continue to improve and create value?'

It is necessary for each business to set **goals** and establish **performance measures** for each perspective.

Gray and Larson (2008) describe the use of the balanced scorecard for **project review**. They suggest that the use of Kaplan and Norton's four perspectives keeps vision and strategy at the forefront of action. They describe using the scorecard to undertake a wide, 'macro' view of project performance, probably five to ten years after project completion. The aim is to establish whether the right projects were undertaken and whether their outcomes support the 'long-range strategic direction of the firm'.

3.2.2 Project management maturity

Earlier in this Workbook we discussed the concept of a **project management maturity model**. The post-completion audit has an important role to play in developing the organisation's capability. The aim of thinking in these terms is not merely for project managers to become better at project management but for the entire organisation to improve and enhance its strategic capability. The five levels of such a model are repeated here for reference.

Level 1   **Common knowledge**
The importance of project management to the organisation is understood and training in the basic techniques and terminology is provided.

Level 2   **Common processes**
The processes employed successfully are standardised and developed so that they can be used more widely, both for future projects and in concert with other methodologies such as total quality management.

Level 3   **Singular methodology**
Project management is placed at the centre of a single corporate methodology, achieving wide synergy and improving process control in particular. A separate methodology may be retained for IS matters.

Level 4   **Benchmarking**
Competitive advantage is recognised as being based on process improvement and a continuing programme of benchmarking is undertaken.

Level 5   **Continuous improvement**
Benchmarking information is critically appraised for its potential contribution to the improvement of the singular methodology.

 ACTIVITY 3

evaluation

Think about project management in any organisation with which you are familiar. Where would you say it was positioned on the project management maturity model? Share your thoughts with any other CIM students you may have contact with.

3.3 Benefits realisation

It is obviously important that the benefits expected from the completion of a project are actually enjoyed. Benefits realisation is concerned with the planning and management required to realise expected benefits. It also covers any required organisational transition processes.

The UK Office of Government Commerce has identified a **six stage procedure for benefits realisation**. This is most relevant to projects aimed at process improvement and changing the organisation's way of doing things

Stage 1 **Establishing benefits measurement**
Measure the start state and record it in the **benefits profile**. The benefits profile defines each anticipated benefit and is used to track progress towards its realisation. Determine how benefit realisation will be measured. Benefits may be complex and spread across departments: designing usable and realistic measures may be difficult.

Stage 2 **Refining the benefits profile**
The benefits profile should be refined and controlled throughout the life of the project. Project managers should conduct regular benefits profile reviews in collaboration with key stakeholders.

Stage 3 **Monitoring benefits**
There should be regular monitoring of benefits realisation. It must be accepted that some projects will only be beneficial in enabling other projects to be successful.

Stage 4 **Transition management**
Projects are likely to bring change and this must be managed in a proper way. Effective communications and will be required as will the deployment of good people skills

Stage 5 **Support for benefit realisation**
Benefits realisation will mainly accrue after the end of the project. Where a project brings changes in methods and processes, there is likely to be a period for settling-down before benefits are fully realised. During this period, costs may rise and problems may occur. Careful management is required to overcome these short-term effects. A philosophy of continuous improvement is required if further benefits are to be achieved.

Stage 6 **Measuring the benefits**
Benefits achieved should be established by comparison with the pre-improvement state recorded in the benefits profile.

Learning objectives	Covered	
1 Utilise a variety of techniques to control project progress	☑	Milestones
	☑	Earned value
	☑	Conflicting requirements
2 Explain the main techniques for reviewing and evaluating project success and failure	☑	Completion meeting
	☑	Completion report

1   What is a project milestone?

2   How is earned value calculated?

3   A single loop feedback control system compares planned and actual achievement so that control action can be taken in the future. What does double loop feedback do?

4   What are the three constraints on project achievement that can be traded off against each other?

5   What options are available for dealing with project slippage?

6   What is the main benefit of carrying out a post-completion audit?

7   What is the highest level in the project management maturity model?

8   How are the benefits brought by a project measured?

1. Days ahead of schedule

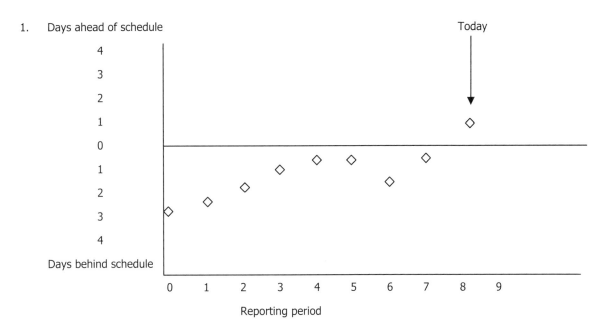

2. Cost variance = EV − AC = £3.46 − 3.95 million = -£0.49 million

    Schedule variance = EV − PV = £3.46 − 4.04 million = -£0.58 million

3. This activity depends entirely upon your personal experience. However, it is unlikely that you will have experience of an organisation that achieves Level 4 or above.

1   A significant event in the life of the project, usually completion of a major deliverable.

2   Earned value is the price of the work that has actually been done.

3   Potentially, double loop feedback can lead to the modification of the plan.

4   Quality, cost and time.

5   Do nothing; add resources; work smarter; replan; reschedule; introduce incentives; change the specification.

6   The opportunity make the management of future projects more effective.

7   Continuous improvement.

8   By comparison with the pre-improvement state recorded in the benefits profile.

Coleman, F. (2009) *'Project deadlines put pressure on security'*, tmcnet.com, 27 April 2009.

Gray, C. and Larson, W. L. (2008) <u>*Project Management: the Managerial Process*</u>, McGraw-Hill, London.

Kaplan, R. and Norton, D. (1992) *'The balanced scorecard: measures that drive performance'*, Harvard Business Review January – February pp. 71-80.

References

Key concepts

Analysis, planning, implementation, control: APIC, 4

Breakthrough project, 149

Business case, 2
Business risk, 118

Completion Report, 206

Correlation, 46
Critical activities, 183
Customer database, 9
Customer service, 4

Databases, 9

Database marketing, 9
Discounted cash flow (DCF), 86
Discounting, 84
Discounting formula, 84
Differentiation, 4

Executive information system, 16

Expert systems, 15
Extranet, 19

Family life cycle (FLC), 75

Forecasting, 67

Gap analysis, 3

Goals, 64
Groupware, 17

Information, 3

Intranet, 18

Knowledge, 12

Knowledge assets, 13
Knowledge management, 13
Knowledge-based economy, 12

Market forecast, 70

Marketing databases, 9
Marketing decision support system, 16
Marketing information system, 7
Marketing intelligence system, 9

Marketing management, 3
Marketing mix, 96
Marketing research, 26
Market segmentation, 71
Model, 69

Negative correlation, 47

Net present value (NPV) method, 86
Network analysis, 183
Non-operational goals, 64

Objectives, 64

Operational goals, 64

Positive correlation, 47

Post-completion audit, 207
Positioning, 94
Present value, 84
Product, 96
Progress report, 198
Project, 142
Project budget, 181
Project management, 143
Project management Plan, 176
Project-oriented culture, 151
Project stakeholders, 167
Project Team, 171
Projection, 67

Qualitative research, 27

Quantitative research, 28

Resource histogram, 191, 195

Resources, 142
Risk, 112, 113
Risk evaluation, 129
Risk management, 126
Risk perspective, 116

Sales potential, 71

Strategic project management, 149

Targets, 64

Target market, 92
Transaction processing systems, 14

Index

Review form & Free prize draw

All original review forms from the entire BPP range, completed with genuine comments, will be entered into one of two draws on 31 January 2011 and 31 July 2011. The names on the first four forms picked out on each occasion will be sent a cheque for £50.

Name: _____   **Address**: _____

_____

_____

1.How have you used this Text?
(Tick one box only)

☐ Self study (book only)

☐ On a course: college_____

☐ Other _____

3. Why did you decide to purchase this Text?
(Tick one box only)

☐ Have used companion Assessment workbook

☐ Have used BPP Texts in the past

☐ Recommendation by friend/colleague

☐ Recommendation by a lecturer at college

☐ Saw advertising in journals

☐ Saw website

☐ Other _____

2. During the past six months do you recall seeing/receiving any of the following?
(Tick as many boxes as are relevant)

☐ Our advertisement in *The Marketer*

☐ Our brochure with a letter through the post

☐ Saw website

4. Which (if any) aspects of our advertising do you find useful?
(Tick as many boxes as are relevant)

☐ Prices and publication dates of new editions

☐ Information on product content

☐ Facility to order books off-the-page

☐ None of the above

5. Have you used the companion Assessment Workbook?   Yes ☐   No ☐

6. Have you used the companion Passcards?   Yes ☐   No ☐

7. Your ratings, comments and suggestions would be appreciated on the following areas.

	Very useful	Useful	Not useful
Introductory section (How to use this text, study checklist, etc)	☐	☐	☐
Introduction	☐	☐	☐
Syllabus linked learning outcomes	☐	☐	☐
Activities and Marketing at Work examples	☐	☐	☐
Learning reviews	☐	☐	☐
Magic Formula references	☐	☐	☐
Content of suggested answers	☐	☐	☐
Index	☐	☐	☐
Structure and presentation	☐	☐	☐

	Excellent	Good	Adequate	Poor
Overall opinion of this Text	☐	☐	☐	☐

8. Do you intend to continue using BPP CIM Range Products?   ☐ Yes   ☐ No

9. Have you visited bpp.com/lm/cim?   ☐ Yes   ☐ No

10.If you have visited bpp.com/lm/cim, please give a score out of 10 for it's overall usefulness   /10

Please note any further comments and suggestions/errors on the reverse of this page.

Please return to: Rebecca Hart, BPP Learning Media, FREEPOST, London, W12 8BR.

If you have any additional questions, feel free to email cimrange@bpp.com

Please note any further comments and suggestions/errors below.

Free prize draw rules

1 Closing date for 31 January 2011 draw is 31 December 2010. Closing date for 31 July 2011 draw is 30 June 2011.

2 Restricted to entries with UK and Eire addresses only. BPP employees, their families and business associates are excluded.

3 No purchase necessary. Entry forms are available upon request from BPP Learning Media. No more than one entry per title, per person. Draw restricted to persons aged 16 and over.

4 Winners will be notified by post and receive their cheques not later than 6 weeks after the relevant draw date. List of winners will be supplied on request.

5 The decision of the promoter in all matters is final and binding. No correspondence will be entered into.